Contents

Introduction

The story of the guitar in blues

The history of blues guitar is almost synonymous with the modern history of the guitar itself. Beginning in the early 1900s, blues guitar players laid the foundation for nearly every style of guitar playing that followed. Jazz guitarists, country guitarists, and of course rock guitarists—all owe a huge debt of gratitude to the original blues pioneers of the early 20th century. It was these players—colorful characters such as Robert Johnson, Blind Lemon Jefferson, and Son House—who brought not only their musical genre, but the instrument itself, to the forefront of popular attention and admiration.

In the earliest days of the recording industry, blues recordings often sold as many as a million copies, and blues performers became widely known to the general public. In addition to the heartfelt, sometimes aching, but often joyous vocals of the early performers, it was the driving rhythms and plaintive cry of the blues guitar that captured the hearts and minds of would-be musicians everywhere. The raw emotions and exhilarating musicianship pouring from their radios and Victrolas inspired guitarists by the score, sparking an increase in guitar sales never seen before. It would be decades later, after the hysteria of The Beatles and early rock, that guitar cemented its place as, arguably, the world's most popular instrument—but that trend began with the blues. Of course it didn't hurt that guitars were largely inexpensive, highly portable, and could serve as the only accompaniment a vocalist would ever need.

And those early amateur blues vocalists had plenty to sing about. Long, hard days spent sweating it out in the cotton fields of Mississippi, Arkansas, and the "Delta" region of the southern United States certainly inspired them to pursue some sort of emotional release, and had many seeking an easier and more enjoyable way to make a living. For many early blues guitarists and performers, their journey began simply as a weekend diversion to help them escape their lowly place in life, and to gain at least some level of notoriety that set them apart from their fellow farm-workers. It was a bonus that they might have earned a buck or two extra spending-cash at a plantation house party or local juke joint.

At the time, extreme poverty was the norm among many of those African-Americans who embraced the emerging blues guitar lifestyle. They largely subsisted on low incomes that they might have earned doing back-breaking work picking cotton or building levees behind a mule-driven plow. Their place in life might have offered them more freedom than their enslaved ancestors of only a few generations before, but they were taken advantage of in nearly every way by the landowners for whom they worked. They may have been paid for their labor, but their plantation landlord and his "company store" kept them as close to broke as a person could be. Fortunately, the music set them free, figuratively at first, and later—after their acclaim grew and they began to earn more playing guitar than working for "the big boss man"—quite literally.

THE
Blues
Guitar
HANDBOOK

Adam St. James

The Blues Guitar Handbook
Adam St. James

To my beautiful wife, Diane, and my wonderful children, Austin and Amber, who went without me many times during the writing of this book, thank you for your love and patience.

A BACKBEAT BOOK
First edition 2011
Published by Backbeat Books
An Imprint of Hal Leonard Corporation
7777 West Bluemound Road,
Milwaukee, WI 53213
www.backbeatbooks.com

Devised and produced for Backbeat Books by
Outline Press Ltd
2A Union Court, 20-22 Union Road,
London SW4 6JP, England
www.jawbonepress.com

ISBN: 978-1-61713-011-3

A catalogue record for this book is available from the British Library.

DESIGN: Paul Cooper Design
EDITOR: John Morrish

Printed by Everbest Printing Co. Ltd, China

11 12 13 14 15 5 4 3 2 1

The blues goes big-time

Blues guitar was, in its infancy, primarily a local phenomenon—and largely confined to the black community. It wasn't until the genre, and the musicians who pioneered it, were "discovered" by a few open-minded or forward-thinking individuals that blues music—and blues guitar—truly took off. One of the key figures in this occurrence is W.C. Handy (1873-1958), the Alabama-born professional musician now regarded as the "Father of the Blues."

Handy, a cornet player, was already a successful songwriter and full-time traveling musician of some acclaim when—as the story goes—he happened across an unfortunately anonymous figure in a train station at Tutwiler, Mississippi. The lanky guitarist he stumbled upon was an early practitioner of slide guitar playing, and Handy immediately took notice of the haunting quality of the music, with its early intimations of the Delta blues. Soon he began to work blues themes into his own compositions, penning the early hits 'Memphis Blues' (1909), 'St. Louis Blues' (1914), and 'Beale Street Blues' (1916). Partly through the success of these hugely popular songs, the blues genre rapidly gained the attention of the general public, moving from a backwater musical style to become one of the dominant musical forms of the modern era.

While Handy's groundbreaking recordings were achieving acclaim, the nascent recording industry was beginning to take shape, and other arts-minded entrepreneurs jumped into the business of making, or facilitating the making, of the music. Early recording studios sprang up in various locales, some literally pay-to-play operations or, in a sense, "starter studios"—places to audition, where working musicians could try their hand at cutting a first record.

One such venture was run by Henry "H.C." Speir (1895-1972), a retail store owner on Farish Street in Jackson, Mississippi. Jackson was the largest city in the Delta, and though Speir was white, his store was located in a black neighborhood. Consequently, he had his finger on the musical preferences of the locals. During the 20s heyday of the classic blues era, Speir had been selling a noticeable quantity of blues records in his general merchandise store. By 1926 he had formed relationships with several record labels, and soon decided to install a metal disc machine to record demos of local musicians.

Speir then sent recordings of the better artists off to established record labels. He soon became known as an expert talent scout with a knack for finding hit songs and noteworthy artists. Naturally, blues musicians flocked to his store from near and far to take their shot at stardom. Speir was responsible for launching the careers of many—if not most—of the Delta's most celebrated blues guitarists, singers, and musicians, including Robert Johnson, Charlie Patton, and Son House, among others.

Robert Johnson with fellow bluesman Johnny Shines

The varying forms of early blues

With much credit due to Speir, the Delta blues, in its most classic format—typically performed by a lone guitarist/vocalist—enjoyed great popularity from the late 20s through the 40s. Some of the earliest Delta blues recordings to gain notoriety featured Ishman Bracey and Tommy Johnson, who were recorded in 1928 by Victor, a major record label. As "Race" records picked up sales—and record labels took notice—more and more major labels began searching for talent, and more and more Delta blues stylists found their way into recording studios. (We'll explore Delta blues guitar playing in detail in Section Eight of this book.)

At around the same time these early Delta blues practitioners and their style of guitar playing were gaining acclaim, players away from the fertile soils of Mississippi and Arkansas took up the instrument and made a name for themselves too. But some guitarists already had their own blues thing going. Texas gave us Blind Lemon Jefferson and Blind Willie Johnson. The highly influential Big Bill Broonzy, originally from Arkansas, moved to Chicago by 1920 and New York City by the early 30s. And the Piedmont region, along the southern Atlantic Coast of the United States—from Virginia, through the Carolinas down to Georgia—chimed in with several noteworthy blues artists as well.

These players in particular put their own spin on the music pouring out of the Delta and the sounds they heard during the female-dominated, band-driven classic blues era. "Piedmont," or "East Coast blues" artists such as Reverend Gary Davis, Barbecue Bob, Blind Willie McTell, Blind Blake, Blind Boy Fuller, Etta Baker, and Brownie McGhee achieved success and notoriety with their own hit songs.

Unlike Delta blues guitar, which relied largely on a driving shuffle rhythm and often featured slide guitar, Piedmont blues guitar playing borrowed liberally from ragtime, 19th-century parlor guitar playing, and a banjo technique known as frailing. The jaunty Piedmont rhythms, punctuated by a constantly alternating bass line not found in most Delta blues guitar playing, worked well in a dance setting. The Piedmont style also enjoyed its heyday between 1920 and 1940, with songs such as Blind Boy Fuller's 'Step It Up And Go' selling nearly half a million records. (We'll be covering Piedmont blues guitar playing—along with other important acoustic blues techniques—in Section Eight of this book.)

The new blues of the post-war period

Together, the Delta and Piedmont musical movements inspired additional guitarists and performers. As time marched on, this acoustic or "country" blues style, often referred to as pre-war blues, began to evolve. Much of the change came about, in part, as a result of the Great Migration. In a trend that had begun as early as 1910, but gained momentum with the onset of World War II, as many as seven million African-Americans left the farms of the Southern United States and headed for the big cities of the north. Many in the black community relocated to Chicago and Detroit, where jobs in the factories cranking out the machines of war were plentiful—and of course, the money was better as well. The change in setting brought about a change in sound too.

Players such as John Lee Hooker, known to make a whole song out of one chord, and McKinley Morganfield, aka Muddy Waters—who was mentored early in his career by the great Son House—launched their careers and scored major hits during or shortly after World War II. This post-war blues may have initially harkened back to its Delta roots, but it carried the urgency of city life in its veins. Waters, in particular, soon took to recording not as a solo guitarist/vocalist in the Delta tradition, but with a kick-ass band. The acoustic blues soon gave way to a newer form: the electric blues. This new sound fit well with the changing lifestyle of the population, from laid-back country living to up-tempo city dwelling. When radios started blasting out these new sounds, electric blues recordings started flying out of record stores.

OPPOSITE PAGE: Blind Lemon Jefferson (left); Blind Willie McTell (right).
THIS PAGE: The Reverend Gary Davis (top); Brownie McGhee (below)

As families and friends told those they had left behind about all the big city had to offer, more and more left the farming communities of the south, and musicians made the move too. During this mass migration, Chicago, Detroit, and Memphis seemed to land the most influential blues musicians and guitarists. As the 50s progressed, two brothers in Chicago, Phil and Leonard Czyz (soon renaming themselves Chess), seemingly cornered the market on blues greatness with their record label. Chess Records was soon cranking out guitar-driven hit songs by a litany of names we now regard as legendary: Muddy Waters, Howlin' Wolf, Chuck Berry, and many others. (Section Nine of this book delves deeply into this Chicago or 50s electric style of blues guitar playing.)

At the same time, Beale Street in downtown Memphis, Tennessee, became a hotbed of blues activity. Even today, this main drag—just a stone's throw from the Mighty Mississippi—features one blues bar after another, often with three or four different bands cranking out the shuffles from before noon to well into the early hours. But what came first, the chicken or the egg? The scene or the player?

In the early 50s, Memphis was home to Delta slide stylist Bukka White, who, like many of his contemporaries in Memphis, Chicago, and other cities, performed during the day on street corners, busking for a few coins from passers-by. Soon his young cousin, Riley, would move to Memphis from the farming region to try his hand in the local blues scene—and he would become its most renowned player. In fact Riley B. King's nickname at the time was Beale Street Blues Boy, hence the stage name "B.B." His 1952 hit, 'Three O'Clock Blues,' originally recorded by Lowell

Fulson in 1946, launched a remarkable recording career that continues well into the 21st century.

In these heady and prosperous post-war days, players such as B.B. King regularly pushed their name and their talents to wider acclaim via popular radio programs they hosted on stations such as WDIA, 1070 AM, out of Memphis, or KFFA, 1360 AM, out of Helena, Arkansas. The signals from these high-power radio stations reached far into the Delta and beyond, and B.B. King, Sonny Boy Williamson II (Rice Miller), Robert Lockwood, Jr, Pinetop Perkins, Robert Nighthawk, and other hosts or house-band members soon made huge names for themselves. As a bonus, up and coming players such as Muddy Waters, Jimmy Rogers, Little Walter, Hound Dog Taylor, and others would often hang round the studios and sometimes perform on the air. A local kid named Elvis Presley grew up listening to these radio programs, and was hugely influenced by the blues he heard on the air.

Usually only 15- to 30-minutes in length, these radio segments might feature a little bit of live playing, a few record spins, and plenty of mentions of the products of the sponsors—who made it all possible and whom the performers were often responsible for lining up. The legendary live rock music program, *The King Biscuit Flower Hour*, paid homage to the original blues radio show *King Biscuit Time*, sponsored by the flour company of the same name. In fact, the *King Biscuit Time* show is still on the air, and in 2010 broadcast its 16,000th episode—making it the longest-running daily radio program in America.

The blues music B.B. and his peers spun or performed live on these shows was often raw and rockin'. Set against the popular music of the time—largely dominated by white crooners such as Frank Sinatra and Bing Crosby—the blues guitarists and musicians of the 50s provided a welcome antidote to the sometimes sugary, highly-polished sound of the mainstream. These blues artists and their recordings quickly gained worldwide acclaim, and young guitarists and other musicians everywhere took notice.

Influencing the future royalty of rock

Across the pond, over in England, young players, then in their teens, such as Keith Richards, George Harrison, Eric Clapton, Jeff Beck, Jimmy Page, Peter Green, and countless others often purchased early blues recordings mail order, sometimes direct from US-based labels such as Chess. They then proceeded to wear out these vinyl treasures learning the incendiary guitar riffs pouring from the recordings of these Chicago blues masters. And back home in the States, young guitarists such as Jimi Hendrix, Billy Gibbons, Johnny Winter, Michael Bloomfield, Duane Allman, Bonnie Raitt, and Stevie Ray Vaughan also did their homework studying the music of the blues masters. (Section Ten of this book examines how these rockers put their blues roots to work.)

Coming of age mostly in the mid 60s and 70s, these guitarists began to crank out revved-up cover versions of the blues classics, or revamped and re-wrote the blues riffs and motifs into their own songs to help truly bring rock'n'roll music to the forefront of popular taste. The Muddy Waters song 'The Blues Had A Baby And They Named It Rock And Roll,' is certainly right on the money.

Decades later, the fact that Eric Clapton and his generation of now legendary rock stars have repeatedly and steadfastly returned to their blues roots, and

OPPOSITE PAGE: Chuck Berry (top); Robert Lockwood Jr and Sonny Boy Williamson II (below). *THIS PAGE:* Jeff Beck

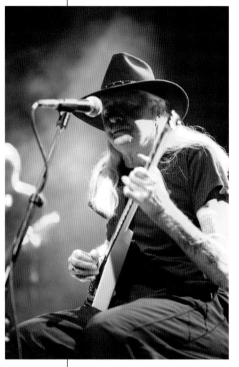

championed their early blues influences, serves to highlight the importance and huge influence of blues music and blues guitar playing. And while they were still alive, often as senior citizens, many a blues legend enjoyed the benefits of this hero worship when artists such as Clapton or The Rolling Stones brought the likes of Muddy Waters or Freddie King up on stage or out on major tours as their opening acts. In the process, these kindly acts of payback introduced the blues elders to millions of potential new fans.

While the electric blues was certainly all the rage after World War II, and well into the rock era of the 60s and 70s, acoustic blues experienced a solid and influential rebirth as well. The American and European folk music revivals of the 50s and 60s resurrected the careers of many an acoustic blues player, including plenty whose stars had faded decades before. These revivals brought pre-war blues players such as Huddie William "Leadbelly" Ledbetter, Son House, Josh White, and others back into the public eye.

This renewed interest in folk music began in part as a political movement, spearheaded by American folk musician and protest songsmith Woody Guthrie. European promoters Horst Lippman and Fritz Rau—who put together the popular and influential American Folk-Blues Festivals which toured Europe throughout the 60s, beginning in 1962—and folk archivist Alan Lomax also deserve much credit for keeping acoustic blues alive. During the early European tours, in particular, future rock stars Mick Jagger, Eric Clapton, Steve Winwood, and Eric Burdon are said to have been in attendance. Led Zeppelin vocalist Robert Plant, who also attended, claims to have been greatly influenced and inspired by these concerts.

Many of the early blues artists who experienced revitalized careers, such as House, had actually given up on music-making long before. Most had taken regular day jobs, sometimes religious in nature, and some had even sworn off music altogether—often torn between their deeply religious beliefs and their love for the Devil's Music, as the blues was often called. House, in particular, was somewhat reluctant to come out of "retirement," but soon warmed to the enthusiastic reception he was given by the primarily white audiences of the blues revival. Renewed recording

areers and world travels often followed, and once-forgotten blues
riginators influenced whole new generations—not to mention another
ace or two—with their music.

Blues in the 21st Century

he blues definitely had its up and downs over the last few decades of the
0th century. The style occasionally jumped to the forefront of popular
ttention—think of Stevie Ray Vaughan introducing his rootsy rock-blues
o millions via mid-80s broadcasts on MTV—before again fading into
elative obscurity behind the pop music of the era. An occasional album,
uch as Eric Clapton's 1994 release, *From The Cradle*, would again drive
ales and renewed interest into much of the blues genre, firing the
maginations of new generations of players, or reminding older players
vho might have left the blues behind what a wonderful, vital, even
elevant style the music remains.

Today blues guitar playing is alive and well, and carried forward by
cores of players, each employing various blues guitar styles in one fashion or another. There are
he traditionalists, such as John Hammond, Corey Harris, Eric Bibb, and Keb' Mo', who model
hemselves after the acoustic fingerstyle greats of the pre-war Delta era. Players such as Charlie
aty (Little Charlie & The Nightcats), Ronnie Baker Brooks (son of 50s blues legend Lonnie
rooks), or George Thorogood reinvigorate the early electric blues of the Chicago blues variety—

OPPOSITE PAGE: Johnny Winter (top); Bonnie Raitt (below)
THIS PAGE: Corey Harris (top); Keb' Mo' (below)

which is of course also still being played by legends such as B.B King, Buddy Guy, Lonnie Brooks, and Wolf/Waters sideman Hubert Sumlin.

The evolution of the style continues as well: blues music is given new life by forward-thinking guitarists such as Derek Trucks, Robben Ford, and Scott Henderson, who twist the blues into a fiery jazz-fusion mix. And blues-based guitar playing is of course kept forever current by rock stars young (Kenny Wayne Shepherd, Jonny Lang, Joe Bonamassa) and old (The Allman Brothers, Johnny Winter, The Rolling Stones, ZZ Top) who either cover blues songs or re-create blues stylings in their own, sometimes unique ways.

From the earliest days of the Delta blues, through the mid century electric blues, and on to today's current crop of rockers, blues traditionalists, blues-jazz virtuosos, and, even mainstream country artists, the sounds and styles of blues guitar playing are not only alive and well, but thriving, and evolving ever onward. Here in the 21st century, blues guitar and blues song formats are arguably the one underlying, constant factor in almost all popular musical styles.

Recording the blues

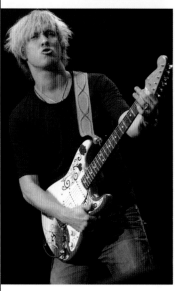

Thomas Edison's invention of a sound recording and playback device in 1877 launched an entire industry that prevails today as one of the prime movers in popular culture, and blues music was a key contributor. Combined with the invention of radio in the 1890s, and the beginning of radio broadcasts in the 20s, recorded music replaced an industry model that, for centuries, had primarily been built on sheet music and live performance.

Sales of radios, phonographs, and consequently, recordings, exploded in the early years of the 20th century. Even when placed in one family's home, early radios were often somewhat of a neighborhood focal point. And fueled by the sounds pouring out of these "community" receivers—where members of multiple households might crowd around to listen to a broadcast—recorded music rapidly came into demand.

Record players had already been around for a couple of decades before radio, but once wireless broadcasts began, sales of players by manufacturers such as Victrola, Zonophone, Gramophone, Grafonola, and Graphophone increased exponentially—as did sales of the discs to play on them. Interestingly, not all of these early records spun at what we now think of as the early standard: 78 revolutions per minute. In the early days various players ran at speeds ranging from 60 to 130

Hubert Sumlin (top); Kenny Wayne Shepherd (below)

PM. The 78 RPM setting eventually became accepted as the average between the two most popular brands of discs, manufactured by Columbia and their competitor Victor. Later that standard was replaced by 45 RPM singles and 33 RPM EPs ("extended play") and LPs ("long players," in other words albums, which did not come along until 1948)—and then of course 8-track, cassette tape, CD, and now mp3 technology followed.

Naturally, with the advent of all this technology came the need for the music itself. And the history of the early record labels and their effect on the musical landscape makes for a fascinating study as well. Some labels were the offshoots of already successful businesses—such as those created by the manufacturers of the actual records and record players. Others sprang up out of the imaginations and hard work of ambitious entrepreneurs.

As the early recording "industry" found its legs, labels such as Brunswick, Vocalion, Decca, Victor, Okeh, Columbia, Paramount, and others routinely bought each other out, created numerous subsidiary labels, helped pioneer still newer recording and playback technologies, and released voluminous amounts of music in every imaginable genre.

Many of these labels have survived—even flourished—well into the 21st century. Columbia records and Victor (later known as RCA Victor) are, of course, major divisions of one of today's largest music industry conglomerates, Sony Music Entertainment. But some of the smaller, lesser-known labels still exist today as well. The Brunswick label is currently distributed by E1 Entertainment out of Canada, for example. Others briefly spring back to life now and then: The Okeh label was resurrected in 1994 as a blues label by Sony Music, only to be retired again in 2000.

The classic blues era

Some of the earliest known recordings date back to the 1880s, but, with the exception of a few early hits (such as the songs of W.C. Handy, mentioned above), the earliest true blues recordings were of the "classic blues" era. This period, which ran roughly from 1920 to 1930, was dominated by female vocalists such as Mamie Smith (1883-1946), Bessie Smith (1894-1937), and Ma Rainey (1886-1939). These three women recorded hundreds of songs, became worldwide celebrities, and achieved a legendary status in the music industry which they retain to this day. They also paved the way not only for other black artists, but specifically for the blues genre as a whole. It was this classic blues that put blues music at the forefront of popular musical taste, largely taking the place previously occupied by the ragtime, early jazz, vaudeville, minstrel, and Tin Pan Alley musical movements.

The classic blues era is largely considered to have begun with Mamie Smith, who may be the first black solo artist ever to have been recorded. Mamie launched her recording career when she entered a studio in 1920 to sing 'Crazy Blues' and two other songs for Okeh Records. 'Crazy Blues' sold more than one million copies in its first year, making Mamie a huge star almost overnight.

No relation to Mamie, Bessie Smith was perhaps the most popular blues singer of the classic blues era. Bessie began her recording career in 1923 with 'Downhearted Blues' and 'Gulf Coast Blues,' tracked for Columbia Records. She went on to record more than 160 songs and became the highest paid black performer of her time, earning her the nickname Empress of the Blues.

A friend and sometimes musical partner of Bessie, Gertrude "Ma" Rainey also began her recording career in 1923, making over 100 recordings for Paramount, who billed her as the Mother of the Blues. Rainey recorded early versions of 'Bo-weevil Blues' and 'See, See Rider,' which wer among the first big blues hits, and also recorded with Louis Armstrong.

All three of these blues legends toured extensively, through the United States and beyond, an enjoyed levels of celebrity akin to that of the biggest blues stars of today. The female-fronte classic blues era served as the introduction to the blues for most listeners, and established the 12 bar framework as the most common blues compositional feature. The good times mostly came t an end, however, with the Great Depression of 1929. By the mid 30s many of the great classi blues singers had either returned home to normal lives, taken day jobs (Bessie Smith worked for while as a hostess in speakeasies), or moved to Hollywood to take their shot at the silver screer Mamie Smith, in particular, appeared in several motion pictures in a movie career that ra through 1943.

"Race records" and the early talent scouts

After the ladies of the classic blues era proved that African-American artists could sell piles c records, labels began to look for more opportunities to capitalize on this source of raw talent. An while Rainey, the Smiths, and other popular blues singers had plenty of crossover appeal wit white audiences, early record label bosses also recognized that blacks bought plenty of recorc themselves. Also, it wasn't just female vocalists the public wanted to hear.

Between the 20s and 50s, much of the male-dominated, guitar-driven blues this book concerned with was released and marketed specifically to blacks under the heading "race records by labels to whom the black music market was simply another profitable business sector. Whi the term race records may seem derogatory, it was a term used proudly by the African-America media at the time, often referring to blacks as "the race." The term eventually faded awa particularly as more and more non-blacks began to purchase these recordings.

Much as they still do today, early record labels relied on talent scouts to find and develop ne artists, whether for their mainstream or their race records releases. Some of these label reps we employees; others worked freelance. H.C. Speir was one of these freelance scouts—a "taler broker" as he referred to himself—and arguably the most important talent scout in blues histor (Speir was honored posthumously with induction into the Blues Hall of Fame in 2005.)

Speir would record demos of unsigned blues artists in his Jackson, Mississippi, store on his met. disc-cutting machine, then arrange for more formal recording sessions if the record labels we interested in what they heard. His finds ended up recording for many of the biggest labels of h day, including Okeh, Victor, Gennett, Columbia, Vocalion, Decca, and Paramount. He would ofte accompany his artists to recording sessions as far away as Texas, Georgia, Wisconsin, and elsewher

Always eager to find his next star, Speir sometimes traveled hundreds of miles in his searc but many a blues artist would simply arrive on his doorstep. Speir was responsible for tl discovery of legendary Delta blues artists including Ishman Bracey, Tommy Johnson, Charl Patton, Son House, Skip James, Robert Johnson, Bo Carter, Willie Brown, The Mississippi Sheik Blind Joe Reynolds, Blind Roosevelt Graves, Geeshie Wiley, and Robert Wilkins.

While his impact would be felt for generations, Speir retired from talent scouting and tl recording industry fairly early in the game. By 1936 he had left the development of musical tale to others. And there were, of course, others who were ready to contribute.

Among them was John Henry Hammond II (1910-1987), who got his start in the music business in the 30s, and was still active through the 80s. Hammond—whose son, John Paul Hammond (born 1942) still performs worldwide as a well-known acoustic blues player—grew up in a privileged household, the great-grandson of William Henry Vanderbilt, the patriarch of one of America's wealthiest old-money families. John Henry played piano, violin, and viola and studied at Yale University in New Haven, Connecticut, class of 1933.

But his university studies were distracted by his more downhome musical interests. While his mother attempted to direct him toward classical music, John had long been interested in more earthy tunes. Growing up rich, John's family had many servants, both black and white, and he took a liking in particular to the music he heard being played or listened to by the black servants in his household. He began to frequent the black music clubs in Harlem (a district in New York City) in his teens, and was highly influenced by a live Bessie Smith performance he attended in 1927. He became the first US correspondent for the UK's influential *Melody Maker* magazine in 1931, and dropped out of Yale around that time to pursue a career in the music industry.

Much to the benefit of the musicians whom he befriended, Hammond sometimes used some of his family's great wealth to fund his musical interests, including recording sessions, live performances of his favorite artists, and more. During the Great Depression, Hammond produced records for Columbia, by jazz greats Fletcher Henderson, Benny Carter, and others. He is said to have helped Benny Goodman get over the color barrier to hire guitarist Charlie Christian and vibraphonist/pianist Lionel Hampton.

The list of his accomplishments, and of the legendary artists he helped make famous during a six-decades-long career is too large to include here, but his influence on the blues must be mentioned. While he worked largely in the jazz realm, Hammond played varying parts in the careers of blues artists such as Sonny Terry, Big Bill Broonzy, Big Joe Turner, and late in his life, Stevie Ray Vaughan, as well as in the revival of the music of Robert Johnson, whom he had planned to showcase at the prestigious Carnegie Hall in New York City in 1938. Unfortunately, Johnson was—as far as we can tell—poisoned by a jealous husband, and died just a month or two before the performance. Hammond instead played recordings of Johnson's music to the largely white audience, during a break from an otherwise live concert, and continued to champion Johnson's music from then on.

Naturally, scouting for talent among the African-American blues community was not only a white man's activity. Chicago-based entrepreneur J. Mayo "Ink" Williams (1894-1980) is perhaps the most successful early black talent scout and record producer on record, and was the best selling race records producer of his time. He gets credit for the discovery of classic blues star Ma Rainey, and Papa Charlie Jackson, whose 1924 recordings of 'Papa's Lawdy Lawdy Blues,' and 'Airy Man

Big Bill Broonzy

Blues,' were the first successful, self-accompanied blue recordings by a male performer.

Ink apparently got his nickname from his ability to get blac musicians to sign his contracts. In a lengthy career which included work for Paramount, Vocalion, Decca, and Brunswick– along with his own label imprints, Chicago Recording Compan and its Black Patti label—Ink Williams worked with blues great Blind Lemon Jefferson, Tampa Red, Mahalia Jackson, Blind Bo Fuller, Blind Blake, and many others. His career lasted throug the early 70s. Interestingly, Williams is not only an inductee c the Blues Hall of Fame, but also the National Football Leagu Hall of Fame—he was one of only three black (American) footba players active in the first year of the NFL, when he played for th Pros out of Hammond, Indiana.

Country blues and the
guitar recordings of the 30s and 40s

It was figures such as Speir, Hammond, and Williams who wer the prime movers in the recording of many of the country blue artists we now regard as legendary. It was often through thes talent scouts' recommendations that a player landed in recording studio for the first time. Admittedly, the scouts had financial incentive to round up marketable new talent, but they clearly carried a love of the musi as well. Either way, they took their work seriously, and brought a lot of now household names int the spotlight.

Early recording engineers and producers took their work seriously too, though they were c course limited by the technologies available. The records credited to early blues singer/guitaris such as Barbecue Bob (1902-1931), a best selling artist for Columbia in the late 20s, or Ishman Brace (1901-1970), who first recorded for Victor in Memphis in 1928, came about during record compan field trips, and in sessions at small studios where the act of recording was still being pioneered.

Microphones, as we know them, were not invented until the mid 20s, and did not come int widespread use until later, and so early recordings were made direct-to-disc. Direct to disc was process by which the artist sang or played into a large sound collecting "horn"—the sam prominent feature we see on 20s and 30s record players. While the artist was performing, th recording machine literally cut the "groove" into a metal disc, capturing the performance, i effect, live. If the artist made a mistake, the recording of that song would have to begin again wit an unused disc. Artists routinely ran through a song a couple of times, which is one reason w often find alternate takes of early blues songs. The recording quality left much to be desired.

The metal discs these sessions created were then used as masters in the manufacture c duplicates. Though we now largely refer to vintage records as vinyl, many of the early records wel manufactured from other materials. Early 78s contain a core made of ceramic, powdered slate, c other materials, covered in shellac, and are somewhat fragile. Vinyl records did not appear unt he late 30s, and did not come into widespread use until World War II, when supplies of shellac were restricted.

Also, these early 78 RPM discs limited an artist to roughly three- to three-and-a-half-minutes per "side," which is why so many early songs are relatively short, and often do not include much in the way of instrumental improvisation. A typical Robert Johnson guitar solo, for instance, may last only a few seconds before he begins to sing again. And though we think of the 78 RPM era as one of singles (usually referred to as sides, as in, "Ma Rainey cut more than 100 sides during her career") popular artists did release "albums," in a sense, consisting of several 78 RPM records packaged and sold together. This type of album packaging was replaced in the 50s by the LP vinyl record, typically consisting of a dozen or so songs on one disc, which set the standard for what most people still think of as albums.

As sales of race records increased, and early country blues artists began to have success, more and more record labels brought these musicians into the studio. Memphis, Atlanta, Chicago, and New York had busy recording studios, but not all recording was done in the big cities. Robert Johnson made his recordings in a hotel room in San Antonio, Texas. And many a Delta blues artist made the drive from Mississippi to Grafton, Wisconsin, about 30 miles north of Milwaukee, to record at a studio operated by Paramount Records.

In a story which does not differ much from the beginnings of the Victor or Brunswick labels, Paramount Records sprang from a manufacturing background. The label was a division of the Wisconsin Chair Company, which had made some early phonographs. The company eventually began to press its own records, and then contracted with other record labels to press their records as well. Paramount enjoyed a large mail order business in the early 20s, and by the late 20s began to bring artists up to its Grafton facility to record. H.C. Speir sent several of his finds to record for Paramount, including Charlie Patton, Willie Brown, and Son House—who all accompanied each other during one session in 1930.

Unfortunately, the way these early recording stars were treated represents a bit of a black eye on the recording industry. They often weren't paid much for their efforts—sometimes just a few dollars per track, with no ensuing royalties. The artists were still eager, because they recognized that a commercially available record or a hit song could increase their live performance earnings potential; and the lure of stardom a record might bring was certainly better than life back home on the farm.

But with an unfortunate penchant for shortsightedness, they usually just took the money offered, laid down their songs, and went on their way—often signing contracts that forfeited all future earnings they may have been able to enjoy. Race records producers were certainly aware

OPPOSITE PAGE: Stevie Ray Vaughan. *THIS PAGE:* Charlie Patton

that these uneducated country musicians knew little if anything about copyrights, royalties, o contracts, and routinely took advantage of them—often feeding on their weakness for alcoho while putting a contract in front of them.

Field recordings and the Lomax family

Fortunately not all the early record producers used dollars and cents as their primary motivation or a lot of early music would have faded into silence long ago. Much of what we know today a the blues—particularly the early country blues—would never have been recorded if not for the hands-on approach taken by archivists. These museum-minded folk had a passion for preserving musical glimpses into the lifestyles and cultures of the Delta farm-workers and laborers, among other groups. Consequently, these fervent individuals routinely loaded recording equipment into their cars and criss-crossed the backroads of the nation looking for down-home and amateu musicians to record. In many cases, it wasn't talent scouting they were up to, unlike the Speirs Hammonds, and Williamses of the world, but rather the concept of capturing for posterity the actual songs and stories of the common people they met and interacted with on their journeys.

This type of archival work is known as field recording, and John Avery Lomax (1867-1948) and

his son Alan Lomax (1915-2002) are regarded as two of the world's most important field recording archivists of folk music styles, no only in America (John), but internationally (Alan).

John Lomax spent much of his life on college campuses—he earned a degree in English Literature from the University of Texa at Austin, and a Master of Arts degree from Harvard University. He worked as a college professor (Texas A&M) or administrator (The University of Texas). It was during his time a Harvard, under the tutelage of famed folklorists Barrett Wendell and George Lyman Kittredge, that Lomax found his true calling making field recordings of folk musicians and preserving their music and their memories. An early collection of cowboy songs, published in 1910 in a book titled *Cowboy Songs And Othe Frontier Ballads*, with an introduction by President Theodore Roosevelt, earned John Lomax national fame.

Lomax soon hit the lecture circuit and wa instrumental in the founding of folklor societies throughout the United States. A these appearances he often sang the songs he had collected, and his influence greatly enhanced efforts to preserve folk music styles nationwide, if not around the globe. All of John Lomax's early work, however, would be only a warm-up for his greatest achievement: his collection of more than 10,000 recordings for the Archive of American Folk Song, under the auspices of the United States Library of Congress. This is considered to be the most complete collection of folk music in the world.

In 1934 John was named honorary consultant and curator of the Archive of American Folk Song by the Library of Congress, a title he held until his death in 1948. With the help of his wife and all four of their children, but particularly his eldest son, John Jr, and younger son Alan, John Lomax Sr began traveling the countryside with portable recording equipment, capturing live performances from as many folk musicians as possible. Early childhood experiences had given him a special interest in African-American music, and it is through his work in the 30s and 40s, recording black musicians throughout the South, that we first heard much of the music we now know as the early blues.

Many of the Lomax recordings were done in prisons, such as the "Parchman Farm" (Mississippi State Penitentiary), because they found there, particularly among the great number of African-American inmates, a sort of time capsule of folk music. Some of the prisoners earned great recognition from or following their Lomax recording sessions, and a few went on to successful music careers after their incarceration ended. One of their great early finds was 12-string guitarist Huddie Ledbetter, also known as Leadbelly. Another early Lomax find was a pre-Chicago Muddy Waters.

After John's death in 1948, his son Alan carried on his great work, eventually traveling worldwide to record folk music, including plenty of musical genres outside the blues realm. Alan's recording excursions reached out to the islands of the Caribbean, and to Ireland, Great Britain, Italy, and Spain. Besides his collecting work and books, Alan eventually produced recordings, concerts, and radio programs, and was instrumental in the folk—and blues—revivals in Great Britain and the United States in the 40s, 50s, and 60s. One of Alan Lomax's great finds was bluesman Mississippi Fred McDowell.

The post-war blues and recordings of the 50s

As important and historic as the Lomax field recordings were, the tracks being laid down in actual recording studios were to become even more dominant in the advancement of the blues during the post-war period. Recording techniques and technologies had greatly improved by the 40s and 50s. With the relocation of a large number of leading blues artists to major population centers such as Chicago, Memphis, and Detroit (and to a lesser extent, New York, Los Angeles, and San Francisco) at the latter end of the Great Migration, the leading artists of the time found themselves in more highly equipped studios, capable of capturing truly professional audio. Sound and recording quality improved radically, as did the construction of the instruments on which the players made their music. Recordings made during this period have stood the test of time, and

OPPOSITE PAGE: Leadbelly. *THIS PAGE:* Mississippi Fred McDowell

many a modern recording engineer or producer seeks to re-create the sound of these records today.

As for the instruments, guitar manufacturers Fender and Gibson began to dominate the electric guitar and bass marketplace, with both Gibson and the C.F. Martin company making some truly well-built, mellifluous, and popular acoustic guitars. Electric guitar amplifiers had improved not only in sound quality, but in size and power as well. Microphones came into their own too, with many from this period still in use and greatly prized today. Also, by this time, recording had switched from direct-to-disc to a much superior reel-to-reel, magnetic tape technology, and multi-track recording began to enter into the picture, thanks in large part to inventor/musician Les Paul.

While some of the old guard of record labels continued to put out influential recordings, several new companies arrived on the scene in the 40s and 50s, some making a huge and still-resounding impact. It didn't hurt that the radio industry—and by then the television industry—were booming. Music marketing by the labels had also blossomed into a highly-developed art form of its own. In short record label reps had learned how to sell more music.

Modern Records, based in Los Angeles and founded in 1945 by the Bihari brothers (Jules, Saul, Lester, and Joe), largely made its name with John Lee Hooker. Other well known blues artists who recorded for Modern include Lightnin' Hopkins, Etta James, Floyd Dixon, and Pee Wee Crayton (thought to be the first blues guitarist to favor a Fender Stratocaster). As did many record labels, Modern created several imprints or subsidiary labels, including Crown, RPM, Flair, and Yuletide—and of course Meteor Records, out of Memphis, for whom Elmore James recorded.

Another noteworthy blues label during this era was Vee Jay Records, out of Gary, Indiana—a blue-collar industrial town and practically a south-side suburb of Chicago. Vee-Jay, launched in 1953, was a black-owned label founded by husband and wife team Vivian (Vee) Carter and James (Jay) Bracken. The label had early success with artists Jimmy Reed, Memphis Slim, and John Lee Hooker (Hooker, as did many artists, made his way to many labels during his early career, sometimes using pseudonyms and aliases to get around contractual obligations). Vee-Jay would eventually score even bigger successes in the rock'n'roll genre—the label had some early Beatles songs in its catalog through a licensing deal with EMI—before succumbing to financial mismanagement. Today some Vee-Jay releases are being re-issued online through Collectables Records.

Many other small labels played roles in the development of the blues, including Aristocrat (for which Muddy Waters recorded in 1947), Parrot (Lowell Fulson and Albert King), Aladdin (Clarence "Gatemouth" Brown, Lightnin' Hopkins), Excello (Lonnie Brooks, Lightnin' Slim), Cobra (Otis Rush, Magic Sam, Willie Dixon, Buddy Guy) and others too numerous to list. Some of the output of these record labels is now owned and/or distributed by major entertainment companies, such as EMI (Aladdin), and Universal Music Group/Vivendi (Cobra). Sadly, many other blues recordings and record labels have gone completely out of print and out of existence.

One name which will probably never fade out of existence, however, is that of the most successful and well-known blues label of the 50s and 60s. Chess Records scored more hit songs, by a longer list of prominent names, than any other blues label, past or present. Brothers Leonard and Phil Czyz (pronounced and later changed to "Chess"), built this all-important music machine after Leonard had bought into the fledgling Aristocrat Records label. He took over the label by 1950, and after bringing in his brother Phil, changed the name to Chess Records.

In its heyday, Chess Records was home to many of the biggest names in the field of the blues. It's no wonder that 50s era electric blues is commonly referred to as Chicago blues, even if the artist in question was not necessarily Chicago-based. But then Chess had a huge advantage over other labels, in that it had an incredible pool of local talent—performing nightly in the many bars and nightclubs around the city, and on the street corners of the city's famed Maxwell Street Market—from which to choose.

The Chess roster certainly reads like a Who's Who of 50s blues legends, and a family atmosphere often prevailed around the label offices—for better or for worse. The label's biggest stars, Muddy Waters and Howlin' Wolf, engaged in a sometimes less-than-friendly competition to see who was the biggest name on the label. Toward the end of the decade, players such as Chuck Berry and Bo Diddley saw their Chess recordings launch the rock'n'roll era. In between, everyone from Sonny Boy Williamson (II) to Jimmy Rogers to John Lee Hooker recorded blues for Chess. Little Milton and Memphis Slim had hits for Chess. Etta James, Lowell Fulson, Big Bill Broonzy, J.B. Lenoir, Junior Wells, and Little Walter called Chess their home at one time or another.

One of the key elements in the success of Chess and its artists may have been the label's house band. Many recordings by the label's biggest stars feature the same backing group, with bassist/producer/talent scout and songwriter extraordinaire Willie Dixon (1915-1992) often running the in-studio show. Along with Dixon, the most celebrated version of the Chess house band often featured Buddy Guy or Hubert Sumlin on guitars, Willie "Big Eyes" Smith on drums, and occassionally Pinetop Perkins or Otis Spann on piano.

OPPOSITE PAGE: Pee Wee Crayton (top); Jimmy Reed (below). *THIS PAGE:* Buddy Guy

Chess—and its subsidiary labels Checker and Cadet—operated out of several different locations in Chicago through the years, but the most famous address, memorialized in song by The Rolling Stones, was at 2120 S. Michigan Avenue, just south of Chicago's Loop business district. Today that hallowed ground is the home to blues great Willie Dixon's Blues Heaven Foundation, and operates as a blues museum and non-profit organization promoting young blues artists, and providing welfare for senior blues musicians. The Chess Records catalog is currently owned and distributed by Universal Music Group, with management of the music by Geffen Records.

Sixties blues and the birth of blues-rock

The 60s brought a lot of social change to America and the world, and that change was reflected in the music of the times. Beginning back in the late 40s, *Billboard* magazine, the leading American music industry journal, had changed the name on its chart of black-oriented hit songs from Race Records to Rhythm & Blues, or R&B for short (this genre is often referred to as soul music, of which soul blues is a sub-genre). As the 60s moved along, it seems that the "blues" aspect of that R&B genre began a decline which it has only occasionally reversed. For many young music fans of the 60s, the blues reflected the sounds and attitudes of an older generation—their fathers' music, so to speak. With the rise of the light-hearted and bouncy Motown Sound, a more danceable, pop-oriented musical style came to replace previous black listening preferences, blues songs topping the charts became more and more infrequent, and the overall market for blues began to diminish.

Add to this the boom in the popularity of rock'n'roll—symbolically launched in 1956 with its hip-shaking Memphis King, Elvis Presley, and furthered in the early 60s by the raucous sounds of California's sunny surf music, and ultimately with the "British Invasion" of the Beatles, The Who, and The Rolling Stones, among others—and the days of true blues music dominating the charts, or the attention of the public, were numbered.

Many of the blues labels reacted to these evolving musical tastes and rolled with the changes. Chess Records, for one, continued to crank out hits, sometimes leaning toward the rock market with the music of Chuck Berry and Bo Diddley, or the R&B/soul market, where they scored a series of hits with lesser-known artists. It is interesting to note that the Chess house band for its soul recordings featured the founding members of 70s funk superstars Earth, Wind & Fire: drummer Maurice White and bassist Louis Satterfield.

That is not to say that many great and highly influential blues recordings were not made during the decade, however. Freddy King (he used the spelling Freddie after 1968) scored a huge hit with his instrumental 'Hide Away' in 1961, which was covered a few years later by bandleader John Mayall with Eric Clapton. Buddy Guy's guitar playing on harmonica star Junior Wells' 1965 album *Hoodoo Man Blues* astounded everyone who heard it, as did his playing on the early-60s American Folk Blues Festival tours in Europe and the accompanying record releases. Led Zeppelin's Jimmy Page has cited it as hugely eye-opening, saying: "It influenced everyone."

B.B. King's 1965 concert recording, *Live At The Regal*, is routinely credited by rock stars and other celebrity guitarists—country star Dwight Yoakam's guitarist and producer Pete Anderson once told me the album had been a huge influence on his playing—as an essential, must-hear blues recording. And of course another landmark blues recording of the time was Albert King's 1967 *Born Under A Bad Sign*, recorded for Memphis label Stax with Stax house band Booker T & The MGs. The album was the blockbuster follow-up to (and included) King's 1966 hit 'Crosscut Saw,' which— in addition to the title track—was also eventually covered by Clapton.

New labels Arhoolie and Delmark also released a lot of great blues records during this period, some done field-recording style, some in studio, and with Arhoolie in particular re-releasing out of print records and archive material from other labels. California-based Arhoolie, founded by blues and roots music impresario Chris Strachwitz, largely concentrated on acoustic blues by players such as Mance Lipscomb and Lightnin' Hopkins. Strachwitz also recorded or re-released music from Big Joe Williams, Lil' Son Jackson, Big Joe Turner, Mississippi Fred McDowell, and Lowell Fulson during the 60s.

Delmark Records, founded by Bob Koester, run out of his famous Chicago retail record shop (Jazz Record Mart), and known for its roster of jazz stars, seemed to make its blues reputation by either beating cross-town rival Chess to the Chicago nightclub bandstands, or picking up noteworthy artists Chess had ignored. Delmark released excellent blues recordings by Junior Wells, Luther Allison, Jimmy Dawkins, Magic Sam, J.B. Hutto, Otis Rush, Little Walter, and many others, in a string of solid blues recordings that continued on into the 70s (and beyond— the label is still active).

Capitalizing on both the increased interest in early blues brought about by the folk and blues

OPPOSITE PAGE: Freddie King.
THIS PAGE: Lightnin' Hopkins (top); Otis Rush (below)

revival movements (and concert tours), plus the respect publicly paid to the blues by rising new rock stars such as The Rolling Stones, The Beatles, Eric Clapton, and others, many record labels began to crank out compilation albums or posthumous releases which themselves became highly influential. Chess records released a series of recordings in the 60s under the title *The Real Folk Blues*, with separate albums highlighting the music of Muddy Waters (1965), John Lee Hooker (1966), Howlin' Wolf (1966), and others. And the 1961 Columbia Records release *Robert Johnson: King of the Delta Blues* brought the original Delta blues star's music to a whole new set of ears.

New blues luminaries came onto the scene too. Some of the artists we first heard in the 60s who are now considered legendary performers include "Queen of the Blues" Koko Taylor; Taj Mahal; and Paul Butterfield, with guitarist Michael Bloomfield—two of the first white blues stars. In England John Mayall put together a variety of band lineups and recorded seminal blues recordings such as his 1966 release *Blues Breakers With Eric Clapton*, which landed in the Top 10 on the UK charts and remains essential listening for blues and rock fans to this day. And of course The Rolling Stones, named after a Muddy Waters song, included covers of many classic blues tracks on their first few albums. In fact, Mick Jagger and Keith Richards renewed an earlier childhood friendship as teenagers when they saw each other on a London train, Jagger carrying Muddy Waters and Chuck Berry albums he had purchased mail order from Chess Records. Later, Marshall Chess, who eventually took over the Chess family business from his father and uncle, claimed to have remembered shipping records to the then-unknown Jagger and Richards when he was working in the label's mail room. Mick and Keith eventually tapped Marshall to head their Rolling Stones record label.

The British blues movement

Hugely important catalysts in both keeping blues music alive during the 60s, and in its role as the primary "clay," so to speak, used in the modeling of rock'n'roll music, were the English musicians, bandleaders, and musical mentors Alexis Korner, Cyril Davies, and the aforementioned John Mayall. Largely through the actions and encouragement of these player/promoters, the "British blues" movement, as it was called, gave birth to many of the most important and influential rock bands in music history.

Throughout the 60s and into the 70s, blues aficionado Mayall brought a stream of young new

OPPOSITE PAGE: John Lee Hooker (top left); Howlin' Wolf (top right); Taj Mahal (below left); Michael Bloomfield (below right). *THIS PAGE:* Alexis Korner

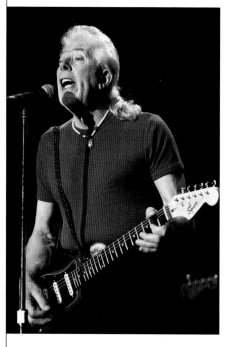

talent into the spotlight with his band and recordings, including future rock royalty such as Eric Clapton and Jack Bruce (who left together to form Cream); Mick Fleetwood, John McVie, and Peter Green (who left to form Fleetwood Mac); and Mick Taylor (who left to join the Stones). Guitarist and nightclub promoter Korner, along with his business and musical partner Davies, deserves credit for mentoring and developing most of The Rolling Stones, Rod Stewart, and Robert Plant, among many others. In Blues Incorporated, the group he formed with Davies, Korner encouraged these young musicians in all things musical, with a heavy dose of blues appreciation. He is often referred to as a founding father of the British blues and later went on to a lengthy radio career, always championing the blues.

Cyril Davies also had a hand in the launch of yet another hugely important rock band with roots in the British blues movement: The Yardbirds. Serving as his backup band at times, The Yardbirds gradually shifted from a blues cover band to a rock/pop outfit, and helped launch the careers of Eric Clapton, Jeff Beck, and Jimmy Page. In fact, Clapton, who featured on the band's first million-selling single, 'For Your Love,' in 1963, left the band to join John Mayall's Bluesbreakers in protest at The Yardbirds' move away from blues and toward pop music. The Yardbirds are considered

pioneers in the use of distortion, feedback, and modern amplification, and of course were a big influence on many American rock acts of the 60s and 70s.

The blues had a baby

Clearly, from the early-60s on—and continuing to this day—blues and blues guitar playing has been unbreakably linked to rock music, rock guitar playing, and many (if not most) of rock's most successful and legendary figures. The blues truly did have a baby named rock'n'roll, as Muddy Waters sang in 1977.

And as black interest in the blues waned in the 60s, white audiences became more interested, in part due to the changing faces on the bandstand. As young white guitarists such as Clapton, Beck, Page, Richards, and The Beatles' George Harrison fell in love with the blues and began to mold it into the early sounds of rock, white audiences fell in love with *their* music—and also in their roots.

American guitarists were listening too, both to these new English blues-rockers, and to the originators of the blues sound. From Seattle, James Marshall Hendrix—a touring sideman who backed artists such as Little Richard, Sam Cooke, Jackie Wilson, and The Isley Brothers on the Chitlin' Circuit of black-friendly clubs and theaters in the early to mid 60s—is said to literally have taken notes in the front row of many a Buddy Guy show. After perfecting his own songs and playing style, and making a quick move to London, Hendrix shook the music world with a blues-rock sound that still resonates today. There's a reason *Rolling Stone* magazine recently named Jimi Hendrix the Number One most important guitarist in their list of the top 100 six-stringers of all time.

In turn influenced by Hendrix, British blues acts such as The Bluesbreakers, Yardbirds, Stones, Cream, and Led Zeppelin, and of course the classic blues artists who started it all, now legendary rock acts such as Z.Z. Top, The Allman Brothers, Johnny Winter, Aerosmith, Van Halen, Lynyrd Skynyrd, and countless others have thrilled untold millions with their blues-based jams. Famous for their female-fronted pop/rock, Fleetwood Mac began as a blues-rock outfit. Australian rockers AC/DC are, in many regards, simply a high-volume blues band. Robin Trower, Foghat, George Thorogood, Bad Company, Humble Pie, and a countless list of classic rock heroes simply fused their blues interests with harder edged and more amplified sounds.

While, stylistically, true blues music has taken a back seat to blues-rock over the past few decades (which has itself been eclipsed by more modern forms of popular music since the 70s), there have been occasional blues resurrections, so to speak. One of the most important in recent memory began during the golden age of Music Television (MTV), circa 1984, when a young blues

OPPOSITE PAGE: John Mayall (top); Fleetwood Mac (below), featuring Peter Green (second from left). *THIS PAGE:* Jimi Hendrix

guitarist by the name of Stevie Ray Vaughan, out of Austin, Texas, lit up the small screen with entertaining music videos for his hits 'Cold Shot,' 'Pride And Joy,' and 'Couldn't Stand The Weather.'

Seemingly overnight, this soft-spoken hotshot guitarist brought blues and blues guitar crashing right through the pop music noise to the forefront of the music scene. He never failed to credit as influences his big brother (and Fabulous Thunderbirds founder) Jimmie Vaughan and a string of blues heroes whom he not only emulated but also routinely jammed with, including Albert King, Buddy Guy, and many more. Though he died tragically in 1990, Stevie Ray Vaughan has scores of imitators to this day, and his legacy is continually added to with DVD and CD boxed set releases which continue to inspire blues *and* rock guitarists worldwide.

Another big year for the blues came in 1994, courtesy (once again) of Eric Clapton. With the release of his return-to-the-blues album *From the Cradle*, Clapton again re-fired guitarists around the globe to dig into the blues roots from which he—and many of his listeners—sprang. Fueled by the Top 10 hit and Freddie King cover, 'I'm Tore Down,' the album reached the coveted Number One spot on *Billboard* magazine's chart of the Top 200 albums, something no other blues album had done in decades.

Over the next few years Clapton followed up that release with album and DVD releases paying tribute to Robert Johnson, a duet album with B.B. King, and several huge concert events featuring not only many of the biggest rock stars of the past 50 years, but also calling many of the living blues legends—such as B.B. King, Hubert Sumlin, and Buddy Guy—up to play right alongside the rock and blues stars they influenced. These concerts, which Clapton aptly dubbed Crossroads, have in turn opened the eyes of yet millions more music fans to the blues artists who initially made EC himself want to play guitar.

The state of the nation—where blues is today

At this juncture, blues music, blues guitar playing, and blues recordings have found relatively steady ground on which to stand. No longer the chart-topping genre it was a few generations ago, the blues is nevertheless stable, with plenty of originators still going strong, and plenty of fresh blood moving the music forward. Since the 70s, record labels such as Alligator out of Chicago, Blind Pig out of San Francisco, and Rounder out of Burlington, Massachusetts, have continually released great blues music. Relative newcomers to the blues scene include labels such as Fat Possum out of Mississippi, founded in 1992; Ruf Records out of Germany, founded in 1994; and NorthernBlues out of Toronto, which released its first album in 2001.

On the technical end, the digital recording revolution has played a part in the proliferation of blues music as well. Affordable home studios have enabled countless nightclub musicians and hobbyist weekend warriors to record and release their own blues albums within a reasonable budget. Digital recording has even caused the expense of recording in some professional studios—typically those which feature old-school analog tape decks—to come down, allowing more players to lay down tracks. And of course the internet, and now social media, have given blues artists known and unknown easy access to promotion, and allowed new generations of fans to discover blues music.

And what they're discovering is that all the varieties of blues—including many never dreamed of by the blues originators of a century ago—are keeping the music alive. Chicago blues, Delta blues, West Coast blues, East Coast blues, soul blues, jazz blues—there's an active blues sub-category for just about every taste.

Tools of the trade: the early instruments

As guitarists, we are often obsessed with the makes and models of instruments played by our favorite artists, and with capturing the exact tone of their specific gear. Early blues performers might chuckle at that notion, as they often played whatever instrument they could afford; and, given that many rose from very impoverished situations, those instruments were not usually of very high caliber. Still, there is a mystique and a certain charm to playing the blues on an instrument that may once have passed through the hands of an early Delta or Chicago bluesman. The vintage guitar market is driven by this type of magic.

The origins of the guitar can literally be traced back thousands of years, to Asia, India, and the Middle East, with plenty of evolution along the way. The guitar as we know it began to take a more familiar form perhaps as long as 1,000 years ago, probably inspired by the four-string oud and the six-string lute, which are often depicted in carvings and other artwork as early as the 8th and 9th centuries. In the 16th and 17th centuries, the Spanish vihuela, with six strings tuned in fourths, as is our modern guitar, may have been the immediate predecessor to the instruments of today.

However the instrument did evolve, it has been largely the same for at least two or three hundred years, though construction and manufacturing techniques and technologies have continued to move forward. While modern guitar manufacturing is largely handled by machine today, most instruments were, of course, handmade in days of old.

Naturally, handmade guitars were not being cranked out by the thousands every week, as they are today. As such, they were not as readily available in remote farming regions, far from a major city, such as in most locales in the Mississippi Delta. Also, because transportation of goods was not as efficient in the early 20th century as it is today, and demand wasn't what it is today, guitars simply weren't on display in stores in most communities. In fact, music stores then were few and far between. Consequently, many early musicians relied on instruments that could be purchased via mail order. Fortunately, these instruments could be acquired by the often poverty-stricken, full-time farm worker/part-time musician for a few dollars.

The American retail outfits Sears, Roebuck &

Blind Boy Fuller

Company and Montgomery Ward were hugely successful early catalog sales companies, with much of their clientele ordering from rural areas where local stores typically carried only the essentials of life. Montgomery Ward began to sell guitars through its catalogs by 1893; Sears first began selling guitars in 1894. Harmony, Washburn, and Lyon & Healy were among the first brands of guitars sold through these catalogs, with prices ranging from $4.50 to $26. Prices actually dropped a bit in the early years of the 1900s, with starter guitars going for as little as $2.45 (as a point of reference, $5 in 1930 would equal approximately $65/£40 today). By the early 20th century, Sears was the largest retailer of guitars, and many an early bluesman certainly learned or performed on Sears-bought guitars.

It's interesting to note that these catalog retailers advised that the earliest guitars be strung with "silk and steel" strings. Until the end of the 19th century, the three bass strings on a guitar were made of a silk core with a fine wire wrapping. The three treble strings were typically made of "catgut," though no cats were harmed in the making. Farm animals, however, were not so lucky, as catgut strings were typically made from the intestines of sheep or goats. They were expensive to make and did not stay in tune very well. With the rise of manufacturing around the end of the 19th century, steel guitar strings—which were less expensive to manufacture—began to gain in popularity. Unfortunately, using the newly created steel strings could damage the instrument and would void the warranty. Guitars of this period were often sold with replacement tailpieces, probably in recognition of the fact that guitarists would use the steel strings despite the possibility of damage and a voided warranty.

It's likely that, pre-amplification, early performers preferred the steel strings for their sheer volume, as compared to the silk or gut strings that had been in use for generations. Steel strings were also cheaper, lasted longer, and stayed in tune better. The out-of-tune recordings we often hear from this era may be due, in part, to the fact that these early instruments were not built to handle the tension of steel strings. Truss rods were not in use at this time either, so early guitars could easily have suffered from warped necks, especially if they were designed for gut and silk strings, and then fitted with higher tension steel strings. And for the players from the Mississippi Delta, and other areas of the American South, heat and humidity would have played havoc with the intonation and tuning of their instruments.

Prior to getting their first real guitar, it was not uncommon for early blues practitioners to get started with a cigar box guitar or a diddley bow. The cigar box guitar was born of necessity, with down-home craftsmen—those who couldn't afford to buy an instrument—literally using an empty cigar box as the body of their guitar, fitting it with some sort of neck and stringing it up to play. Cigar box guitars make for fun and creative home projects.

Primarily an American invention, the diddley bow was derived from a West African instrument which may have been brought to America centuries before the era of slavery. This simple musical instrument could be easily constructed using a wire and a couple of nails, possibly adding a bottle as a bridge. This is the way some early blues musicians got their introduction to stringed instruments. By nailing one end of a wire to the side of their house, and the other to the floor of their porch, and then plucking the wire while sliding a bottle or pocket knife up and down the "string" to change pitch, their musical journey was off and running. Chicago blues great Buddy Guy once told me he enjoyed toying with a diddley bow in his youth.

Slides and slide guitars

Perhaps these early interactions with the diddley bow played a part in making slide guitar so prevalent in the blues, especially early acoustic blues. If guitarists had grown up finding melodies with a slide on a diddley bow—a common childhood pastime of the era—then applying that same slide to an acoustic guitar would be a logical next step.

The art and craft of slide-making is long the lore of legend as well. While pocket knives were often employed as slides—and any metal tool might suffice—many a Delta blues man crafted a slide from the broken off neck of a glass bottle, hence the synonym bottleneck for slide. Of course, they would grind down the sharp edges before slipping their finger into their new slide! With so many quality slides available today, you really don't need to try this inherently risky do-it-yourself project at home, but if you must, there are instructions available online. Please use proper glass cutting tools and techniques if you want to attempt this procedure, and be careful!

One of the most popular glass slides of all is actually a small medicine bottle. Coricidin was a popular cough remedy (not to mention a potentially deadly recreational drug) of the mid 20th century. As Allman Brothers Band founder Duane Allman discovered in the 60s, the bottles in which this tonic came were perfectly sized to fit a guitarist's finger. Manufacture of the actual glass Coricidin bottles was discontinued in the early 80s, but shatter-proof replicas of these bottles have been made since the mid 80s, and are sold at music stores worldwide. In fact, due to the danger of breakage, modern "glass" slides are often made of shatter-proof Pyrex, or ceramic, porcelain, or other less fragile materials.

Of course the big debate among slide players will probably always be, "Which has the better tone, metal or glass?" Some say glass slides have a warmer sound; metal slides have a distinctive bite, and can sound quite trebly or even buzzy. The tone of either a glass or metal slide can be shaped to the user's liking easily enough using modern amps and effects. Many a player has used a simple socket wrench as a metal slide, including Paul Barrere of the band Little Feat, who told me he buys his slides in the Sears hardware department. (Barrere uses ⅜-inch sockets; he got the idea from Little Feat founder Lowell George, who used ¹¹⁄₁₆-inch sockets.) Small pieces of pipe will also do, and plenty of other items will work in a pinch as well, such as a cigarette lighter, a beer bottle, a shot glass, a stone—or anything that resonates.

Slide guitar—as is much early acoustic blues—is usually played fingerstyle, and commonly with the use of fingerpicks. Early fingerpicks were made of metal, and these bright sounding accoutrements are still very popular, though fingerpicks are also manufactured of various types of plastic today. Fingerpicks typically provide a brighter, cleaner sound than fingertips alone, and an

Duane Allman

increase in volume as well—which would have served a pre-amplified performer well in a loud and rowdy Delta juke joint. They take some getting used to, but they save on wear and tear on your fingertips and nails as well.

It is also important to note that, in the late 1800s and early 1900s, guitar often competed with banjo for a spot on stage. Banjos, by nature of their construction, could be heard over a crowd of boisterous club-goers (not to mention horns or percussion instruments), while early guitars might be less audible. As such, pre-electric guitarists would appreciate any new technology that would provide them with more volume. One such advancement was the introduction, in the late 20s, of the resonator or resophonic guitar. Any discussion of blues guitar—especially early acoustic blues—would be incomplete without mention of this still-popular instrument. Son House, Bukka White, Bo Carter, and Blind Boy Fuller, among many other bluesmen, were fond of playing resonator guitars throughout much of their careers.

Resonator guitars were initially constructed with metal bodies, and a built-in "speaker" system which would amplify, albeit acoustically, the sound produced by the guitar. This amplification was provided by a spun metal cone or cones, typically either one or three, which were attached to the bridge and placed inside the body of the guitar. Naturally, depending on their construction, resonator guitars are usually referred to as either single- or tri-cone (with a third designation, biscuit, denoting yet another design alternative). The resonator guitar did provide more volume than that of a traditional wooden-bodied guitar—not to mention a very distinctive sound—and quickly became popular.

Later versions of resonator guitar included wooden bodies fitted with the metal cones. Both are in use today, with blues players leaning toward the tri-cone metal bodies, and the wooden-bodied, single cone resonators often favored by bluegrass pickers. Resonator guitars are also available with either square or rounded necks, with the square-necked versions typically played lap-steel

Bukka White (top) and Eric Clapton (below) playing resonator guitars style—laid flat on the player's lap and with the slide held in the hand rather than worn on the finger.

The history of the resonator guitar is not without intrigue. The instrument was invented and first brought to production in 1927 by John Dopyera, at the request of steel guitarist George Beauchamp, with whom Dopyera founded the National String Instrument Corporation. Just a year later Dopyera left National to form the Dobro Manufacturing Company. The ensuing path of both of these companies—and the involvement of Dopyera and his brothers Rudy, Emile, Robert, and Louis—became complex over time.

Through the decades the names National and Dobro have come and gone, and production of resonator guitars by these companies has stopped and started—while other manufacturers took up production of the instruments. At various times the name Dobro was actually owned by guitar manufacturers Mosrite and Regal. Today the name Dobro is owned and aggressively defended (from a trademark standpoint) by the Gibson Guitar Corporation. Dobros and other brands of resonator guitars are readily available in various price ranges and with varying designs. Of course the pre-war (before 1941) Nationals are highly sought after today, and can be very costly to acquire.

The age of amplification

Eventually, of course, the benefits of volume provided by resonator guitars were made obsolete with the invention of the electric guitar and amplifier. Various tinkerers and musically-minded inventors had been dabbling in the electrical amplification of guitars and other stringed instruments—and filing patents—from as early as the 1910s.

George Beauchamp, he of the National resonator guitar company, developed an electrically amplified guitar in 1931, and with the help of a National director, Adolph Rickenbacker, brought the guitar to production in 1932. The Rickenbacker Electro String Instrument Corporation was founded in 1934, and soon afterwards National, Dobro, Epiphone, Gibson, and other manufacturers jumped into the mix and started producing their own electric guitars

The first electric guitars were typically archtop or acoustic guitars fitted with the newly invented transducers or pickups (as we know them). Big-band guitarists were early adopters of this new technology, as they quickly found the electric guitars could finally compete with the volume of a big-band horn section. Gibson's still sought-after ES-150, favored by Charlie Christian of the Benny Goodman Orchestra, was introduced in 1936, with the "150" representing the $150 for which the guitar sold. T-Bone Walker, a big-band guitarist with a bluesier take than Christian, was another early proponent of the electric guitar, as were Big Bill Broonzy and Tampa Red.

A few incarnations of solidbody electric guitar showed up almost right away as well, with the first "Spanish" style (the standard guitar body shape) electric appearing courtesy of the Vivi-Tone company by 1934. Audiovox may have produced various incarnations of solidbody electric guitars in the mid 30s too, and Rickenbacker started to market in 1935 a solidbody made of Bakelite, an early plastic.

Of course with the first electric guitars came the first electric guitar amplifiers. Early models of guitar amp may be traced to the use of modified PA amplifiers. By the mid 30s, Gibson and Rickenbacker were producing amplifiers specifically intended for use with an electric guitar, naturally to pair up with the electric guitars they were building and marketing.

As time marched on, guitar and amplifier manufacturing clearly became big business. By the 40s and 50s, quality had improved and new technology evolved. The Fender Electric Instrument Company, founded by radio repairman and inventor Leo Fender in the mid 40s—and initially earning success with lap-steel guitars during the Hawaiian music craze around World War II—created its first electric guitar amplifier in 1945, then pioneered in 1950 with its Esquire solidbody electric guitar. The Esquire was soon followed by the Fender Telecaster (which started production as the Broadcaster and, briefly, the so-called "No-Caster") and Stratocaster model solidbody electric guitars. Muddy Waters played a Fender Telecaster through much of his career.

Gibson was not to be outdone, however, and answered in the early 50s with the Gibson Les Paul, designed by and named after the already successful musician and inventor who also had much to do with the creation and early development of multi-track recording. To this day, the Gibson Les Paul, along with the Fender Tele and Strat (and arguably a few hollow or semi-hollow body guitar styles, such as Gibson's ES-335) are the uncontested champions of electric guitar body styles, copied by many competing manufacturers. In the decades that followed this Golden Age of guitar manufacturing, countless variations on guitars, amplifiers, and the related accessories and tools of the trade have arrived on the scene.

Modern blues players now have nearly 100 years of musical instruments to choose from, and their decisions on what gear to play naturally stem from the style of blues in which they specialize. A traditionalist, focusing on the music of the early Delta blues players, may have an old weather-beaten acoustic or National resonator in their collection. A proponent of the Chicago blues scene of the 50s may prefer an archtop electric and a Fender Bassman amp. A jazz-blues pioneer, readily moving the genre forward in the 21st century, may covet any number of modern guitar makes, and a digital modeling amp—replete with endless combinations of effects pedals. The choices are endless, but that same obsession with capturing the perfect, magical tone remains.

Muddy Waters (top); Mick Taylor in John Mayall & The Bluesbreakers (below)

Fifty blues guitarists you should know and hear

Limiting this list to 50 of the top players was frustrating—there are so many others who deserve mention, and who arguably could have made the list of the "Top 50 Most Influential Blues Guitarists of All Time." Who to include? Who to leave off?

As such, this list can't necessarily be considered the definitive "Top 50 Most Influential," but rather a pretty solid list of candidates, covering multiple genres of blues guitar playing. By the time you've acquainted yourself with the music of even a handful of these artists, you'll no doubt discover similar artists not mentioned here who might make your list.

Enjoy the music, and the journey, while you get started with this list of 50 really important blues guitarists.

ROBERT JOHNSON (1911–1938)

Style(s): Delta blues, acoustic blues

Robert Johnson is known as the King Of The Delta Blues, and is perhaps the single most important blues guitarist to have played and recorded during the original Delta blues heyday of the 30s. While he recorded only a scant 27 tracks, his music has been covered and covered again by countless artists, including The Rolling Stones and Eric Clapton—who dedicated an entire CD and DVD to Johnson's music. If you only hear one Delta blues guitarist, it should be Robert Johnson.

BIG BILL BROONZY (1893–1958)

Style(s): Country blues, acoustic blues, folk blues

Broonzy began his recording career in the 20s in Chicago, with a bit of a ragtime feel, but soon moved in a more bluesy direction. He had numerous hit songs through the 30s, and then, when electric blues made his music passé, he reinvented himself as a folk-blues revivalist. One of the first blues artists to tour Europe, he opened the door for the great folk-blues revival tours that influenced so many future rock stars.

SON HOUSE (1902–1988)

Style(s): Delta blues, slide blues, acoustic blues

Son House predates even Robert Johnson as one of the earliest blues stars. His slashing slide style influenced Johnson, Muddy Waters, and later generations. After recording in the 30s, House disappeared from the public eye for decades, but his career was revived with the 60s folk blues revival movements, when promoter Dick Waterman found him and brought him out of retirement.

CHARLIE PATTON (1887–1934)

Style(s): Delta blues, acoustic blues

Charlie (or Charley) Patton was one of the first Delta blues stars and a huge influence on those who followed, including Robert Johnson. A contemporary of Son House as one of the earliest blues guitar heroes, Patton lived the life of a rock star—and died like one, succumbing to alcohol poisoning before the age of 50. Patton lived at the famous Dockery Plantation, but traveled throughout the South performing showman-style guitar gymnastics that would have made Jimi Hendrix proud.

BLIND LEMON JEFFERSON (1897–1929)

Style(s): Delta blues, acoustic blues, Texas blues, slide blues

The original Texas blues guitar hero, Blind Lemon Jefferson recorded more than 100 songs—and died under mysterious circumstances befitting a blues star—before the 30s even began. His playing influenced later Texas bluesmen Lightnin' Hopkins and T-Bone Walker, and his many hit songs encouraged other male singers to play blues during the female-dominated classic blues era.

HUDDIE "LEADBELLY" LEDBETTER (1888–1949)
Style(s): Delta blues, acoustic blues
Known for his clear voice and 12-string guitar prowess, Leadbelly found fame after an Alan Lomax field recording trip discovered him at the Parchman Farm (Mississippi State Penitentiary). Leadbelly was pardoned shortly afterward and became the Lomaxes' driver, and a featured performer at many a 40s folk blues revival festival and coffeehouse concert. His music has influenced many folk and blues guitarists who followed.

MISSISSIPPI FRED MCDOWELL (1902–1972)
Style(s): Delta blues, slide blues
Discovered by archivist Alan Lomax in 1959, and later tracked down and recorded by Arhoolie Records founder Chris Strachwitz, life-long farmer McDowell found fame and life as a professional musician in his sixties on the 60s folk blues revival circuit—but he probably should have been recording since the 30s. Bonnie Raitt and The Rolling Stones have covered songs by McDowell, who was fond of saying, "I do not play no rock'n'roll, just the sweet and nach'l blues."

REV. GARY DAVIS (1896–1972)
Style(s): Delta blues, acoustic blues, Piedmont blues
Blind from early childhood, Blind Gary Davis was a Carolina-based multi-instrumentalist who began a recording career in 1935, and is a key figure in the early Piedmont blues style.

His fingerpicking influenced Bob Dylan, The Grateful Dead, Jackson Browne, Keb' Mo', and many others. Davis played ragtime- and Gospel-influenced blues, and enjoyed a resurgence in popularity during the 60s folk blues revival, performing at the Newport Folk Festival, and having his music covered by the likes of Peter, Paul, and Mary.

BARBECUE BOB HICKS (1902–1931)
Style(s): East Coast blues, Piedmont blues, slide blues
Columbia Records' best selling blues guitarist between 1927 and 1930, Barbecue Bob—so called because he was discovered by a Columbia talent scout cooking and playing guitar at a barbecue—was Atlanta's premier guitarist in his time. Bob played 12-string guitar, often with a slide, and recorded more than 70 songs.

SKIP JAMES (1902–1969)
Style(s): Delta blues, country blues
Nehemiah "Skip" James was an early star for Paramount, for whom he had recorded 26 sides in 1931. His music is eerie, full of creepy lyrics and otherworldly moans. He favored minor keys and used a D minor tuning, playing his guitar with a banjo style finger-picking technique. After leaving the music industry for 20 years, James was rediscovered in time for the 1964 Newport Folk Festival, and thereafter enjoyed a full time musical career until his death.

MICHAEL BLOOMFIELD (1943–1981)
Style(s): Chicago blues, electric blues, slide blues
Michael Bloomfield was one of the first white blues stars, and one of the first blues-rock guitar heroes. He grew up in Chicago and made himself at home as a teenager in the

black blues clubs on the south side, where he became a regular (not always invited) sit-in player with the likes of Muddy Waters, Howlin' Wolf, and other blues greats. He played on Bob Dylan's *Highway 61 Revisited*—and with Dylan at Newport when Bob infamously "went electric"—but is perhaps best known for his work in the Paul Butterfield Blues Band.

WILLIE DIXON (1915–1992)

Style(s): Chicago blues, electric blues
Technically, bassist Willie Dixon doesn't belong in this list of guitar players. But his influence on the entire Chicago and electric blues genre—and subsequently on rock'n'roll—is so huge, he cannot be overlooked. Dixon was the songwriter and producer (not to mention bassist) of many of Muddy Waters' and Howlin' Wolf's biggest hits, including 'Spoonful,' 'I'm Your Hoochie Coochie Man,' 'Little Red Rooster,' 'I Ain't Superstitious,' and too many classics to list here. Dixon's songs have been covered by countless rock stars, including Rod Stewart, Jeff Beck, Cream, The Rolling Stones, and many others.

BUDDY GUY (1936–)

Style(s): Chicago blues, electric blues
At the time of writing, Buddy Guy is arguably the world's second most important living blues guitarist, after his friend and mentor B.B. King. Guy initially made a name for himself as a Chess Records session guitarist, backing many of the Chicago blues greats during the early 60s. He was a huge influence on Jimi Hendrix, Eric Clapton, and many of the British blues-rock stars of the 60s, and later Stevie Ray Vaughan. Guy has cranked out a steady stream of hot blues records of his own over the past 50 years, tours incessantly, and is the proud owner of—as well as both a regular fixture and performer at—Chicago's most famous and popular blues club, Legends.

JOHN LEE HOOKER (1917–2001)

Style(s): Acoustic blues, electric blues
The master of one- and two-chord blues, John Lee Hooker made an entire career out of the incessant boogie groove that drove his first single, 'Boogie Chillen,' to the top of the charts in 1948. Influencing just about everyone who followed, Hooker recorded under a half-dozen or more aliases, almost always playing the same basic song. He was beloved by rock stars and movie stars alike—see his foot-stomping performance in *The Blues Brothers*—and appeared on major tours (with The Rolling Stones) and even major television commercials (Pepsi) before his death at the age of 84. A well-deserving member of both the blues and rock'n'roll halls of fame.

SAM "LIGHTNIN'" HOPKINS (1912–1982)

Style(s): Acoustic blues, electric blues, Texas blues
Lightnin' Hopkins successfully covered a wide range of blues styles during a music career that lasted from the early Delta through the MTV eras. In a worthwhile roots-style mentorship, Hopkins served as the eyes and chauffeur for Blind Lemon Jefferson, then played blues on the Texas club circuit for a couple of decades before finally finding the inside of a recording studio in 1946. But despite scoring some minor hits, Hopkins didn't seem fazed by success, and didn't like to travel, preferring to stay rooted in the dive bars of his Houston hometown. The folk blues revival tours of Europe in the 60s, however, seemed to bring him out of his shell. He's remembered for his low-down electric blues playing and sometimes nasty wah-wah work.

ELMORE JAMES (1918–1963)
Style(s): Electric blues, slide blues
The King Of The Slide Guitar, Elmore James was both a contemporary of Robert Johnson, and a kingpin of the early Chicago blues scene. His tone was monstrous—he rewired his own amps for more volume and distortion—and far more raucous than any heard before. Elmore's lick from 'Dust My Broom,' updated from his mentor Robert Johnson's version, is a must-know slide guitar lick.

ALBERT KING (1923–1992)
Style(s): Chicago blues, electric blues
Albert King played his guitar upside down and backwards, with the thick strings toward the floor, but that didn't stop him from playing some of the biggest bends in the blues. Albert was revered by Hendrix and Clapton, and copied extensively by Stevie Ray Vaughan, whom he mentored and with whom he recorded—listen to both their recordings of 'The Sky Is Crying' back to back and you'll hear the unmistakable influence. He is one of the "Three Kings" of the blues, along with B.B. and Freddie. Albert's 1967 hit 'Born Under a Bad Sign' has long been a blues jam standard.

B.B. KING (1925–)
Style(s): Chicago blues, electric blues
"The King Of The Blues" is still going strong as of this writing, performing hundreds of shows per year well into his eighties, and is the only remaining member of the "Three Kings." Possibly the most influential guitarist of all time, B.B. King even has a must-know pentatonic scale guitar position named after him in "B.B.'s Box." He scored his first hit in 1953 and hasn't looked back since. B.B.'s 'The Thrill Is Gone' may be the most well-known blues song on the planet.

FREDDIE KING (1934–1976)
Style(s): Chicago blues, electric blues
The other member of the unrelated "Three Kings," Freddie (spelled Freddy early in his career) was the youngest, but is nearly equally hallowed by rock royalty. Beginning in 1961 Freddie scored several rare instrumental hits with 'Hide Away,' 'San-Ho-Zay,' and 'The Stumble,' and later recorded a classic version of 'Goin' Down.' These songs soon became blues standards, and have been covered by the likes of Clapton and Beck, among others.

ALBERT COLLINS (1932–1993)
Style(s): Chicago blues, electric blues, Texas blues
Known as "The Iceman," Collins scored a million-selling instrumental hit called 'Frosty' in 1962, and then named almost every subsequent album after something based on the concept of ice and cold, hence the nickname. He played with his bare fingers and used a capo on a Fender Tele tuned to a minor key, pulling out blistering licks almost effortlessly. Collins was a big beneficiary in the renewed interest in the blues brought on by Stevie Ray Vaughan in the mid 80s, recording well received major label albums, touring extensively, and enjoying high-profile media exposure until his death of cancer at age 61.

MUDDY WATERS (1915–1983)
Style(s): Chicago blues, electric blues
If B.B. hadn't already laid claim to the title King Of The Blues, it would belong to McKinley Morganfield, aka Muddy Waters. He grew up in the Delta, but relocated to Chicago in time to become the most revered figure in the Chicago blues movement of the 50s and 60s, dueling it out constantly with Chess Records label-mate Howlin' Wolf for the top of the charts. Waters more or less invented the

electric blues band (and by extension, the modern rock band) format, and the Muddy Waters Band featured a Who's Who of legendary blues sidemen. He sang with authority, and played a mean slide guitar with a haunting quality that can sometimes be hard to re-create.

T-BONE WALKER (1910–1975)
Style(s): Electric blues, jump blues, jazz blues
Aaron Thibeaux "T-Bone" Walker grew up in a musical household and was playing professionally by age 15. He was mentored by family friend Blind Lemon Jefferson, and later by jazz guitar great Charlie Christian, and was possibly the first major player to use an electric guitar (some say it was Christian). In turn, Walker was one of the biggest influences on B.B. King, Chuck Berry, and Jimi Hendrix. Walker recorded as a teenager for Columbia, but it is his 1947 hit, 'Stormy Monday,' by which most modern guitarists remember him, and which was most famously covered by Bobby "Blue" Bland and The Allman Brothers.

OTIS RUSH (1935–)
Style(s): Chicago blues, electric blues
Otis Rush is yet another of the Chicago blues greats who launched their careers in the 50s heyday of the genre. More a West Side performer (like Magic Sam, Buddy Guy, Freddie King), than a South Side player (like Muddy Waters, Howlin' Wolf), Rush's blues and recordings have a slightly more up-town feel. His 1956 hit 'I Can't Quit You Baby,' was famously covered on Led Zeppelin's first album a dozen or so years later, and his 'All Your Love (I Miss Loving),' a blues jam standard, was covered by John Mayall's Bluesbreakers with Eric Clapton in 1965.

BROWNIE MCGHEE (1915–1996)
Style(s): Acoustic blues, folk blues, Piedmont blues
The acoustic duo of singer/guitarist Walter Brown "Brownie" McGhee and his long-time musical partner, harmonica player Sonny Terry, were kings of the folk blues revival of the 50s and 60s. Both had been protégées of Piedmont blues legend Blind Boy Fuller. McGhee and Terry performed and toured together for nearly 40 years, working 11 months per year and releasing dozens of albums between 1958 and 1980. McGhee's guitar style has influenced scores of Piedmont and country blues style players, including instructional legend Happy Traum who recorded McGhee in 1971 for a popular instructional guitar course.

JIMMY REED (1925–1976)
Style(s): Electric blues
Based on his many hit songs recorded for Vee-Jay Records during the 50s and 60s, Jimmy Reed could easily have been a much bigger star, but rampant alcoholism kept him from achieving all that he could. His hits 'Big Boss Man,' 'Baby What You Want Me To Do,' 'Bright Lights, Big City,' and many others were covered by the likes of Elvis, The Rolling Stones, The Grateful Dead, and many other rock greats. Reed was featured on the 1968 European American Folk Blues Festival and was inducted into the Rock & Roll Hall Of Fame in 1991.

HUBERT SUMLIN (1931–)
Style(s): Chicago blues, electric blues
Hubert Sumlin served as right-hand man and lead guitarist for Howlin' Wolf through most of Wolf's career—and also, for a time, played with Muddy Waters as well. As one of the few remaining elder statesmen of the original

Chicago blues scene of the 50s, former sideman Sumlin is enjoying renewed interest in his playing. He recently recorded an album that featured both Eric Clapton and the Stones' Keith Richards, and has appeared in the finale jam sessions at Clapton's "Crossroads" concerts. Sumlin's unforgettable guitar lines in Wolf's 1964 'Killin' Floor' (which also featured Buddy Guy on acoustic guitar) were famously re-created in 1969 by Jimmy Page on *Led Zeppelin II* with the cut 'The Lemon Song.'

LUTHER ALLISON (1939–1997)

Style(s): Chicago blues, electric blues
Another of the Chicago West Side greats, Allison mixed rock, funk, and even a touch of reggae with his blues. He recorded for a variety of labels, including Motown (one of a few blues artists the label signed), but by the late 70s, he was finding his biggest audiences in Europe. Allison moved to Paris in 1984 and lived there most of the rest of his life. He recorded a string of solid albums for Alligator Records in the 90s on which audiences can hear the fire and passion in his playing. He is survived by his son Bernard, a monster slide player in his own right.

FRANK "SON" SEALS (1942–2004)

Style(s): Chicago blues, electric blues
Born in Arkansas and playing music professionally by age 13, Seals spent time on drums (before switching to guitar) behind Robert Nighthawk, and also jammed with Albert King, Rufus Thomas, and Bobby Bland. Seals relocated to Chicago in 1971, where he was discovered by Alligator Records founder Bruce Iglauer playing in a South Side club. Seals was a fiery lead guitarist and gravel-voiced singer who recorded and performed live until his death due to complications of diabetes.

LONNIE BROOKS (1933–)

Style(s): Chicago blues, electric blues, swamp blues
Born Lee Baker, Jr, and playing and recording initially as Guitar Junior, Brooks got his start in zydeco king Clifton Chenier's Red Hot Louisiana Band, then began scoring his own regional hits in Texas and Louisiana in 1957. Brooks spent time in Sam Cooke's touring band before settling in Chicago in 1959 (where a previously established Guitar Junior forced his name change). Brooks has been a mainstay of the Chicago blues scene, and has toured worldwide ever since, with guitar playing sons Ronnie and Wayne as part of a family band. Brooks has headlined the Chicago Blues Festival (the world's largest blues fest), and his songs have been covered by the likes of Johnny Winter and The Fabulous Thunderbirds.

ERIC CLAPTON (1945–)

Style(s): Blues-rock, electric blues, acoustic blues, British blues
It would be no stretch to call Eric Clapton the most popular, successful, and well-known blues-rock guitarist in music history. His early 60s beginnings with The Yardbirds and John Mayall's Bluesbreakers established him, while still a teen, as the new blues whiz kid, and five decades later—despite all his mainstream rock success—it is still the blues that Clapton seems to return to over and over. He is probably the most important champion of the music on Earth, using his huge worldwide stature to keep the blues in our sights, routinely and repeatedly recording the music of his blues heroes, and bringing them on stage with him at nearly every opportunity.

JIMI HENDRIX (1942–1970)

Style(s): Blues-rock, electric blues
Perhaps the most influential guitarist of all

time, Jimi Hendrix—known for his rock pyrotechnics—was at heart a blues guitarist. He grew up listening to his father's Muddy Waters records, learned all he could at the feet of Buddy Guy, and was playing lead guitar for John Hammond, Jr, just before Chas Chandler, star bassist of The Animals, took him to London, hired Mitch Mitchell and Noel Redding to back him up, and made him a star. If you doubt he belongs in this book, listen to his recording of 'Red House' again.

ROBERT CRAY (1953–)
Style(s): Electric blues, soul blues
Robert Cray plays a smooth, R&B or soul-blues style that has scored him mainstream acclaim, hit songs, and high-profile opening spots and multiple guest appearances on Eric Clapton tours and at Clapton's "Crossroads" concerts. Cray's hotshot lead guitar-playing blends well with his soulful singing style to create a modern version of the classic 60s electric blues. The timing of his first big hit, 'Smoking Gun,' in 1986—along with the ascendancy of Stevie Ray Vaughan—deserves credit in helping to spur an 80s blues revival.

STEVIE RAY VAUGHAN (1954–1990)
Style(s): Electric blues, blues-rock
The smokin' hot blues and blues-rock guitarist from Austin, Texas, who almost single-handedly brought blues music back from the brink of death during the 80s. Vaughan's incendiary approach to traditional blues guitar playing rubs some purists the wrong way, but there is no denying his high-profile career—including hit songs, major tours, and popular MTV videos—brought blues music to the attention of more people and guitarists than anyone since the mid-60s British blues movement.

JIMMIE VAUGHAN (1951–)
Style(s): Electric blues, blues-rock, Texas blues
A founding member of the Texas blues-rock outfit The Fabulous Thunderbirds, and big brother (and mentor) to the late, great Stevie Ray Vaughan, James Lawrence "Jimmie" Vaughan has enjoyed a lengthy solo career since leaving the T-Birds in 1990. Initially rubbing shoulders with the likes of Jimi Hendrix in 1969, and later touring with the Stones and Clapton during the 80s, Vaughan has enjoyed a leisurely release schedule, with albums seemingly coming out only when he isn't busy working on his hot rods. A noteworthy proponent of Texas blues, with a lot of highly placed friends, such as Eric Clapton, who fortunately keep him from forgetting about guitar altogether.

TAJ MAHAL (1942–)
Style(s): Acoustic blues, electric blues, blues historian
A multi-instrumentalist and avid blues and music historian, Taj Mahal—born Henry Saint Clair Fredericks—has spent the past five decades blending the blues with roots-based music from Africa, the Caribbean, the South Pacific, and beyond. His work as a musician sometimes seems to be secondary to his work as a roots music preservationist, and he pulls both off in an educational and entertaining way. From his early recordings with Ry Cooder to his most recent releases, Mahal has woven traditional Delta, Piedmont, soul-blues, electric blues, reggae-tinged blues, Georgia Sea Islands-infused gospel, and every possible combination of blues-this and blues-that into his own fun and enlightening mix.

BONNIE RAITT (1949–)
Style(s): Acoustic blues, electric blues, blues-rock, slide guitar

Bonnie Raitt's blues slide guitar playing was considered a strong point long before she hit the major commercial success she achieved in the late 80s with her multi-million selling album *Nick Of Time*. She earned her stripes in the 60s blues revival circuit under the mentorship of promoter Dick Waterman, playing alongside the likes of Howlin' Wolf and Mississippi Fred McDowell. Raitt has long championed traditional blues artists and her slide playing has influenced generations of players.

KENNY WAYNE SHEPHERD (1977–)
Style(s): Electric blues, blues-rock
Kenny Wayne Shepherd found his way to the blues while still a child, and was performing regionally around his hometown area of Shreveport, Louisiana, by his early teens. A worldwide blues-rock star by the age of 16, Shepherd has proven his mettle since, with a string of successful blues-heavy rock albums, a half-dozen hit singles, and more guest spots on stage with blues legends, such as B.B. King and Eric Clapton, than many rock stars twice his age. Shepherd plays largely in the style of Stevie Ray Vaughan, with a kick-ass rock style that nevertheless is firmly rooted, song after song, in the blues.

DUANE ALLMAN (1946–1971)
Style(s): Electric blues, blues-rock, slide blues
Founding member of the Allman Brothers Band, Henry Duane Allman played slide guitar with a spark and expertise that is still revered to this day. Allman was just shy of his 25th birthday when he died in a motorcycle accident, but his legacy lives on, and 40 years later he is still regarded as one of the most influential blues-rock guitarists in history (*Rolling Stone* magazine named him second only to Hendrix in their recent list of the top 100 guitarists of all time). His incomparable

bottleneck work courses throughout the early music of the band he founded with brother Gregg, but perhaps his most celebrated track is that of the dueling slide parts he played with Eric Clapton on 'Layla,' one of the most popular rock songs of all time.

DEREK TRUCKS (1979–)
Style(s): Electric blues, blues-rock, slide blues
Carrying on ably and humbly in the footsteps and huge shadow of Allman Brothers Band founder Duane Allman, young Derek— nephew of the band's drummer Butch Trucks—is perhaps the most capable slide guitarist of the early 21st century. Derek's work with the ABB has always honored Duane's legacy while adding his own jazzy, world beat influenced guitar style. Trucks' playing with his Derek Trucks Band, which he started when he was 15, takes his blues slide guitar playing to an even loftier locale, bringing in the influence of jazz great John Coltrane and the ragas of Indian music, while still retaining a heavy blues flavor.

GEORGE THOROGOOD (1950–)
Style(s): Electric blues, blues-rock, slide blues
George Thorogood boogies in the style of John Lee Hooker, and attacks his slide playing much in the vein of Elmore James. His many blues-rock flavored hits, such as 'Bad To The Bone' and 'I Drink Alone'—and the accompanying videos—portray a larger-than-life persona of the loner, bad-ass bluesman, and Thorogood plays it to the hilt. His good-time boogie blues, and particularly his bottleneck work, have done much to keep slide blues alive over the past 30 years.

ROBBEN FORD (1951–)
Style(s): Electric blues, blues-rock, jazz blues
Beginning in the 70s, Robben Ford has worked

with such diverse artists as Miles Davis, Joni Mitchell, Jimmy Witherspoon, Charlie Musselwhite, and jazz fusion pioneers LA Express and Yellowjacket. But it is almost always the blues to which he returns. Since early in his career Ford has routinely released killer albums mixing traditional blues motifs with his capable jazzy riffing, not to mention a big dose of rock guitar-hero techniques. His style sets the tone for a more advanced look at blues music for all future artists to consider.

JOHNNY WINTER (1944–)

Style(s): Electric blues, blues-rock, acoustic blues, slide blues

A Texas bluesman who crossed back and forth over the blues and rock border early in his career, Winter has primarily focused on blues since the late 70s. He performed at Woodstock, alternately shared the stage (and studio) with the likes of Rick Derringer and his keyboard-playing brother Edgar, and revived the career (and finances) of Muddy Waters as producer of a trio of great Waters albums during the late 70s. A monster slide player on either electric or resonator guitar.

KEB' MO' (1951–)

Style(s): Acoustic blues, Delta blues, electric blues

Almost a quarter century passed between Kevin "Keb' Mo'" Moore's first recordings, backing Jefferson Airplane violinist Papa John Creach on four albums, and Mo's 1994 debut album. In between he served as a staff songwriter for A&M Records and as a demo producer. His first solo album featured two Robert Johnson covers, and Mo' has never strayed too far from the acoustic blues since.

JOHN HAMMOND, JR (1942–)

Style(s): Delta blues, acoustic blues, slide blues

The son of famed blues and jazz impresario John Henry Hammond, John Paul Hammond, Jr, has created a legacy of nearly 50 years worth of solid Delta and acoustic styled blues recordings. In his 60s Greenwich Village days, Hammond actually had both Jimi Hendrix and Eric Clapton in his band, albeit for only a matter of days. Hammond routinely performs on resonator guitar, and is primarily a blues traditionalist, certainly worthy of more acclaim than he has achieved.

JOHN MAYALL (1933–)

Style(s): Electric blues, British blues

Though Mayall is a solid blues guitar player and vocalist in his own right, he belongs on this list as a bandleader and talent scout, and a kingpin of the British blues movement. If not for Mayall setting his ego aside and hiring the likes of Eric Clapton, Peter Green, John McVie, Jack Bruce, Mick Fleetwood, Mick Taylor, and later players such as Walter Trout and Coco Montoya, the blues and blues-rock guitar worlds would have been a very different place. Mayall's performing and recording career, which began in the 50s, continues to this day.

CHUCK BERRY (1926–)

Style(s): Electric blues, Chicago blues, blues-rock

Chuck Berry signed with Chess Records in 1955 and quickly released 'Maybellene,' which went to Number One on the R&B charts that September. A quick string of still-classic hits followed—'Roll Over Beethoven,' 'Rock And Roll Music,' 'Johnny B. Goode'—and Berry secured his place as one of the main links in the chain between blues and rock'n'roll. Nearly 60 years later, Chuck Berry-style riffs are everywhere—from blues to rock to country to heavy metal. Indeed, "all of Chuck's children are out there, playing his licks," as Bob Seger put it.

DUKE ROBILLARD (1948–)

Style(s): Electric blues, Chicago blues

A former member of Roomful Of Blues, and in 1990 the replacement for Jimmie Vaughan in The Fabulous Thunderbirds, Robillard has now enjoyed a lengthy solo career including dozens of worthy releases peppered with spicy blues licks. Overall Duke plays in a style reminiscent of T-Bone Walker or Freddie King, but his voluminous discography includes excursions into almost every imaginable blues sub-genre. A masterful player.

BO DIDDLEY (1928–2008)

Style(s): Electric blues, Chicago blues, blues-rock

Ellas Otha Bates McDaniel, aka Bo Diddley, grew up on Chicago's South Side and got much of his early playing experience at Chicago's famed Maxwell Street Market, where he performed on street corners during World War II with Earl Hooker and others. Recording for Chess, he hit the top of the R&B charts with the song 'Bo Diddley' in 1955, followed by a string of other hits. Diddley played a unique rectangular guitar, and helped bridge the gap between blues and rock. His "Bo Diddley beat" is required knowledge for any rock or blues guitar player.

LITTLE CHARLIE BATY (1953–)

Style(s): Electric blues, Chicago blues, blues-rock, jazz blues, jump blues

Founder of (and now retired from) Alligator Records artists Little Charlie & The Nightcats, Baty is one of the key living links to the playing of T-Bone Walker. Baty's Chicago-meets-jump-blues fretwork is sometimes also mixed with western swing and even surf, but he is truly a West Coast blues monster. Now pursuing jazzier varieties of his favorite genre, Baty is a modern blues master who really must be heard.

BILLY GIBBONS (1949–)

Style(s): Blues-rock, electric blues

The driving force behind blues-rock heavyweights Z.Z. Top, the "Reverend" Billy Gibbons channels John Lee Hooker, B.B. King, and Albert King on a nightly basis. With his favorite Les Paul, "Pearly Gates," a host of other custom and weird guitars, and an ever-changing collection of overdrive pedals, Gibbons has cornered the market in beefy tone and cool pinch harmonics. Routinely re-inventing his image, the leader of the "Little Ol' Band from Texas" nevertheless has kept down-and-dirty blues at the heart of the group's sound since the very beginning.

Tutorial
PART 1
BLUES GUITAR BASICS

Getting started

Before we dig in to the specifics of blues guitar playing—no matter which type of blues you are interested in learning to master—this section of *The Blues Guitar Handbook* will cover some helpful equipment basics. In this section you'll find suggestions on what type of guitar to get started with, whether you should practice standing or sitting, how to choose the right guitar pick, and general information on gear, including amplifiers, effects, and more. Let's get the journey started!

Guitars

Many first-time guitar students question whether acoustic or electric guitars make for better first instruments. The definitive answer is … it depends. It depends on the style of music you ultimately wish to play. If you're aiming at learning the styles of Robert Johnson or Keb' Mo', an acoustic guitar is probably the way to go. If you're more interested in playing in the style of Buddy Guy or Eric Clapton, an electric guitar is probably a better choice.

But either way, as a guitarist, you should know that acoustic and electric guitars are pretty much the same instrument—and that as a guitarist, you'll probably end up owning both an acoustic and an electric guitar (or more than one of each) in the long run. While it seems most people choose to start on acoustic guitar, electric guitars often prove to be easier for total beginners to play.

One main reason electric guitars are sometimes easier to play is because electric guitars often use a thinner or "lighter" gauge string, which is easier to press down on the fretboard. Of course, if you already have an acoustic—and if you've ever felt that it was difficult to play, or if it even hurt your fingers to press down on the strings—try putting a set of light gauge electric guitar strings on your acoustic. Pros do it to make acoustic lead guitar playing easier, so there's no reason you can't do it as well.

How much to spend

If you've got a spare $75,000 or so to spend on a vintage 1957 Gibson Les Paul, go for it. But these days you can get a decent starter guitar in the $100 price range, and sometimes even less. Many music stores also offer "starter packs" which include an inexpensive electric guitar, plus a small amplifier, and the cords with which to plug in. This is a great way to get started making music.

A word of warning: You should know that guitar players often become afflicted with GAS, or Gear Acquisition Syndrome. In other words, once you start on the journey of guitar playing—particularly electric guitar playing—you'll probably start wanting to buy new gadgets and accoutrements to go along with your electric guitar and amp. It's a fun, but potentially expensive proposition. My advice is just to go for it and enjoy the ride.

I often tell students to get started on a less expensive instrument, and then upgrade after you've made some progress. This gives you time to be sure you are really going to put in the requisite number of hours you thought you were going to devote to guitar playing before buying an expensive instrument. It also gives you time to become familiar with a variety of guitars before settling on one particular model.

Many guitarists find that, over time, they end up wanting to own at least one each of several different classic guitar models, typically including a Gibson Les Paul, Fender Stratocaster and Telecaster, some sort of hollowbody electric, and a nice acoustic guitar. There are many other great guitar manufacturers making popular guitars today as well, and a Paul Reed Smith, Guild, Gretsch, Rickenbacker, or other make and model guitar may eventually find its way on to your wish list too. Simply learning about and researching all these different guitars—and the amps and effects that eventually go with them—is part of the fun.

Take a look at the makes and models played by your favorite artists, and do some research before heading out to a music store to try out a few guitars. A good rule of thumb for guitar shopping is, if it feels right, it is right. But when you pick up a guitar in a store—no matter how cool or pretty it looks—if it doesn't feel right and comfortable to play, it probably isn't the guitar for you. Also be aware that the same model of guitar may come with different neck shapes, or there may be a difference in the way two otherwise identical guitar models feel to you. Go with your instincts, and don't just buy a guitar based on its looks.

This is why you should actually play as many guitars as possible before committing to a purchase. Also, for this reason, I don't recommend buying guitars online for anyone who isn't already quite an experienced player, unless that online purchase is so inexpensive that it won't matter if it turns out to be less than the perfect guitar. I have bought perfectly good guitars online—without playing them—for less than $50.

Still, I recommend that most players stick with purchases from real music stores where they can actually play the guitar on which they are about to spend money. And don't be shy about your playing ability. If you're there to spend money, make sure you spend a couple of minutes playing each guitar, trying out all the different guitar techniques you know on each instrument.

Once you have your guitar

OK, you've got the guitar home. Now what? It's very helpful to set up a practice area, some place comfortable where you can leave your guitar set up on a stand, ready to play at a moment's notice—and any time the inspiration hits you. You're far more likely to pick up the guitar and play if it is out and visible, rather than locked away in a case, under your bed, or in your closet.

Your practice station should include a comfortable chair—one without arms—a music stand on which to put this book, and of course your guitar and amp. Also essential is some type of music playback device, whether that be a CD player, a small stereo, your mp3 player's docking station, or your computer. In the 21st century, many players find that practicing in front of their computer provides many benefits, including access to music-related software, the internet, the ability to pop in an instructional DVD, CD, CD-Rom, or to plug in your mp3 player to jam along with. Consider these options when setting up your practice area. You will also need an electronic tuner or you can use the tuning tones on the *Blues Guitar Handbook* CD (Track 1).

CD TRACK 1

Also, it is important to know that guitars prefer comfortable temperature and humidity, much the same as humans. Keep your guitar at room temperature as much as possible, and away from sources of heat or cold, including sunny or drafty windows, and heating and air conditioning vents. Never leave your guitar out in the cold or hot garage or car, or the instrument may be damaged, and will almost certainly develop tuning problems. You may also need to run a humidifier or de-humidifier depending on the conditions in your home.

Playing position

Most players prefer to practice sitting down when playing and practicing alone. If so, the body of the guitar should rest comfortably on your right thigh if you are right-handed, or on your left thigh if you are left-handed. You want your thigh parallel to the floor so the guitar does not slip away from you while you are playing. Use some sort of footrest if necessary. Holding on to the guitar should not be a struggle. If there's a problem, fix it now so you can concentrate on playing the guitar, not holding the guitar.

Try to keep the neck mostly parallel to the floor as well, or slightly tilted upward. However you hold the guitar, you do not want your fret-hand wrist to be in an awkward position. If your wrist is bent too much, try changing the position of the guitar neck. Also, your fret-hand elbow should not be pressed tightly against your body, but should instead be out away from your body. Adjust your playing position if necessary to make this right.

If you play in a band you might find yourself rehearsing standing up. The choice to stand or sit is ultimately yours, as is the way to wear your guitar if you are standing. No one can tell you how best to adjust a guitar strap—how high or low to wear a guitar while standing is strictly a personal decision. Try starting with the top edge of the guitar just above your belt buckle and then move it up or down depending on your comfort level.

SECTION

What about guitar strings?

Much like your preference for a certain playing position, a player's preference for a certain brand, style, or size of guitar string is mostly a personal decision. With experience, and over time, you will come to understand the differences and form your own opinions on these matters.

Overall, you should do what feels comfortable to you, not what another player or a manufacturer's ad with some cool looking rock star or sexy model tells you to do. There are dozens of string manufacturers, and most buy their raw materials (steel wire, etc.) from the same sources. I have had major string manufacturer representatives admit this to me. You don't need to spend a fortune on guitar strings to get a good quality string.

As for sound, the various string brands all sound pretty similar to all but the most picky listener. As a novice guitarist, you shouldn't worry about brand, but instead should focus on string gauge. The basic rule of thumb with guitar strings is, the thicker the string, the better the tone (and the more volume). However, thinner gauge strings are much easier to play.

You can always work your way up to heavier gauge strings over time, as your playing becomes more advanced, and your fingers build strength and stamina. It's not fun to play on heavy gauge strings if you aren't conditioned to them. If you're fighting against strings that are uncomfortably stiff and rigid, a sure sign they are too heavy for you, you won't want to practice on those strings. Change to a lighter gauge string if thick strings are causing you to avoid playing and practicing.

Brand new acoustic guitars typically come with a set of "light gauge acoustic" guitar strings, which usually range from .012 (12 thousandths of an inch) or .013 on the thinnest string (the high E-string), to approximately .052 for the thickest string (the low E-string). Acoustic guitars also come with a "wound" third (G) string. Wound strings are not easy to bend, and in lead guitar playing—particularly blues-based lead guitar playing—the third string needs to be bent frequently (bending is a technique we will cover in this book).

A brand new electric guitar is typically strung with a set of "light gauge electric" strings, which typically range from .009 to .042, or even .046 on the thickest string. Also, sets of electric guitar strings usually come with an "unwound" third string, making it much easier to bend. Naturally, it is easier to play on these lighter gauge electric strings—for most players, and certainly for beginners—than on regular acoustic guitar strings.

Don't be afraid to put a set of light gauge electric guitar strings on your acoustic guitar to make playing that guitar easier and more fun. Again, as your strength and stamina build, you may eventually return to regular acoustic strings—or not. Guitarist Lurrie Bell, son of 50s Chicago blues harmonica great Carey Bell, once released a father and son album featuring some incredibly hot acoustic lead guitar playing. When I spoke with Lurrie about this he told me he recorded that album using an acoustic guitar strung with light gauge electric strings. If he can do it, so can you and I. Of course you should not put metal guitar strings of any kind (acoustic or electric) on a nylon-stringed "classical" guitar. This could tear the bridge off the guitar, warp the neck, and ruin the instrument.

What kind of guitar pick should I use?

A player's choice of guitar picks is also a personal matter. Picks come in all shapes, sizes, thicknesses, colors, designs, and materials. As an inexperienced player you should audition a variety of different plectrums before settling on a particular brand or design. You may find that playing comes easier to you with something other than the pick you started with—or not. But you owe it yourself to shop around a bit.

Early guitar picks were almost always made of celluloid, and many players still use those picks. Celluloid guitar picks frequently tear, however. There are other materials, such as vinyl, used to make guitar picks that never tear, though they do eventually wear out. There are also exotic guitar picks available, made of materials such as felt, bone, metal, or stone, among others.

Some players debate whether a thicker or thinner guitar pick is better. Again, it's a matter of personal opinion. However, you might find that thin guitar picks work well for simple strumming, as you might do on an acoustic guitar if you are primarily a rhythm guitar player. Lead guitar players may find that a thicker, stiffer pick works better, particularly if the player is prone to faster playing.

Once you decide on a certain design of guitar pick, you might want to find a way to buy those picks in bulk to get a better price. You can even get custom-designed guitar picks printed with your name or artwork on the pick—but you might want to wait until your album release party to shower those on your adoring fans.

Also, I've found that the simple act of putting a guitar pick in your pocket every morning will lead to more guitar playing. A lot of players seem to be forever without a readily accessible guitar pick, and thus don't take advantage of all the opportunities to play guitar or try out a new instrument when that opportunity presents itself. These players lose valuable chances to experience new guitars, and end up practicing less. Just get in the habit of putting a guitar pick in your pocket every morning, and you'll end up playing more guitar—and improving faster.

What about fingerpicks?

If your preferred guitar style leans toward Delta blues, you may want to begin using a comfortable set of fingerpicks. These are guitar picks that fit over your fingertips, as a sort of extension of your fingernails. Again, just like regular picks (sometimes referred to as flat picks), fingerpicks come in all shapes, sizes, designs, and materials—and you should try out a variety of these before settling on the set which works and feels best for you. Fingerpicks definitely take some time to become accustomed to, but they give your playing a bright and aggressive tone you simply won't get from your fingertips alone. They also spare your fingernails from wear and tear.

Some players—particularly country guitar pickers—use only a thumb pick, and they use their bare fingertips for any other fingerpicking needs. Resonator (steel-bodied) guitar players tend to use fingerpicks on their thumb and first two or three fingers. Again, that choice is a matter of personal opinion. Shop around and try out a variety of fingerpicks, and consider not just playing comfort, but tone as well, when you audition the various models. You'll notice that metal fingerpicks have a brighter tone than vinyl fingerpicks. The choice is yours.

What is a capo?

A capo is a small, inexpensive device that clamps across the fretboard of your guitar, raising the pitch of the notes played, much like fretting a higher note. Many players use a capo to facilitate easier playing up the neck of the guitar. Albert Collins was a well-known blues guitarist who frequently used a capo in his playing.

With a capo, a player can use the basic guitar chord shapes far beyond the "open position" in which we play when not using a capo. This makes it easy to change keys between songs—something you might need to do to accommodate a particular singer's vocal range—even with limited guitar skills. Also, if a player is not fluent with barre chord shapes, which are the typical technique a guitarist uses to play higher on the neck, a capo can help overcome this deficiency.

But capos are not used only to overcome playing issues. They can also provide a guitarist with a certain tone which differs from either an open-position or a barre-chord guitar tone. Just like with your choice of a certain brand, or particular gauge of guitar string, or style of guitar pick, the use of a capo is a personal decision. You may find that you almost never use a capo, but that simply putting one on your guitar once in awhile can spur new creative ideas you wouldn't otherwise have achieved.

Amplifiers and effects

After finding that dream guitar, an electric guitarist immediately starts fantasizing about amplifiers. Over time you may discover that, though you can spend thousands on a "boutique" guitar amplifier, you may actually prefer the sounds you can get from a tiny practice amp. Many a famous recording was made using the smallest and least expensive of guitar amps. Jimmy Page of Led Zeppelin famously recorded most of the great blues and rock tunes on his band's first two albums using little more than a 10 watt Fender Princeton amp, cranked up real loud in a room with great reverberation.

Your purchase of a guitar amplifier probably has more to do with budget than anything else, but rest assured there are a great many options available, and in all price ranges. The amp that comes with an inexpensive guitar starter pack is often perfectly suitable for years of good times. Add to that some basic effects pedals (more on those in a minute), and you may have all the amp you'll ever need.

There are a few classics, though, and you should know at least a little about some of them. The aforementioned Fender Princeton is a great little amp. Fender Twin amplifiers, along with that company's Bassman and Showman models have long been favorites among guitarists. These are examples of "combo" amps, which include the speakers and electronics in one component. Most amplifier manufacturers make combo amps. Marshall, Vox, Mesa Boogie, and Peavey all make popular lines of combo amplifiers.

Players who want something bigger—typically for live concerts—may opt for a separate speaker cabinet and an amplifier "head." A classic example of this head and speaker cabinet combination is the Marshall "stack" or "half stack" which was at one time favored by Jimi Hendrix and Eric Clapton (in Clapton's Cream era). You won't need this much wattage or this many speakers, however, unless you're playing in very large clubs or auditoriums, or you just happen to enjoy hearing ringing in your ears.

Amplifiers new and new-old

"New-old? What in the world is that?" I hear you asking. By new-old I mean amplifiers that are built brand new either to the exacting specifications of a particular model of old—we call them vintage—amplifier, or amps that are built using new technology, such as digital, to emulate the sound of vintage amps.

A key element to amps built to vintage specs, is whether or not the amplifier uses good old vacuum tubes to generate tone and power. Players typically feel that tube-driven amps (as opposed to solid state or digital) have a richer tone than those built without tubes. For many years—largely from the late 60s until the early 90s—amp manufacturers moved away from tubes. Public outcry, and possibly common sense, eventually brought tubes back into favor, however.

There are also amplifier purists out there who say they can hear the difference between an amp that is "hand-wired" and amps built using modern manufacturing techniques. Hand-wired amps are, as the name suggests, built entirely by hand—as was done in the Golden Age of the classic guitar amps, for instance the 1959 Fender Bassman amp. Many sought-after vintage amps were hand wired, one at a time, before amp manufacturers began using modern assembly line and later computerized manufacturing techniques.

If you are one of these purists, you can find small amp manufacturers who build amps to the original designs, using as many of the original parts (or parts made to the same specs) as possible. Amplifier builders such as Victoria, Matchless, or Tone King have specialized in these new-old amps over the years.

The other new-old I've mentioned pertains to digital amplifiers that use modern technology to "model" the sounds of vintage amps. These digital modeling amplifiers, as they are called, such as a Fender CyberTwin or a Roland Micro-Cube, can crank out some amazingly authentic tones, and are well-deserving of a listen.

Another benefit of digital modeling amps is that, in addition to a plethora of classic amp sounds, they typically include a wide selection (an impossibly rich selection in the more expensive models) of effects. This is also something to consider before purchasing either an amplifier or any effect pedals or other such devices.

Effect pedals and other tone-altering devices

Most electric guitarists eventually tire of a simple, stock clean or dirty amp sound, and begin to long for other tonal options. By this I mean they end up buying effects pedals to alter the sounds coming out of their amp, beyond simply twisting the knobs on the amplifier itself. This can become an addictive and expensive habit—but it's a ton of fun trying out these devices in a guitar shop.

For the tone junkie, as many guitarists might be labeled, there are signal-altering devices out there to suit just about every taste and every budget. Most players start with an overdrive or distortion pedal, then progress to some sort of chorus, reverb, or delay. Along the way they may opt for a wah-wah pedal (think of the opening notes in 'Voodoo Child,' by Jimi Hendrix), a roto-vibe (think of the swirly sound in many Stevie Ray Vaughan songs), or a tremolo (that shimmery thing going on in some blues tunes).

Any one of these pedals can cost you a pretty penny, and you may end up needing or wanting only one—or a whole stageful. Start with an overdrive pedal, such as the classic Ibanez Tube Screamer—a favorite of Stevie Ray Vaughan and many a blues guitarist—to add a little crunch to your playing. If you are leaning toward multiple pedals, you might want to consider purchasing a multi-effects unit, such as something from the popular Digitech RP series or the Line 6 Pod series. Or, as I mentioned in the section above about digital modeling amps, you may opt for a new amp which includes built-in effects. Again, the choice is yours.

Guitar diagrams and musical concepts

Guitar players are faced with a variety of sometimes confounding musical diagrams, charts, and graphics. This section of *The Blues Guitar Handbook* will explain the basics of deciphering these useful tools and will give you a solid foundation on which to base all your future guitar studies. In this section you'll learn how to read chord diagrams, scale diagrams, guitar tablature, and sheet music.

The old saying is true: knowledge is power. The more you know about guitar, and about music in general, the better player you will become. Many guitarists shy away from basic musical concepts that really aren't so difficult. Don't be one of those lazy players—you'll just limit yourself. If you're reading this book, you know you're better and smarter than that. Besides, most musical concepts are not as complex as the uninformed think they are.

There is a basic set of skills you should spend a little time with, and you'll find you are probably able to understand many of these essential concepts almost as soon as you learn them. Your playing will improve with the learning of these ideas and rules of thumb, and it will improve again each time you apply these concepts to the music you play and practice.

At the most basic level, essential skills include the understanding of the various diagrams used to teach guitar, including neck or "block" diagrams and both musical notation and tablature. Also, you should learn basic counting and how the different types of musical notes and time signatures work. And you should learn at least some general music theory, and a little about the scales from which music theory originates. I'll throw in a few other helpful and important concepts in this section of the book as well.

Don't be afraid to come back and re-read this section a few months down the road, or a year or two from now. Understanding musical concepts is a bit like fine wine: both improve with time. I also advise that you have patience while it all soaks in. Don't get hung up trying to understand something that doesn't at first make sense, letting a mental roadblock stop you from playing the instrument. Strive to keep your fingers moving while your brain grapples with new information.

Understanding musical concepts sometimes creeps up on you over time. You'll have plenty of "Aha!" moments if you let them come naturally. Just keep up the physical end of playing the guitar and the brain will catch up.

So let's make a deal, shall we? If you'll make a promise to yourself to dig in and not give up too quickly, I'll do my best to make things easy for you.

The four basic diagrams for guitarists

There are really only four graphic diagrams guitarists must concern themselves with, chord diagrams, scale diagrams, guitar tablature (or "tab" for short), and sheet music notation. Maybe you're already familiar with one or all of these, but just to be sure, let's take a quick look at all four, and then I'll explore in more detail where necessary.

Chord diagrams

These are diagrams of the actual guitar neck, showing the strings, the frets, and typically either dots or numbers showing where to put your fingers. When numbers are shown, rather than dots, they are there to indicate exactly which finger goes where. Stick close to these fingering suggestions whenever possible, but if another fingering just works better for you, go for it. In some cases an exact fingering has a very certain purpose; other times it can be treated as a suggested fingering. If it's really important to use a particular fingering, I'll let you know why.

The low E-string (the thick string) is on the left, and the high E-string (the thin string) is on the right. An "o" above the diagram indicates that the string should be played open. An "x" above the diagram indicates the string should not be played. A horizontal line between two or more dots indicates that those notes should all be played with one finger, as with a barre chord. Most of the time this will be the first finger, but not always. A number to the left of the diagram indicates a starting or positioning fret number if the diagram is showing a chord or group of notes to be played higher on the neck.

Scale diagrams

To show a scale we use a horizontal neck diagram—similar to a piece of tablature. In this case, the low E-string will be at the bottom of the diagram, and the high E-string at the top. The black dots show where to place your fingers. The white dots show that the string is played open, ie, not fretted.

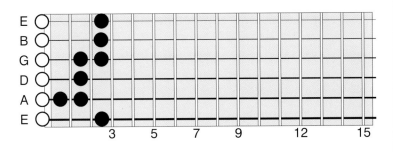

Tablature

The next sets of diagrams that guitarists need are tablature, or tab, and sheet music. Which should you learn to read? Understanding at least a little of both may be the best way to go. Either method of guitar transcription (the notating of how a song is to be played) contains valuable and helpful information, and either method can take some time to master—though tablature definitely allows for a quicker start toward true music-making.

Guitar tab is very popular these days, and with good reason. It may be the quickest and easiest way for guitarists to understand where and when to place their fingers on the fretboard. Tablature has actually been around for hundreds of years, and is used for most stringed instruments, not just guitar and bass.

Tablature is a valuable tool, and an easy diagram to learn and understand. It does have its limitations, however: unlike standard sheet music notation, most tablature does not include any rhythmic information. It shows you on what strings and frets to put your fingers, and in what order, but it does not give you any indication of how the rhythm of the guitar part is to be played. With tablature, if you don't already have a pretty good idea of the rhythm of the song, you're out of luck. In other words, you have to have heard the song before using the tablature or you won't be able to get the rhythm right.

This would not be the case if you were able to read sheet music. Also, reading highly-detailed tablature for a complicated guitar part takes almost as much skill as reading the same part on sheet music, except the tablature doesn't supply the rhythmic information. In the long run, most musicians would be better off learning to read sheet music. It takes time and effort to become a high-level sight-reader; but once there, you can play any music, whether you have ever heard it or not. Chip away at learning to read sheet music a little at a time, and don't be afraid to begin with the most basic reading exercises, such as in a beginners' guitar instructional book.

Still, tablature is a very useful tool, with some advantages sheet music does not include. For example, there are many situations in which, even with the skill to read sheet music, you may want to refer to the accompanying tablature to see exactly where on the neck that particular part is to be played. With guitar, there are almost always many different places to play the same note or riff, and the tablature can actually clarify something that sheet music does not provide.

Tablature is closely related to the scale diagrams shown on the previous page—with the thick E-string at the bottom—but it includes the additional element of time going by in the song. A scale diagram shows you where to put your fingers. But it is static in time, showing only one moment of a fingering.

Tablature shows you on which string and frets to put your fingers too, but it does so in a timeline fashion. We read the timeline from left to right, just as we would read sheet music. So you play the notes in order, starting from the left and proceeding to the right. In the following tablature, we would play the third fret on the sixth string four times, then play the fifth fret on the sixth string once.

Example 2.1

Like sheet music notation, professionally produced tablature does include bar lines, which separate a song into measures. You should be aware that free internet tab, created by untrained transcribers, often does not include bar lines or break the song into the proper measures. In a typical blues, rock, or pop song, there are four beats per measure (using 4/4 time as an example), so a piece of tablature in 4/4 time, with a simple quarter-note (crotchet) beat played for four measures divided by bar lines, might look this:

Example 2.2

Basically, if the fret numbers in a piece of tablature are close together, it means those notes are to be played close together in time, whereas tablature showing notes with a lot of space between them indicates those notes are held out longer, or that we rest between notes. In the following example, the first two measures include notes played close together in time (in this case, the notes are eighth-notes/quavers), followed by two measures of notes with more space between them (in this case, half-notes/minims):

Example 2.3

In tablature, chords (three or more notes played simultaneously) or intervals (two notes played simultaneously) are indicated by fret numbers stacked on top of each other. When you see fret numbers stacked up, you should hold down all the indicated frets and strings and strum them simultaneously.

Example 2.4

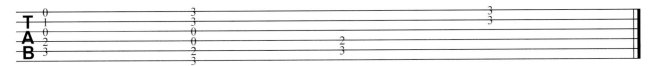

And here's a little trick for reading tab: When you try to play a piece of tablature which includes one note each on adjacent strings, played one after another, analyze the entire group of notes to see if it actually includes all the notes in a

Example 2.5

particular chord shape. If so, you may want to simply hold down that chord (as if the notes had been stacked in the tablature), and then pick the individual strings. In the following example, the tablature spells out an A minor chord:

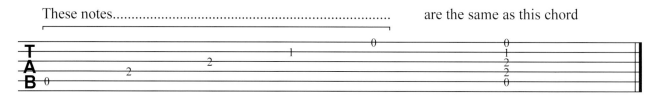

So in this example, rather than playing the first note, then removing that finger from the fretboard before playing the second note, and then the next note, etc, it would be better to simply hold down the chord, then pick each string individually, as in an arpeggio. Not "seeing the chord for the threes," as I like to joke, is a common mistake made by novice tab readers. But now you know to look for this type of thing.

Guitar playing involves many types of articulations, such as bends, slides, hammer-ons, pull-offs, and vibrato, among others. These have their own special symbols. The following tablature shows how some of the most common articulations are notated in professionally transcribed tablature:

Example 2.6

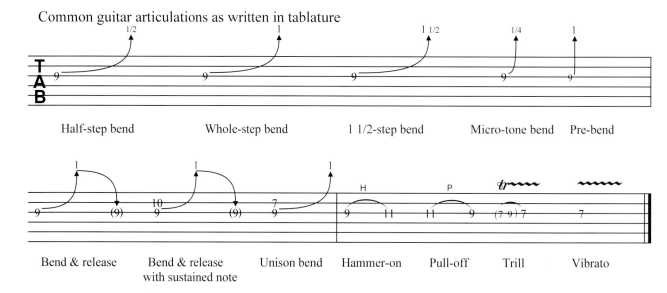

Sheet music

Learning to read sheet music can be a bit frustrating, but a steady effort toward a long-term goal will pay huge dividends. Even being able to read sheet music at the level of an elementary school student will definitely help an adult musician understand music better and advance on their instrument more quickly.

Space does not allow this book to serve as a complete primer on sight-reading, but I'll touch on a few basics. Some of the essential skills of musicianship are to be learned here, whether or not you actually apply them to sight-reading, such as understanding what is meant by a "quarter-note bass line" or how to count the 12 measures in a 12-bar blues song.

The musical staff looks very similar to tablature, but these two transcription devices have absolutely nothing to do with each other. The six lines of tablature represent the six guitar strings, but the five lines of the musical staff have no relation to guitar strings whatsoever (or the strings of any instrument for that matter). The five lines of the musical staff are simply the backdrop for a coded language that millions of musicians the world over have learned to read—probably tens or hundreds of millions throughout the course of history. And if all those people have done it—including millions of children—you can do it too.

We can use both sheet music and tablature together, too. While the sheet music shows exactly how the song goes, including the rhythmic information missing from tablature, we can use the tablature to see exactly where on the neck to play the song.

On the musical staff, each line and each space between the lines represents a musical note. There is a simple way to memorize these lines and spaces. The four spaces spell the word FACE, starting with the bottom space and going upward. The five lines, starting with the bottom line and going up, are E-G-B-D-F, which many people the world over memorize with a mnemonic phrase: Every Good Boy Does Fine, or all kinds of fun variations, such as Empty Garbage Before Dad Flips, or Elvis's Guitar Broke Down Friday.

Example 2.7

The study of sheet music begins with notes on or between these five lines, but eventually we need more notes. To represent all the notes on the guitar, we will also need to learn to read notes both above and below the staff. These notes are shown using "ledger" lines when necessary. While it can be tricky to learn to read these, the same mnemonic phrases that applied to the notes within the staff can be applied to the notes above or below the staff, except that they are flipped.

Both above and below the staff, the *lines* can be memorized as FACE, and the *spaces* as Every Good Boy Does Fine. Here's how that works:

Example 2.8

Example 2.9

At the start of each piece of music is a key signature, showing which notes are sharpened or flattened in that particular key. In the key of A major, for instance, the lines and spaces for C, F, and G have sharp signs on them, indicating that the key requires the notes C♯, F♯, and G♯. If any note in a piece is not in accordance with the key signature, it will be preceded by a natural (♮), flat (♭), or sharp (♯) sign. This indication stays in force for the rest of that measure, after which the note returns to the pitch indicated by the key signature.

In addition to which musical pitches to play, sheet music includes other vital information. Perhaps the most important has to do with rhythm. Every song has a time signature, which tells us what kind of beat the song has. The most common time signature is 4/4, but 3/4, 6/8, and 12/8 are also common, especially in blues music. In most songs, the time signature indicated at the beginning of the song lasts throughout the song.

The top number indicates how many beats per measure, in this case, four beats per measure.

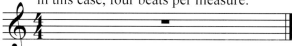

The bottom number indicates what type of note gets one beat, in this case, a quarter-note.

What does all that mean? First, notice that we're using simple fractions. Each of these fractions tells us how we will divide each measure of music. The top half of the fraction tells us how many beats are in each measure. So in 4/4 time, we're going to count to four in each measure. In 3/4 time we'll count to three. In 6/8 time we'll count to six, and, of course, in 12/8 time we'll count out 12 equal parts in each measure.

The bottom half of the fraction tells us what type of note gets one beat—in these examples either a quarter-note (in 3/4 or 4/4 time) or an eighth-note (in 6/8 or 12/8 time). The common rhythmic values you need to know include whole notes, half-notes, quarter-notes, eighth-notes, and 16th-notes (semibreves, minims, crotchets, quavers, and semiquavers in British terminology).

Whole notes get four beats. Half-notes get two. Quarter-notes get one beat. It takes two eighth-notes to equal one quarter-note, so you might think of eighth-notes as getting a half-beat each (in 3/4 or 4/4 time). It takes four 16th-notes to equal one quarter-note.

Continuing with this logic, and using 4/4 as our time signature, it would take one whole note to complete a measure (meaning that would be the only note we played in that measure). It would take two half-notes to complete that same measure of 4/4 time. We could also complete a measure of 4/4 time with either four quarter-notes, eight eighth-notes, 16 16th-notes, or any combination thereof.

Example 2.10

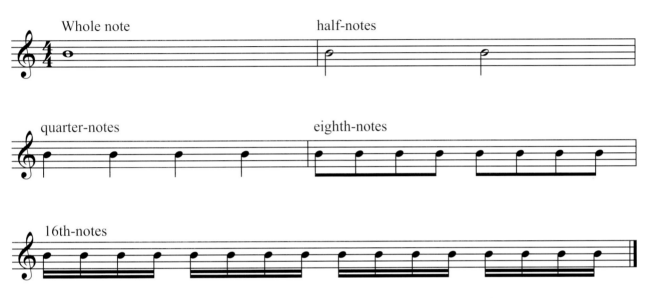

Not all songs are in 4/4 time however. Let's examine the other common blues time signatures, starting with 3/4 time. In 3/4 or waltz time, we use a quarter-note as our basis of counting, but we only count to three in each measure. In 3/4 time we might see either three quarter-notes, six eighth-notes, or 12 16th-notes. A whole note, which gets four beats, is too big for a measure of 3/4 time. But in its place we commonly see what is called a dotted half-note in 3/4 time. A dot after a musical note increases that note's rhythmic value by half, so a dotted half-note equals three beats—just enough to fill a whole measure in 3/4 time.

Example 2.11

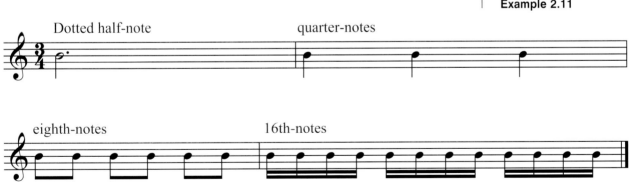

Both 6/8 and 12/8 are common blues time signatures, and both use the eighth-note as their basis of counting. So, in a measure of 6/8 we would have six eighth-notes (or some combination of notes equaling six eighth-notes, such as three quarter-notes), and we would count to six. In 12/8 we might see 12 eighth-notes, and we'd count to 12 in each measure. Typically, in 6/8 or 12/8 time, we accent the first of each group of three beats, as in **1**-2-3 **4**-5-6 or **1**-2-3 **4**-5-6 **7**-8-9 **10**-11-12. Accenting these beats feels quite natural after a while, and neatly breaks these time signatures into easier groups of three.

To simplify the above mumbo-jumbo, you really don't have to worry much about what type of note gets one beat (quarter-notes or eighth-notes). You simply have to count to either three, four, six, or 12 in each measure. And that ain't so hard.

Then there are triplets. Triplets are a very common rhythmic element of blues and blues-rock music. Quarter-notes, eighth-notes, and 16th-notes can be played as triplets, which is a way of playing three notes in a space normally reserved for two. An example of this would be three eighth-notes, played as a triplet, in the space of one beat—where we would normally play only one quarter-note or two eighth-notes.

Example 2.12

Counting basics

Ok, now that you've taken all that in, let's talk about how to count. Counting is an essential musical skill, whether you ever become a serious sight-reader or not. If you can't count and stay on beat, you're going to have a very hard time playing with other musicians, or even playing music satisfactorily on your own. Fortunately, learning to count musical beats is not rocket science.

Most of the time simply counting to three, four, six, or 12 in each measure—depending on the time signature—will be good enough. Sometimes when trying to reproduce a tricky part in a piece of music we may need to break each beat into its eighth-notes, 16th-notes, or triplets.

Example 2.13

Here is a diagram showing how you would count various beats:

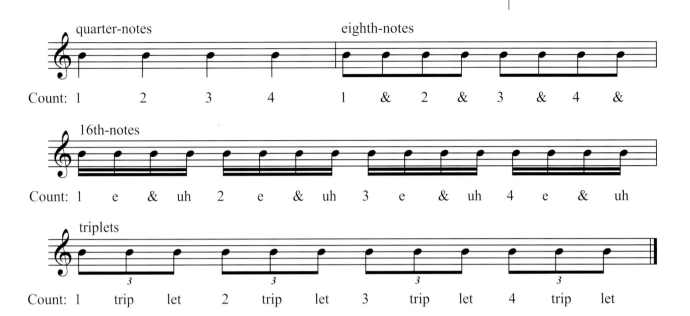

Example 2.13 *(continued)*

Also as a guitarist, you should know that alternate picking (a consistent down-up motion with your pick) helps you play in time, almost as if your pick is the swinging pendulum of an old-fashioned pyramid-shaped metronome. When you are playing a measure of eighth-notes, your pick should go down on the beat, and up on the "and." When you are playing a measure of 16th-notes, you will go down on the beat and the "and," and up on the "e" and the "uh." Even when a beat is skipped, you want to maintain this steady alternate picking.

You also need to know about rests. Rests are a pause in the music, and have the same characteristics as notes. Music commonly includes whole note rests, half-note rests, quarter-note rests, eighth-note rests, and 16th-note rests. When you encounter a rest, you simply stop your guitar from making sound for as long as the rest indicates. Here are some examples of how rests might appear in a piece of music:

Example 2.14

A song may sometimes include multiple measures of rest, such as during a drum solo. In the event of a multiple-measure rest, you'll want to lay out (keep your guitar silent), while counting out the measures before you begin playing again. Here is an example of how a section of multiple measures of rests might appear in a piece of music:

Example 2.15

This is a multi-measure rest indicating the player should not play for four complete measures

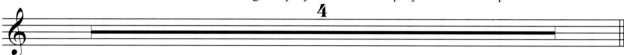

Here's a helpful trick for counting multiple measures: Instead of saying 1, 2, 3, 4 in each measure, and then trying to keep track of how many measures have gone by, substitute the measure number for 1 each time. So for a four-measure pattern you would count: 1-2-3-4, 2-2-3-4, 3-2-3-4, 4-2-3-4.

A tie combines two note values. When you see a tie in music, you play the first note and let it ring for the entire duration of both tied notes. You do not play the second note. Ties often cross bar lines. You might see a quarter-note on beat four of one measure tied to a quarter-note on beat one of the next measure. In this case, you would play the note on beat four, and let it ring all the way through beat one of the next measure, stopping that note on beat two.

Example 2.16

Ties combine the rhythmic value of notes

Articulation marks in sheet music

In the tablature section above I showed you a variety of the most commonly used guitar articulations—such as bends, hammer-ons, vibrato, etc—and how they appear in tablature. Opposite, I show you how the same markings appear in sheet music (and I've combined the tablature with each to make it more clear).

Example 2.17

Rhythm slashes

Some sheet music takes a bit of a shortcut and, rather than showing you accurate notation, uses "rhythm slashes" instead. Typically, chord names will be indicated above the staff (such as G7 or C9, etc.), with the rhythm to be played shown in slashes rather than complete note-heads. Here is an example of a guitar part using rhythm slashes:

Example 2.18

Repeats and second endings

After you've learned the basics of reading sheet music, from the standpoint of individual measures, you'll also want to know how to follow sheet music from the beginning of a song to its end. Most sheet music does not show an entire song written out completely measure after measure—this would usually take too many pages—but instead uses repeats, codas, first and second endings, and other indicators to guide you through the composition. There are a small handful of important symbols and instructions you'll want to know to help you navigate a piece of music.

A repeat sign, a double thickness barline with two dots either before or after it, indicates that you are to go back to the beginning of the song, or to repeat a section of the song. A repeat at the beginning of a song will often include only a repeat sign at the end of the section to be repeated, meaning you should go back to the beginning of the song and repeat from there. A repeat in the middle of the song will include both a beginning and ending repeat sign, indicating that you repeat only those measures enclosed within the repeat signs. Often, there may be additional instructions in the music, typically written in *italics,* which tell you how many times to repeat that section. If there are no such instructions, you should only repeat that section once before moving on to the next section of the song.

Example 2.19

Repeat from beginning   Repeat between repeat signs

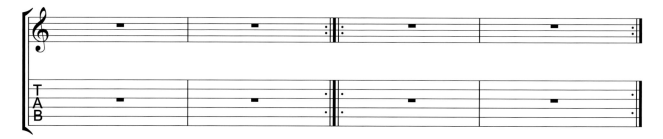

There is also a repeat symbol, which indicates that you are to repeat the previous measure. A special repeat sign straddling two bars, with the number "2" above it, indicates that you are to repeat the previous two measures.

Example 2.20

Repeat previous measure   Repeat previous two measures

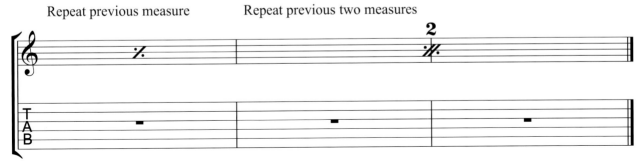

Often a section of music being repeated has a different ending the second time through the repeat. This is usually indicated by the numbers "1" and "2" under a bracket. In the following example, the repeated section is four measures long, but the second time through, you are to replace the measure under the bracket, marked "1," with the measure under the "2."

Example 2.21

First and second time bars

Play this measure first time   Play this measure second time

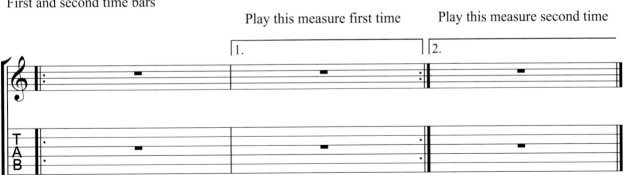

Other common instructions that indicate movement from one section of a song to another include the *dal segno, coda,* and *da capo* indicators. These markings often work together to help us navigate through a song.

Sometimes we are asked to jump forward or backward in a song, or to repeat a certain previous section of a song using the *dal segno* (often abbreviated "D.S.") marking, which means "from the sign." When you see the *D.S.* marking, you then look back through the music for the sign and repeat from there. *D.S al Fine* means you repeat from the sign to the end (sometimes marked *Fine).*

At *D.S. al Fine*, go back to the sign and then play to *Fine*

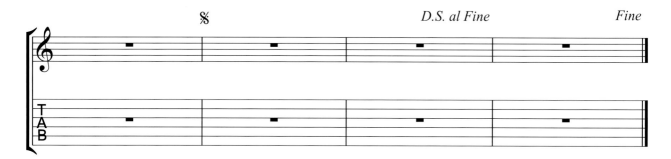

Example 2.22

D.S. al Coda tells you to repeat from the sign to the coda symbol and/or the words "*To Coda*", and then jump to the coda (marked with the coda symbol and found at the end of the sheet music.) The coda is a section at the end of the song, the outro, if you will.

At *D.S. al Coda*, go back to the sign, then at *To Coda* jump to the Coda symbol at the end of the music

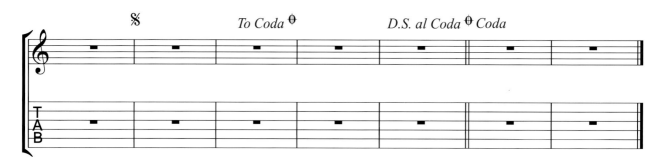

Example 2.23

Da Capo, which is Italian for "from the head," means from the beginning. When you see the abbreviation "*D.C.*" it means to start over at the beginning of the song. And once again, you'll need to know where to repeat to. Just like the *dal segno* (D.S.) marking, there are two common markings which tell us where to go after repeating from the beginning of the song: *D.C. al coda*, and *D.C. al fine*. As with the *D.S.* markings, the *D.C. al fine* marking instructs you to play from the beginning of the song to the end of the song or the *fine* marking.

PART **1** SECTION 2

At *D.C. al Fine*, go back to the beginning and then play to *Fine*

Example 2.24

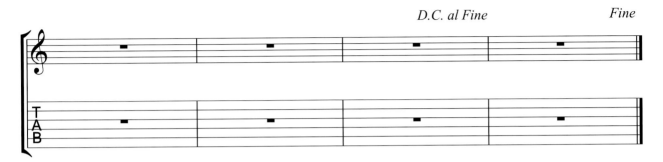

D.C. al coda tells you to repeat from the beginning of the song to the coda sign, at which point you would jump to the coda at the end of the song.

Example 2.25

At *D.C. al Coda*, go back to the beginning, then at *To Coda* jump to the Coda symbol at the end of the music

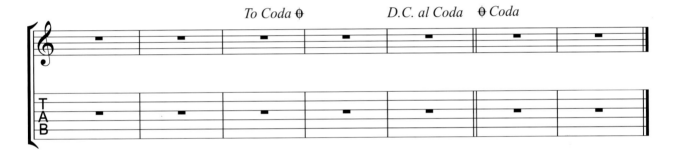

The basics of music theory

The simple phrase "music theory" sends shivers down the spine of many musicians. But don't be afraid, it ain't rocket science! In Section Three here you'll learn some of the basics of music theory. With time, understanding these concepts will help you make more sense out of the songs, chords progressions, and lead guitar patterns you learn throughout *The Blues Guitar Handbook*, and throughout your life-long guitar playing adventure.

Basic concepts

Learning a little music theory goes a long way for any musician. I want to help you understand a few basic concepts that will bring into much clearer focus how music and songs work. Don't be reluctant to read this section a few times over the next few months.

Half-steps and whole-steps

At its most basic level, understanding music theory involves understanding the simple concept of half-steps and whole-steps (semitones and tones). On the guitar, the movement from any one fret to the next fret is called a half-step. This would be the equivalent of playing any two adjacent keys on a piano, regardless of whether they are black or white. A half-step is the most basic unit of pitch measurement in music theory.

Two half-steps—a movement of two frets—is called a whole-step. Musicians often talk about half-steps and whole-steps, and as guitarists we might talk about a "bend of a step and a half, or two steps"—especially if you're studying the blues lead guitar playing of Albert King. Over time, you should (and probably will) become able to hear and recognize half-step and whole-step movement.

Example 3.1

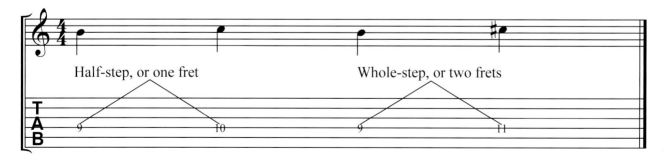

Half-step, or one fret   Whole-step, or two frets

PART **1**   SECTION 3

As we'll discover shortly, all music theory relates to scales. And musical scales can be defined by their pattern of half- and whole-steps. While it is not essential to memorize these formulas, it is helpful to know of their existence. As musicians become more advanced, and start to add exotic scales into their repertoire of musical abilities, it is the scale formulas of half- and whole-steps that will help them understand the difference between, say, a major scale and the commonly used and really cool-sounding Mixolydian mode. Similarly, the formulas will help them change from a natural minor scale to the fun and frequently used Dorian mode.

Compare the following diagrams showing how basic major and minor scales—plus the two modes I've just mentioned—can be looked at in terms of their formula of half-steps and whole-steps.

The formula of half-steps and whole-steps for a major scale is Whole-Whole-Half-Whole-Whole-Whole-Half. It might also make sense to think of the major scale as having a half-step between the third and fourth notes, and between the seventh and eighth notes.

Example 3.2

The formula of half-steps and whole-steps in a major scale

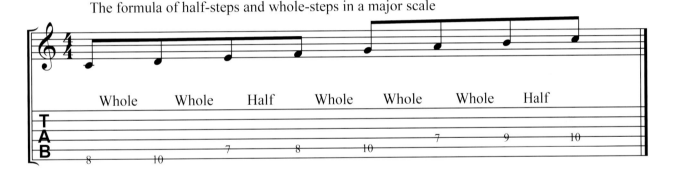

The formula is slightly different for a minor scale. The minor scale formula of half and whole-steps is Whole-Half-Whole-Whole-Half-Whole-Whole. You might find it helpful to think of the minor scale as having a half-step between the second and third notes, and between the fifth and sixth notes. (This is the natural minor scale. There are other minor scales.)

Example 3.3

The formula of half-steps and whole-steps in a minor scale

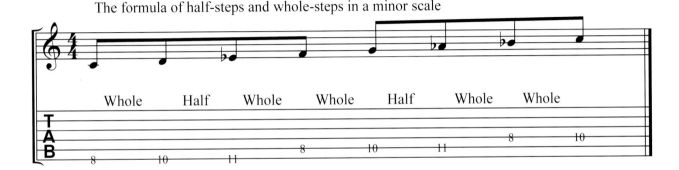

SECTION 3   PART **1**

Example 3.4

The formula for the popular Dorian mode closely mirrors that of a minor scale. The formula for the Dorian mode is Whole-Half-Whole-Whole-Whole-Half-Whole.

The formula of half-steps and whole-steps in the Dorian mode

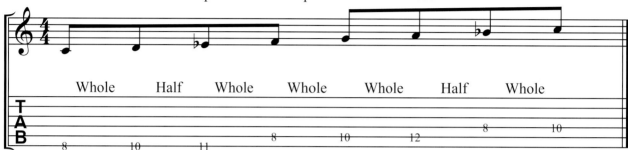

Example 3.5

The Mixolydian mode is very similar to a major scale. The formula for the Mixolydian mode is Whole-Whole-Half-Whole-Whole-Half-Whole:

The formula of half-steps and whole-steps in the Mixolydian mode

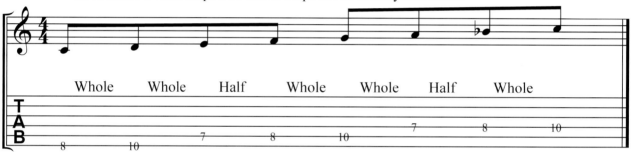

Intervals, octaves, and the chromatic scale

An interval is the distance between two notes. We also use the term interval to refer to two notes played simultaneously. When we play two notes together, we refer to them by the interval between them, as in a third, or a fifth, which we determine by counting up the scale from the lower note to the higher. Thus C and E are a third apart. C and G are a fifth apart. Thirds and fifths are quite common in blues music, and there are other common "intervallic" riffs we'll explore later in this book as well.

Opposite are all the intervals, starting on C, and including the octave. An octave refers to the interval between notes that share the same name, but are not the same pitch. From the sixth-string eighth-fret C to the fourth-string tenth-fret C is one octave. The C on the first string at the eight-fret is another octave higher.

PART **1**   SECTION 3

Example 3.6

Intervals and their common names

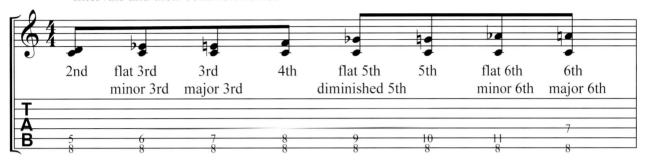

2nd	flat 3rd	3rd	4th	flat 5th	5th	flat 6th	6th
	minor 3rd	major 3rd		diminished 5th		minor 6th	major 6th

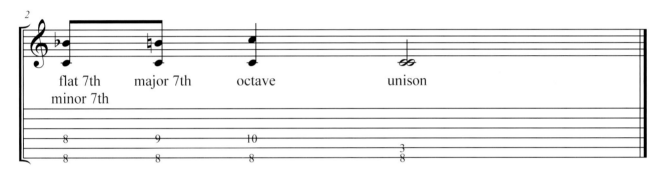

flat 7th	major 7th	octave	unison
minor 7th			

An octave is a basic unit of musical measurement, and one all musicians must know. One octave includes 12 half-steps. If you play your low E-string open, then play E at the 12th fret on that string, you have moved one octave—or 12 half-steps—higher.

If you were to play every note in between these two E notes, you could be said to have played a "chromatic" scale. Chromatic scales are not commonly used in blues music, but it is important to know what is meant by the term chromatic.

Example 3.7

A chromatic scale starting on C

Often musical movement is referred to as chromatic, which simply means that—on guitar—we might play a series of notes each one fret above or below the previous note, temporarily ignoring, in a sense, the appropriate scale for that song. Here is an example of chromatic movement as it is often seen in a blues turnaround:

Example 3.8

A common chromatic phrase in a blues turnaround

The major scale dominates musical theory

Now that you know a little about half-steps, whole-steps, and chromaticism, we can talk about scales, and bigger and more important musical concepts. All music theory is based on the major scale, with slight reference to the chromatic scale. For example, chord names, such as C13 or E7♯9 refer to chords (C and E, in this case) that include specific additional notes indicated as they relate to that chord's root note. The root note of a chord or scale is the note the chord or scale is named after—ie, a C13 chord has a C note as its root. The root note of the chord is also the root note of the scale from which come all the funny numbers.

So, to understand the basics of these numbers, you should study the major scale, and the numbers assigned to the notes in that scale. A major scale includes seven notes per octave, and a seven-note scale is sometimes referred to as "diatonic." Here is a C major diatonic scale, covering two octaves, with the scale steps or intervals numbered:

Example 3.9

A two-octave major scale with common interval numbers

Notice that some tones in the scale change name depending on whether they fall in the first or second octave above our starting note. In the key of C, the first D we come to is known as the second, but the D an octave higher is called the ninth. This is because the D in the second octave above our starting note is nine scale steps above that starting note. The same holds true for the 11th and 13th, which are named differently in the first octave (fourth and sixth).

However, some (really important) notes never change their name, regardless of what octave they fall in. The root note is always referred to as root or one. Thirds, fifths, and sevenths in the scale are always referred to as thirds, fifths, and sevenths, no matter which octave they fall in.

But let's get back to those wacky chord names and figure out what in the world is meant by "♯9." When you see a chord name with a ♭5 or ♯9, or similarly mysterious title, you are dealing with something called an "altered" tone. These notes come from the chromatic scale, but the name we give that altered tone— sharp this or flat that—is a name given in reference to the nearest note in the diatonic major scale. In this example we would take the ninth of the major scale and raise it a half-step to make it a sharp ninth (♯9); or we would take the fifth of the major scale and flatten it (lower it a half-step) to make it a flat fifth (♭5).

Knowing that all note names are given in reference to the seven-note major scale, let's take another look at the 12-note chromatic scale. Notice that any note that wasn't present in the major scale is denoted as a flat or sharp or some kind of altered scale step, in deference to the major scale. This is where all the weird

Example 3.10

A two-octave chromatic scale with common interval numbers

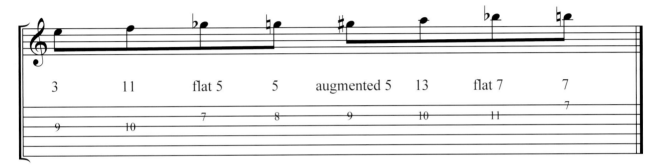

numbers come from in chord names, and these same altered tones sometimes come into play when talking about the scales used to play melodies or guitar solos.

While the major scale dominates music theory, it does not necessarily dominate the actual music we play. Not all music is major. In blues we often use a minor scale, pentatonic scales, the blues scale, or modes such as Dorian and Mixolydian, instead of a straight major scale. When we talk about one of these scales or modes, we again make reference to the major scale, evidenced by the flat third and flat seventh of the minor scale (which are flat compared to a major third or major seventh from the major scale).

Another type of scale pattern you must know and understand to master blues is the pentatonic scale. Pentatonic scales are hugely important in blues guitar playing and blues music in general, arguably more important than the diatonic major or minor scales, and particularly so in older or more traditional blues.

Pentatonic scale patterns are simply subsets of major and minor scales. As the name "penta"—which is Greek for five—suggests, the pentatonic scale has only five notes per octave, as compared to the seven notes per octave in a major or minor scale. Pentatonic scales are therefore easier to learn and memorize, and are often the first scale pattern a guitarist learns.

Example 3.11

An A minor scale with common interval numbers

An A minor pentatonic scale...   and A blues scale

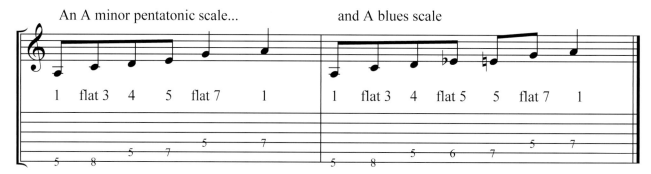

Closely related to the pentatonic scale is the blues scale, which simply adds a flat fifth to the pentatonic scale.

The example above shows these three types of scale. The numbers underneath each one illustrate how the scale relates to the major scale.

The Dorian and Mixolydian modes are commonly used in blues music and are very closely related to the diatonic major and minor scales, with the scale formulas altered only slightly. The Dorian mode is identical to a natural minor scale, but with a "raised" or sharpened sixth scale step. Compare an A natural minor scale to the A Dorian mode:

Example 3.12

An A minor scale with common interval numbers

And an A Dorian scale

The Mixolydian mode is identical to a major scale, but with a flat seventh scale step. Compare an A natural major scale to the A Mixolydian mode:

Example 3.13

An A major scale with common interval numbers

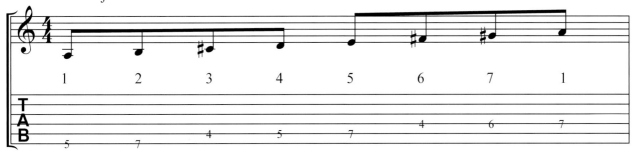

And an A Mixolydian scale

Example 3.14

Again, each scale or mode has its unique formula of half-steps and whole-steps. It's not important to memorize these formulas, but it is helpful to see the big picture of how changing a note here or there by a half-step can dramatically change a scale. There are literally dozens of exotic scales a musician might want to learn, but in *The Blues Guitar Handbook* we will stick to just a few, and only those commonly found in blues music. And better yet, you may already know some of these: the major scale, the minor scale, the pentatonic scale, and the blues scale. And since the Mixolydian and Dorian modes are commonly used in blues music, we'll touch on those throughout this book as well.

How chords are built

Chords are built using notes from scales. A basic major or minor chord is comprised of a root note, a third (flat third for the minor chord), and a fifth. These notes—or scale steps—are found in a scale beginning on the root note of the chord, ie, C for a C chord, A for an A minor chord, etc. Fortunately it is easy to memorize root (the "one" of the scale or chord), third, and fifth. You need to remember this; it's the basis for almost all chords.

Example 3.15

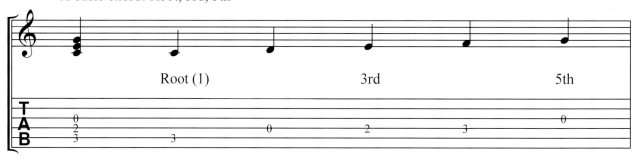

A basic chord: Root, 3rd, 5th

If a major or minor chord is built using a root, third, and fifth, can you complete the pattern to create a seventh chord? If you said "root, third, fifth, seventh," you are correct. We can continue on in this fashion to create a ninth chord, 11th, and 13th.

Example 3.16

A type of 7th chord: Root, 3rd, 5th, 7th

Special chord rules

There are, of course, a few extra rules and circumstances a musician needs to learn about building chords. I'll touch on just a few of the more important issues here. A deeply detailed understanding of chord construction is beyond the scope or needs of this book, so I'll stick to some basics.

Let's start with seventh chords: There are basically three different types of seventh chord: major sevenths, dominant sevenths, and minor sevenths. The most common types of seventh chords used in blues are the dominant seventh (which most people just call a seventh chord), written C7, and the minor seventh chord, written Cm7 or Cmin7. Both of these chords feature a root, third (flat third for the minor chord), fifth, and a flat seventh. Major seventh chords, written Cmaj7, include a root, third, fifth, and major seventh, and have a pretty sound that isn't often used in blues.

SECTION 3 PART 1

Here are the three main types of seventh chord:

Beginning on any note, a root, major 3rd, 5th, and major 7th make a major 7th chord:

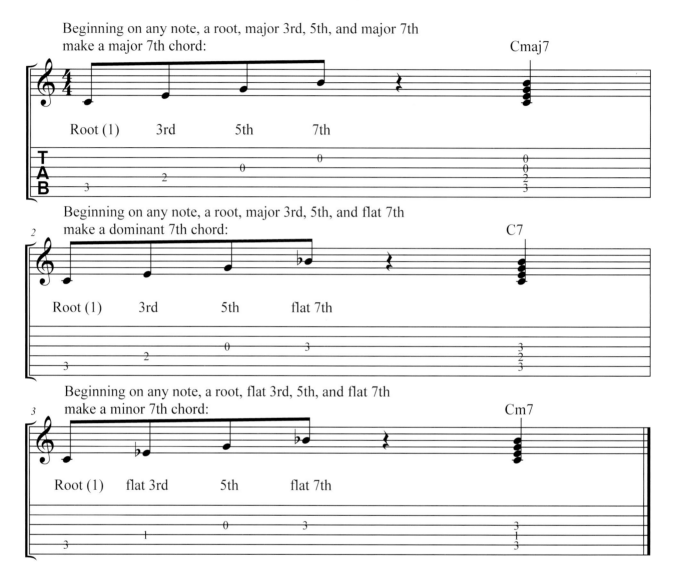

Example 3.17

Occasionally we leave a note out of a chord. It is not required that every chord include the root, third, fifth, seventh, etc, particularly if another instrument in the band (often the bass or piano) is playing that note. For example, if the song calls for an A7 chord, and your bass player is playing the A root note, you don't necessarily need to play that note on the guitar. You could get away with playing just the third, fifth, and seventh of the chord. This allows a guitarist to play more interesting "voicings" of chords.

Here is a common blues chord shape, played as an A7 chord, with no root note:

Example 3.18

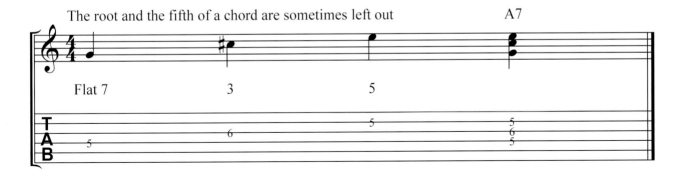

Often in sheet music, we come across chords such as A7/G or D/F♯, sometimes called "slash" chords due to the slash between the letters. These chords are technically known as inversions, and are fairly common. An inversion is simply a chord that is played with a note other than its root note in the bass. The note after the slash is the bass note.

In this example, we would play an A7 chord over a G bass note, or a D chord over an F♯ bass note. Here is notation showing these common inversions:

Example 3.19

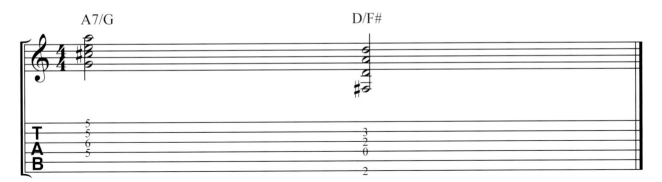

Another type of chord you'll often come across is the suspended chord. Suspended chords are fun and easy, and something every guitarist needs to know. Most guitarists are familiar with the chord D suspended or Dsus4. This is a chord in which we have substituted the fourth of the chord for the third. But this is usually only temporary, as a sus4 chord almost always "resolves" to a regular major chord, the fourth of the chord (the suspended note) releasing its musical tension or resolving to the third.

You can see the fourth resolve to the third of the chord in the example overleaf:

SECTION 3   PART 1

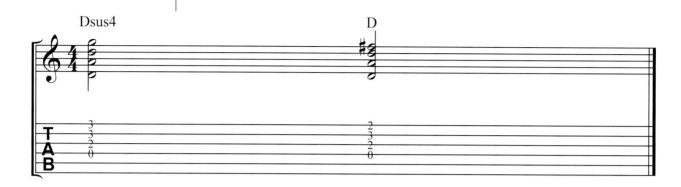

Example 3.20

Chords with confounding names such as flat fifth, sharp ninth and minor seven flat fifth include "altered" scale steps. Remembering that all music theory is based on the major scale, you can understand what is meant by a flat fifth or a sharp ninth. These are chords which include notes that have either been raised or lowered one half-step from the normal fifth or ninth in a major scale.

Altered chords are very common in jazz music, and are found occasionally in blues and other styles of pop music. Fortunately, knowing just a handful will cover most of your blues needs, and you'll find them scattered throughout this book.

Here we show four A chords: a regular A major chord, then an A chord with a flat fifth and a sharp ninth. Notice also that the sharp ninth chord includes a seventh. Then follows an A minor seventh chord and an A minor seventh flat fifth chord, which is simply a minor seventh chord with a flatted fifth:

Example 3.21

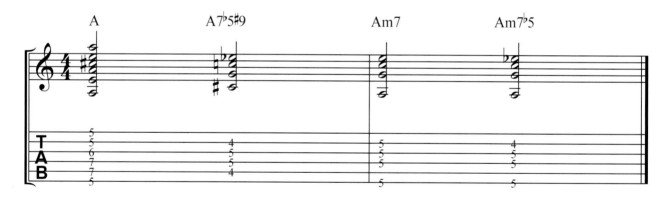

That's all the crazy chord stuff I'll cover here, though you may find some other oddities in various sections in this book. Again, I recommend that you concentrate on playing the music and the guitar parts, and don't worry so much about all the funny names and tricky rules.

Chord progressions, chord scales, and the all-important I-IV-V

As a blues enthusiast, you have probably heard musicians refer to a chord progression as a "one-four-five." What exactly does this mean?

Just like chords themselves, chord progressions are built or based on the musical scale. To understand a chord progression, musicians often ascribe numbers to each chord, just as we assign numbers to the scale steps in the chord. And we use Roman numerals when discussing chord progressions, to differentiate them from chord tones such as a fifth or seventh.

Here is a diagram of a "harmonized" C major scale, that is, a C major scale on which we have built chords on each scale step. Notice that each chord is assigned a Roman numeral. Upper case Roman numerals (I, IV, and V) indicate major chords. Lower case numerals (ii, iii, vi, vii) indicate minor chords.

Example 3.22

Chords in the key of C major

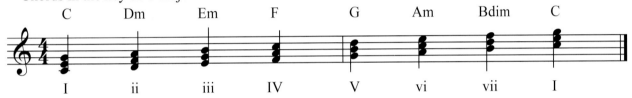

It is also important to be able to understand a chord scale in a minor key. Here is a chord scale for the key of A minor. Notice that the i, iv, and v chords are all minor in a minor key. This would be the basis for a minor blues:

Example 3.23

Chords in the key of A minor

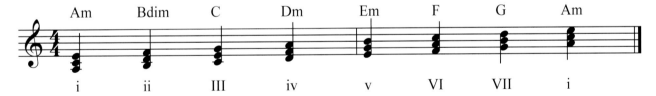

All songs—and all chord progressions—can be analyzed, broken down, and spoken of in terms of these Roman numerals. The one-four-five—written I-IV-V— chord progression is by far the most common progression in all music, not just in blues. But it is completely dominant in blues.

Most blues songs are I-IV-V, though there are several other common chord progression patterns used in the blues, which we will cover in *The Blues Guitar Handbook*.

One such pattern that shows up in the music of the Delta blues, and is a huge part of most jazz music, is the ii-V-I progression. In the key of C major this would

SECTION 3 | PART **1**

Example 3.24

be Dm-G-C. Another common chord progression, sometimes found in a gospel blues tune, is I-iii-IV-V. In the key of C this would be C-Em-F-G.

Common chord progressions, shown in C major

Once you understand this system of numbering chord progressions, you'll find that you can much more easily play in any key, or transpose songs from one key to another. Also, if you are a fairly competent lead guitarist, you'll find that you can improvise equally in various keys using the knowledge of these chord progressions as your guide. Soloing over a I-IV-V blues song is largely the same no matter what key the song is in. As a guitarist, all you have to do is slide your licks and scale patterns up and down the fretboard to land at the appropriate frets for I-IV-V in that key and you're ready to soar.

Relative major and minor keys

Now that you know a little about keys and scales and chord progressions, I want to explain one more thing that sometimes comes into play in blues music—in all styles of music, for that matter. All major keys have a related minor key, and vice versa. These are called "relative" keys. If we were to analyze the formulas of half and whole-steps for both a major and minor scale, and then apply those formulas to all 12 chromatic notes we would find that each major key shares the exact same notes with one specific minor key—its "relative minor."

For example, if we were to start on C and follow the formula of half and whole-steps for a major scale (W-W-H-W-W-W-H), we would get the notes C-D-E-F-G-A-B-C. And we would get those exact same notes if we started on A and used the formula of half- and whole-steps for a minor scale (W-H-W-W-H-W-W). No other major and minor key share these same particular notes, so C major and A minor are relative keys. In sheet music they share the same key signature of no sharps or flats. The

Example 3.25

Relative major and minor keys: C major and A minor share all the same notes.
A two octave C major scale...

...includes all the notes for A minor

relative minor is always three half-steps down from the keynote of the major scale. The relative major is always three half-steps up from the keynote of the minor scale.

For example, G major shares the same notes—and key signature (one sharp, F♯)—with E minor. G major and E minor are relative major and minor keys.

Example 3.26

Relative major and minor keys: G major and E minor share all the same notes. A two octave G major scale...

...includes all the notes for E minor

Relative major and minor keys sometimes come into play during a bridge of a song—though more often in styles of music other than blues. For example, a song in the key of C major may shift to the relative key of A minor during the bridge (typically eight measures), and then back to the key of C major for the remainder of the song. It is important to be aware of this relationship between relative major and minor keys for this reason, and also to understand why a scale pattern you know as A minor pentatonic can also be used as C major pentatonic—as I'll demonstrate later in this book.

Another, somewhat similar occurrence is that of playing in "parallel" major and minor keys. These are the major and minor keys starting on the same note: A major and A minor, for example. It is not unusual for a more advanced guitar player to move back and forth between the major and minor versions of a key when soloing. Many a solo, and many a blues solo, will, for example, play some notes in the key of A major, and then a few notes in A minor, and then slide back to A major again—even possibly touching on a few notes from the A Mixolydian mode or A Dorian mode along the way.

Understanding how to find the parallel and relative minors and majors of a key (not to mention knowing a few other scale tricks, such as playing modally) can seriously improve your guitar playing.

Relax, this isn't a test!

You shouldn't feel that you have to memorize and master all this music theory stuff. Just knowing that it exists will help you understand and play guitar better. Music theory and how it applies to the music you want to play will sink in over time. And rest assured, very few of the blues masters we'll cover in *The Blues Guitar Handbook* knew anything about music theory. If you can buckle down and learn it, it will definitely help you—but don't let *not* understanding it stop you from playing guitar and learning the great blues songs and techniques in this book.

SECTION 3

PART 1

Tutorial
PART 2
MASTERING A BLUES SOUND

Blues rhythm guitar

Every great blues song is based on a solid rhythm. In this section of *The Blues Guitar Handbook* we'll explore playing rhythm guitar in the various forms of the blues, including the ubiquitous 12-bar blues, as well as the lesser known eight-bar and 16-bar blues progressions, blues ballads, gospel blues tunes, and others. We'll also examine common chords, riffs, and fretboard patterns used in blues rhythm guitar playing, with a look at common strumming patterns, blues grooves, turnarounds, and more.

This section of *The Blues Guitar Handbook* includes two halves, covering two interlocking elements of blues rhythm guitar playing: 1) understanding how the songs are laid out, and 2) knowing how to play common blues chords, riffs, and other guitar techniques as used in those songs. The first half of this section examines the blues song formats. The second half demonstrates guitar techniques that can be applied to the various song formats.

Song formats

The 12-bar blues

The most common form of the blues is the 12-bar blues. This 12-bar—or repeating 12-measure—format is the basis for countless thousands of blues songs (not to mention innumerable blues-based rock, country, and jazz songs) and is the meat of the working blues guitarist's repertoire. There are two basic forms of the 12-bar blues, and you should know both.

The first you must learn, and the most common format of 12-bar blues, includes 12 measures (bars) which follow a strict formula: four measures of the I chord, two measures of the IV chord, two more measures of the I chord, one measure of the V chord, one measure of the IV chord, and two final measures of the I chord. (If you don't know what is meant by "I-IV-V" chords, go back and look again at Section Three: The Basics of Music Theory.)

It doesn't matter what key the song is in, the 12-bar blues always follows this format, or something very close to it (I'll show you a couple of slight variations below). Using the key of A as our example, the I, IV, and V chords would be A, D, and E respectively. Here is a 12-bar blues in A:

SECTION 4   PART **2**

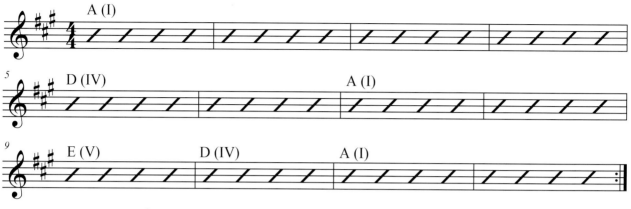

Example 4.1

In the key of E, the I, IV, and V chords are E, A, and B, respectively. Here is a 12-bar blues in E:

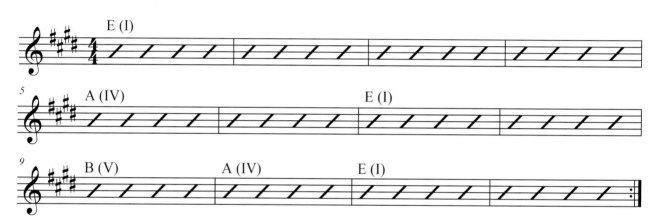

Example 4.2

The second most common form of the 12-bar blues is one musicians call the "quick-change" 12-bar. In the quick-change 12-bar blues we simply replace the I chord in the second measure of the song with a IV chord. This quick change can sometimes trip up the uninitiated, but you're not one of them, because you have now been initiated. Here is a quick-change 12-bar blues in A:

Example 4.3

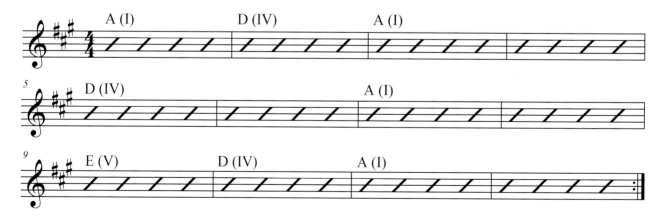

And here is a quick-change 12-bar blues in E:

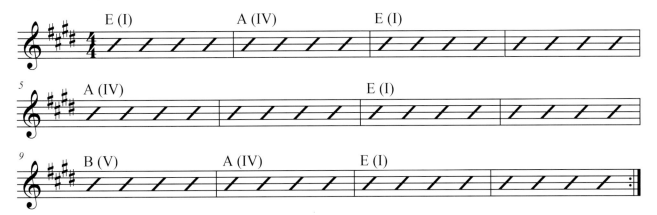

The turnaround

Example 4.4

The final four bars of a 12-bar blues song are known as the turnaround. The turnaround, coming toward the end of the pattern, gives us a strong push back to the beginning of the song, "turning" us around to get us started all over again for another time through the song, or chorus, as each pass is sometimes called (especially by soloists).

The Turnaround: Measures 9 - 12

There are many variations of turnaround that can be substituted for the basic ending shown above, and blues guitarists pride themselves on knowing many. In fact the goal of many a veteran blues guitarist is never to use the same turnaround twice in one night—a tall order, considering they may go through the 12 bars a dozen times in a single song (with singing and solos), and a working musician may play 30 or 40 12-bar blues songs at one gig.

Example 4.5

In this section of *The Blues Guitar Handbook* I will demonstrate a couple of basic turnaround variations, more as concepts than as actual guitar parts. In other sections of this book I will further detail some specific, classic guitar turnarounds as played by the legends of the blues.

SECTION 4

PART **2**

The most basic—and most common—variation on the turnaround shown above involves inserting a V chord in the final measure of the song. This V chord can be played on different beats of that measure, depending on the player and the specific turnaround riff. Here is one common turnaround variation with a V chord in the final measure:

Example 4.6

The Turnaround: Measures 9 - 12

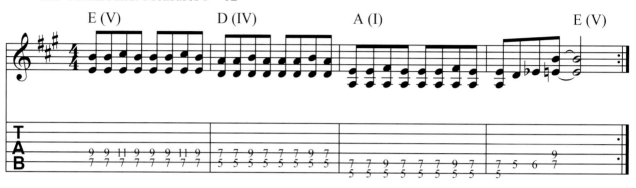

And here is another variation:

The Turnaround: Measures 9 - 12

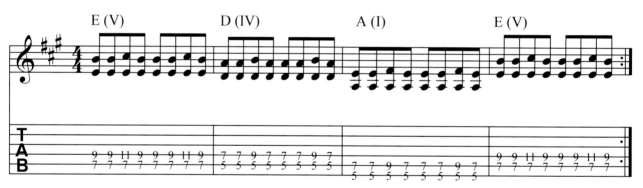

Example 4.7

This final move to the V chord at the end of the 12-bar pattern leaves us with a very strong urge to return to the I chord, either to start the next chorus of the song, or to end the song with one final measure of the I chord (almost all songs end on their I chord). This is because, regardless of the style of music, a V chord, also known as the "dominant" chord in music theory, provides an irresistible need for resolution to its I chord.

Another common occurrence in the turnarounds of 12-bar blues songs is to replace the IV chord in measure ten with a V chord—so that the V chord played in measure nine continues into measure ten, then is followed either by two measures of the I chord (in measures 11 and 12), or by some other variation of the final two measures, as demonstrated above.

The Turnaround: Measures 9 - 12

Again, countless turnarounds have been concocted by blues guitar legends over the years, and since each player had his favorites, many turnarounds can be considered a trademark of a certain legendary player. I'll throw many more at you in the chapters ahead. Some are more challenging than others, but advanced blues guitarists often consider themselves collectors—so to speak—of turnarounds. So start your collection today—that's part of the fun of playing blues guitar.

Example 4.8

The eight-bar blues

The eight-bar blues is less common than the 12-bar blues, but does pop up in the playing of the blues legends frequently enough that you should acquaint yourself with it. 'Key To The Highway' and 'How Long Blues' are examples of blues standards in the eight-bar format.

There are many varieties of eight-bar blues, a few of which are detailed below. The typical eight-bar blues song will often change rapidly from chord to chord, and can easily be confused with a quick-change 12-bar blues—before completely surprising the 12-bar veteran with its sudden turnaround. Still, almost all versions of the eight-bar stick with the I-IV-V chords—the same chords used in a 12-bar blues song—so learning the pattern is simply a matter of learning when to change chords, and which chord comes next.

The most common form of all eight-bar blues progressions is embodied in the blues standard 'Worried Life Blues,' originally recorded by pianist Big Maceo Merriweather (with Tampa Red on guitar) in 1941, and subsequently covered by many blues greats.

Eight-bar blues, 'Worried Life Blues' style: I-I-IV-IV-I-V-I/IV-I/V

Originally made popular in 1941 by Big Bill Broonzy, later a hit for Little Walter, and recorded as an impromptu jam between Eric Clapton and Duane Allman on Derek & The Dominos' *Layla And Other Assorted Love Songs* album, 'Key To The Highway' is one of the most widely known eight-bar blues songs. The song moves quickly from the I to V chords in the first two measures, which will certainly trip up the unprepared.

Example 4.9

Eight-bar blues, 'Key To The Highway' style: I-V-IV-IV-I-V-I-V

Example 4.10

Another popular variation on the standard eight-bar blues shown above can be found in Elvis Presley's 'Heartbreak Hotel.' This eight-bar form starts out much like a 12-bar, with four measures of the I chord, before going into a sudden turnaround.

Eight-bar blues, 'Heartbreak Hotel' style: I-I-I-I-IV-IV-V-I

Example 4.11

Just one more: 'Walking By Myself,' as recorded by Freddie King and many others. This eight-bar format again starts out with four measures of the I chord, just like a 12-bar blues, before moving into its four-bar turnaround.

Eight-bar blues, 'Walking By Myself' style: I-I-I-I-IV-V-I-V

Example 4.12

The 16-bar blues

Yes, there is also a 16-measure format of the blues. 'I'm Your Hoochie Coochie Man,' written by Chicago blues legend Willie Dixon and first recorded by Muddy Waters in 1954—and since covered by a Who's Who of the blues—is an example of a 16-bar blues, as is Albert King's 'Oh, Pretty Woman.'

Again, there are many varieties of 16-bar blues, but perhaps the most common version of the format simply involves playing a 12-bar blues, with a doubling of the first four measures of the song. So instead of playing the I chord for four measures, as in a typical 12-bar blues, we play the I chord for eight measures, before

Example 4.13   continuing through the remainder of a regular 12-bar blues pattern.

16-bar blues, common style: I-I-I-I-I-I-I-I-IV-IV-I-I-V-IV-I-I

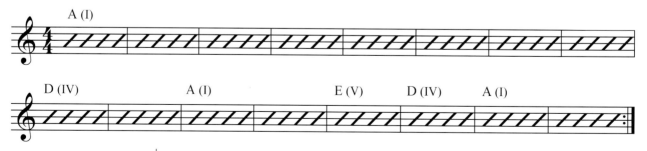

PART **2**   S E C T I O N   4

It is important to note that, in a 16-bar blues song, it is not uncommon for the instrumental sections of the song—as in the guitar solos—to be played as straight 12-bar blues, before reverting back to the 16-bar format when the singer again kicks in with the vocals.

Rather than extending the beginning of the 12-bar format with eight bars of the I chord, some 16-bar blues songs instead extend the turnaround of the 12-bar. In this type of song, the first eight bars are played as in a normal 12-bar blues: four measures of the I chord, two measures of the IV chord, and two measures of the I chord.

But the remaining measures are all doubled. Instead of one bar of the V chord in measure nine, followed by one bar of the IV chord in measure ten, and two bars of the I chord in measures 11 and 12, this type of 16-bar blues consists of two bars of the V chord, followed by two bars of the IV chord, and then four bars of the I chord.

Example 4.14

16-bar blues, extended turnaround: I-I-I-I-IV-IV-I-I-V-V-IV-IV-I-I-I-I

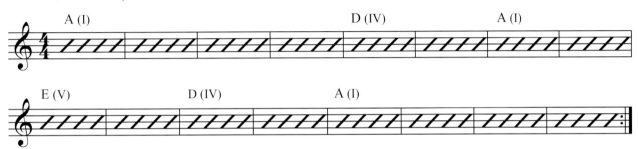

In just a slight variation on the progression shown above, in which the turnaround is doubled, some 16-bar blues songs are created by repeating the V-IV section of a 12-bar blues turnaround, and then extending the final two bars of I chord to four measures.

16-bar blues, repeated V-IV section: I-I-I-I-IV-IV-I-I-V-IV-V-IV-I-I-I-I

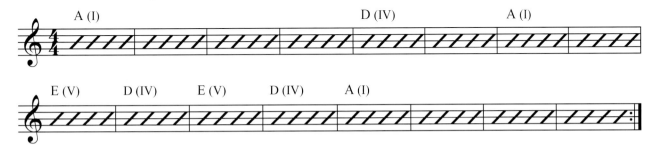

Example 4.15

Also, a 16-bar blues is occasionally based on an eight-bar blues, rather than a 12-bar blues. In this scenario, each measure of the eight-bar blues is repeated. This can be done with any version of an eight-bar blues. Here is one example, using the 'Key To The Highway' format:

16-bar blues, doubled eight-bar blues style: I-I-V-V-IV-IV-IV-IV-I-I-V-V-I-I-V-V

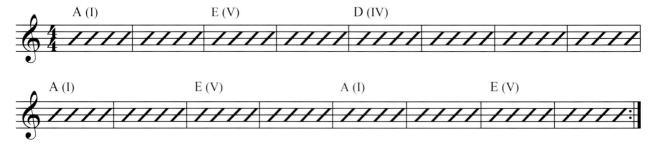

Example 4.16

The shuffle

While the blues song formats shown above may have their differences, they typically have one thing in common: each is usually played with a shuffle beat. Understanding the term shuffle and how a shuffle rhythm feels is essential to playing blues, and in understanding how to shuffle, it can be helpful to have some understanding of the concept of groove.

The groove of a song is an all-important element of music, not just the blues. When musicians talk about groove they are referring to the feel of the song, which can be broken down into two basic parts: first, what type of recurring rhythmic pattern is used to perform the song? For example, is the primary rhythmic figure a funk pattern using 16th-notes; maybe a syncopated Latin jazz rhythm; possibly a straight eighths rock beat? And second, how does the rhythm feel? Is the song's groove laid-back or is it hurried? Is it aggressive or relaxed? Is it on the beat or behind the beat?

Understand also that this is different from whether or not the song is played at a fast or slow tempo. Tempo is the speed of the song, often measured in beats per minute. A slow blues song might have a tempo of just 50 beats per minute, while an up-tempo jump blues may cruise along at 140 beats per minute.

Any variety of groove or feel can be played at any tempo. And like any other groove, shuffles can be played at either a fast or a slow tempo. But regardless of tempo it is the shuffle feel that is at the heart of most blues music. But not all blues music is played with a shuffle groove.

The slow blues or blues ballad

The shuffle may dominate the blues world, but not all blues songs are played as shuffles. The blues ballad—or slow blues—is the main exception. Rather than using the skipping or lurching shuffle groove or even the more rock-like straight eighths beat so popular in up-tempo blues tunes, the slow blues song often employs a triplet feel, or a groove that has a definite **1**-2-3 type of feel, with an accent on the first of each group of three beats.

In fact, slow blues songs are usually written in 12/8 time, which means there are twelve eighth-notes in each measure. We break these 12 eighth-notes down into four groups of three. A measure of 12/8 time is counted **1**-2-3, **4**-5-6, **7**-8-9, **10**-11-12, with a strong accent on 1, and slightly less emphasized accents (called "sub-accents") on beats 4, 7, and 10. At first it may feel slightly awkward to count to 12. But with a little practice, breaking the 12/8 slow blues measure down into four equal sections, each with three beats, comes naturally to most players.

Applying this 12/8 slow blues count to a 12-bar blues pattern, we might play the rhythm this way:

Example 4.17

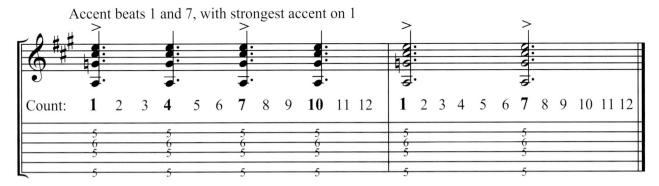

Most slow blues songs don't do anywhere near that much strumming. It is not uncommon to see 12/8 slow blues rhythm patterns written with a strum only on each accent (as when playing quarter-notes in 4/4 time), or only on the first and seventh beats (as when playing half-notes in 4/4 time).

Example 4.17

Regardless of how much strumming is required to complete a given measure in 12/8, you'll still want to keep counting **1**-2-3, **4**-5-6, **7**-8-9, **10**-11-12. If you play with a good drummer, you'll easily be able to lock in with this count. Examples of

SECTION 4 PART **2**

12/8 slow blues tunes include 'The Sky Is Crying,' written by Elmore James and covered by Stevie Ray Vaughan among others, and 'Five Long Years,' a slow blues standard recorded by countless artists, including Eric Clapton on his 1995 *From The Cradle* album.

Other common blues chord progressions

As I've made abundantly clear so far in this book, most blues songs are built on I-IV-V chord progressions (or i-iv-v for a minor blues). Occasionally we get to change things up with some different combinations of chords. One such pattern that shows up in the music of the Delta blues, and is a huge part of most jazz music, is the ii-V-I progression. In the key of C major this would be Dm-G-C.

Example 4.18

A ii-V-I chord progression in C major

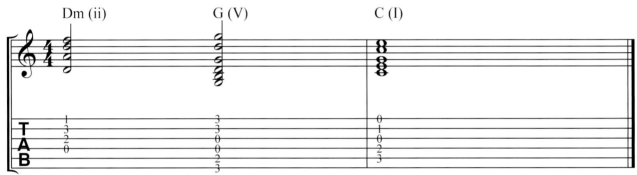

A common method of throwing in the sound of a ii-V-I progression, particularly in fingerstyle blues, is to simply play an alternating bass line off the V chord. In the key of E, with a B as our V chord, a quick move to an F♯ in the bass gives us the ii-V-I sound, without even having to play the full ii chord. Playing the ii chord with a simple alternating bass note off the V chord was a common practice of many Delta and Piedmont blues players.

Example 4.19

An implied ii-V-I chord progression in E major

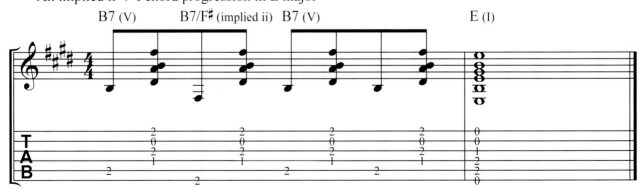

Another common chord progression, sometimes found in a gospel-tinged blues tune, is I-iii-IV-V. In the key of C this would be C-Em-F-G. Freddie King used this progression in his classic 'Palace Of The King,' in the key of D—with the chords D-F♯m-G-A.

Example 4.20

A I-iii-IV-V chord progression in D major

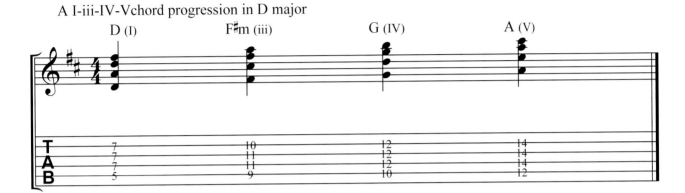

Of course the classic "gospel climb" plays a part in many a blues song, and is a key element in one of the most widely known blues songs of all, 'Stormy Monday,' written by T-Bone Walker and covered famously by Bobby "Blue" Bland and The Allman Brothers. The gospel climb goes I-ii-iii-IV.

Example 4.21

A I-ii-iii-IV "gospel climb" chord progression in G major

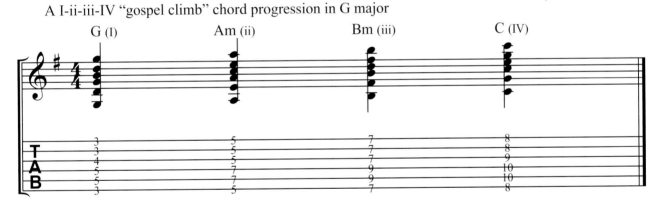

SECTION 4   PART **2**

One more common progression—though in some uses it's just a couple of notes played off the I chord, rather than a series of chords—is the I-III-IV progression, which follows a minor scale (in A minor, A, C, D) but uses major chords or power chords without either a major or minor third. Often played as a boogie—think John Lee Hooker and ZZ Top—this progression can be played with any number of strumming patterns.

Example 4.22

A I-III-IV chord progression in A

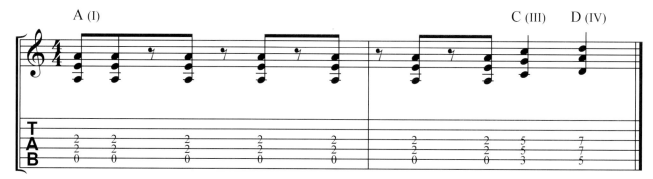

Major or minor chord?

It is not uncommon for a blues song to play major chords where the "chord scale" calls for a minor chord. A very common instance of this is found in a minor blues, in which the IV and V chord are played as major chords rather than minor chords. In the key of A minor, for example, the actual scale calls for a D minor and an E minor chord. But in many songs we change those minor chords to major chords.

Example 4.23

A V-IV-i chord progression in A minor, with the V and IV chords played as major

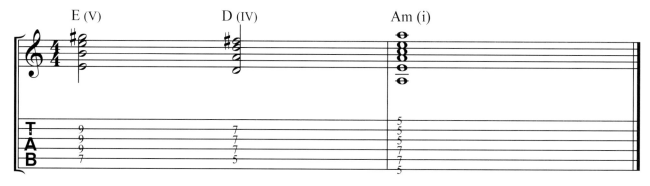

Guitar techniques

The absolutely essential shuffle rhythm

A good shuffle rhythm is fairly easy for most musicians to achieve, though it may take a little practice, especially if the player is coming from a rock'n'roll background. In fact, it is helpful to compare a basic rock rhythm pattern with a shuffle rhythm when learning how to shuffle.

In particular, it is the rock'n'roll rhythm pattern known as straight eighths that is most comparable to a blues shuffle. This type of rhythm is called straight eighths because it includes complete measures of eighth-notes (eight eighth-notes per measure), played in a steady, even flow. Here is a straight eighths rock rhythm:

CD TRACK 2

Example 4.24

A "straight eighths" rock rhythm

Unlike the steady, driving, very even and consistent straight eighths rock rhythm, the blues shuffle has a sort of lurching feel. This feel can be thought of as similar to the human heartbeat (maybe that's why it's such a popular groove), sort of a lub-**dub**, lub-**dub**, lub-**dub**, lub-**dub** feeling, with a stronger emphasis placed on the second of each pair of notes (the "dub"). It is this second part of each pair of notes that actually falls on the beat.

The sheet music for a shuffle pattern is usually written the same way as the rock straight eighths pattern—with solid measures of eighth-notes—but with one important distinction: the blues shuffle sheet music typically will say "shuffle" at the top, and/or might have a notation indicator showing that each beat is to be thought of as a triplet.

S E C T I O N   4   PART **2**

A shuffle rhythm with indication that eighth-notes are to be "swung" or played as a shuffle

CD TRACK **2**

Example 4.25

Playing this groove will come naturally over time, but if you struggle with getting a consistent shuffle going, it may make more sense to see the shuffle rhythm pattern written another way, one in which you can clearly see that one of the notes in each pair is slightly longer than the other.

This can be written as a series of triplets (actually a quarter-note and an eighth-note lumped together on one beat), with each beat having one slightly longer note (the quarter-note) and one shorter note (the eighth-note). The longer note is the "dub" of the shuffle heartbeat, and the shorter note is the quicker, anticipatory "lub," which pushes us quickly to the next beat. Sheet music for blues shuffle songs is sometimes written this way, rather than with the more common eighth-note method shown above.

CD TRACK **2**

Example 4.26

A shuffle rhythm written as triplets, one note clearly longer, no special indication needed

In the remainder of *The Blues Guitar Handbook* I will primarily use the straight-eighths notation rather than the triplets notation to illustrate examples of shuffle blues songs—because it is generally easier to read—but I wanted you to be aware of both notations.

PART **2**   S E C T I O N   4

Common shuffle guitar techniques

Now that you understand the feel of the blues shuffle—and the variety of 12-bar, eight-bar, and 16-bar blues chord progressions routinely used in blues music—it's time to examine some specific guitar moves as they are applied to these patterns. Call them fingerings, voicings, techniques, or what have you, but the following guitar skills can be found in countless blues songs.

The easiest form of blues guitar shuffle requires only two fingers when played in an open position—using open strings for some of the notes. You probably already know how this works. If you do already know how to play this basic blues shuffle, don't jump ahead—instead, stick with me and shift your thinking to concentrate on the simple music theory or the sheet music that goes along with these chord voicings, rather than the fingerings themselves.

Blues shuffle songs played in A and E both routinely use this easy two-finger technique, and I have taught absolute beginners—who had never touched a guitar before—to play this form of blues shuffle song within a matter of minutes. It's so easy, even a child can do it.

I'll show you this basic blues technique in both keys, starting with the key of A. Remember that we are going to be using the I, IV, and V chords—as we will in most blues songs. The I chord in A is, of course, A. The IV chord is D; the V chord is E.

In the key of A we place the first finger on the second fret of the fourth string and strum the open A (fifth) string and the fourth string. This is an A chord (technically it is an A5 power chord, but I'll refer to it as A to keep things simple). We will then alternate between the second fret on the fourth string, and the fourth fret, played with the third finger. The note at the fourth fret is F♯, which is the sixth note in the A major scale. That makes this an A6 chord.

Using the more common, straight eighths style of sheet music notation, we'll be playing and counting "one-and-two-and-three-and-four-and" while we play this shuffle groove. Play the A chord on "one-and." Then play the A6 chord on "two-and." Then repeat this same pattern for beats three and four, with the A chord on beat three and the A6 chord on beat four. We need four measures of this repeating pattern.

CD TRACK **3**

Example 4.27

A typical shuffle guitar pattern. Notice chord change on beats two and four

In measure five of a 12-bar blues we move to our IV chord, in this case, D. The great thing about this easy blues shuffle is that to change from the A chord to the D chord we simply move over a string and play the exact same fingering.

To alternate between the D and D6 chord we'll be playing the open fourth string (D), and either the first finger on the second fret (the D chord), or the third finger on the fourth fret (the D6 chord), using the exact same rhythm and strumming that we used on the I chord.

CD TRACK 3

Example 4.28

The shuffle guitar pattern continues on the IV chord, changing chords on beats two and four

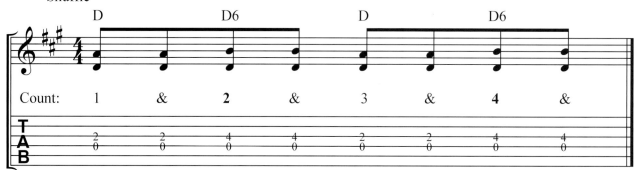

In the 12-bar blues we would return to the I chord (A and A6) for measures seven and eight, and then go to the V chord (E and E6) for measure nine. To play the E and E6 chords we will place our first finger on the second fret of the fifth string and strum the open E (sixth) string and fifth string together, alternating with the third finger on the fourth fret.

CD TRACK 3

Example 4.29

Shuffling on the V chord in A

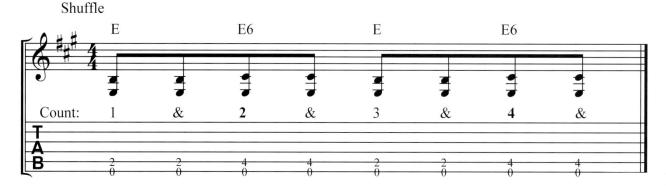

In a typical 12-bar blues we would now return to the IV chord (D and D6) for measure ten, then the I chord (A and A6) for the final two measures. The complete song is shown in Example 4.30 (opposite page).

The complete 12-bar blues shuffle in A

Shuffle

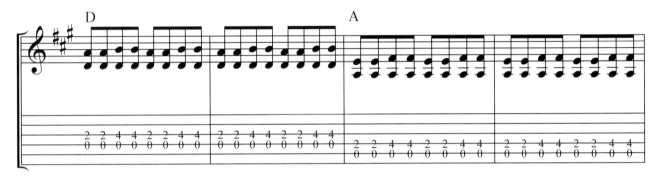

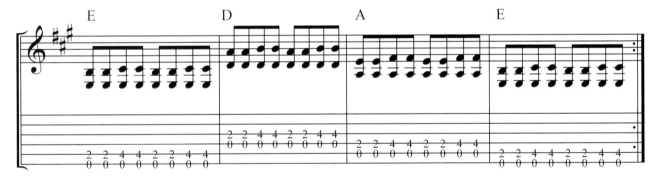

In the preceding song we alternated between two strums of the main chord on beats one and three, and two strums of the 6 chord on beats two and four. In another common variant of this basic blues, which I will demonstrate in the key of E, we will change this up slightly. A I-IV-V blues song in the key of E includes the E (I), A (IV), and B (V) chords.

For this blues shuffle in E we'll start with the E and E6 chords played on the sixth and fifth strings. But we will only play the E6 chord on beat two (not on "two-and") and beat four (not "four-and"). Since we are playing, basically, a straight eighths rhythm—which would include eight eighth-notes per measure—we will be strumming the E chord six times, and the E6 chord only twice per measure.

S E C T I O N 4   PART **2**

Another common shuffle guitar pattern. Notice the 6th chord is played only on the third and seventh strums

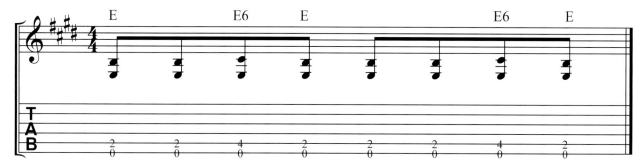

CD TRACK 5

Example 4.31

To play the A and A6 chords we simply move over one string to strum the fifth and fourth strings. Remember to play the A6 chord only for one strum on the second beat of the measure, and for one strum on the fourth beat of the measure.

The shuffle guitar pattern moves to the IV chord.

CD TRACK 5

Example 4.32

CD TRACK 5

Example 4.33

In the key of E, the V chord is B. Unfortunately, we can't play a two finger B6 chord, so we are left with two basic choices: play the B chord as a power chord using the first and third fingers (either at the seventh fret on the sixth string or the second fret on the fifth string) and then use the pinky to change the B to B6; or play an open B7 chord.

The V chord in the key of E is B. Here are three different potential fingerings:

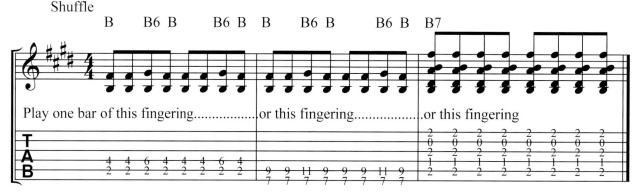

The complete easy blues shuffle in E might look like this:

CD TRACK **6**

Example 4.34

Shuffle

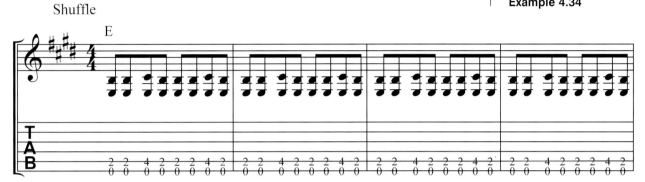

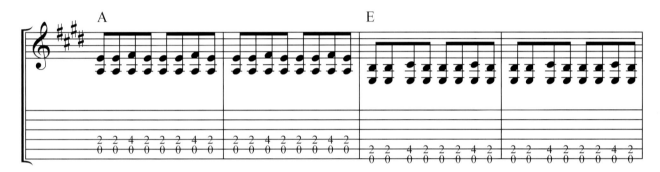

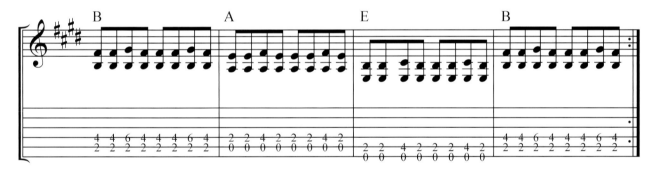

Knowing how to play this easy blues shuffle in both the keys of A and E is an absolute must for all blues players. Countless blues songs are based on these chord progressions, using these fingerings. In fact, knowing how to play this basic shuffle in every key—for which we'll need barre chords (or power chords played up the neck)—is a must. We'll tackle playing this technique up the neck, away from the open positions of E and A, in just a bit, but first …

SECTION 4 PART **2**

The 5/6/flat-7 shuffle

Once you know the easy shuffle shown above, you can quickly learn to spice it up a bit by adding one additional note. As described above, the basic two-finger A chord, which includes the notes A and E, is technically a power chord or A5 chord—because it includes the note A (the root note of the chord), and E (the fifth of the chord).

By adding the F♯ at the fourth fret on the fourth string we changed that A (or A5) chord to A6. Now we'll use our pinky to play the fifth fret on the fourth string. This is the note G, the flat-seventh of A, giving us an A7 chord.

CD TRACK 7

Example 4.35

Notice the rhythm of this song, with two strums for each chord: A on beat one, A6 on beat two, A7 on beat three, and back to A6 on beat four.

A blues shuffle utilizing A, A6, and A7 chords. Play the G in the A7 chord with your little finger.

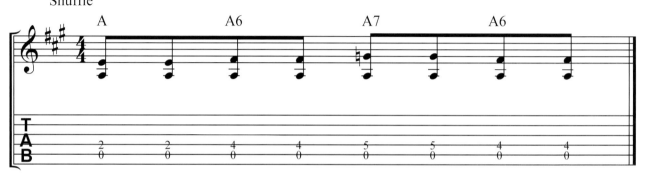

Again, for the IV and V chords we'll use an identical fingering, using our pinky to create the D7 and E7 chords. The entire song might look like this.

The complete 12-bar blues shuffle in A

CD TRACK 8

Example 4.36

PART **2**   SECTION 4

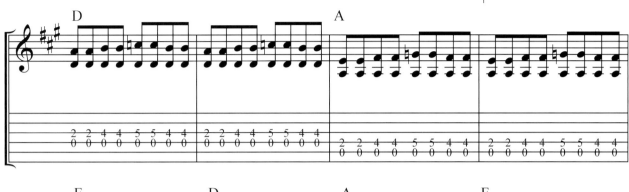

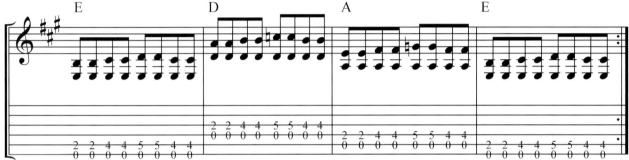

The basic shuffle in other keys

While a huge percentage of guitar-based blues songs are in the keys of E and A—allowing us to play in the open positions shown above—we routinely need to play blues in other keys as well, or sometimes in the keys of A and E, but somewhere other than open position. Many blues songs follow the same shuffle patterns you just learned, but play the chords higher on the neck, using either power chords or barre chords, instead of the open strings.

If you're a veteran barre chord player or basic power chord rocker, you'll have little problem tackling these next examples—though you may struggle to get your pinky to cooperate and stretch out far enough to hit the sixth and flat-seventh notes. It is definitely easier to make this stretch the higher on the neck you play, due to the decreasing distance between frets. For this reason I'll write this example out up at the eighth fret, in the key of C, which would include the C as our I chord, F as our IV chord, and G as our V chord.

Use the eighth-fret barre or power chords for the C (root note on the sixth string) and F chords (root note on the fifth string), and then play the G at the tenth fret (root note on the fifth string.) Pay close attention to the tablature in these next examples to see where you should be fingering these chords. Also notice that in some measures the song calls for the main chord, plus its sixth and its seventh variants, while in other measures the seventh chord is not used. Blues songs routinely change it up from measure to measure in this fashion.

CD TRACK 8
Example 4.36
(continued)

SECTION 4 PART **2**

The 12-bar blues shuffle in C, using barre or power chords

Shuffle

PRO TIP: In general, when playing chords up the neck on the guitar, it is a good habit to play full barre chords rather than power chords most of the time. However, when faced with the pinky moves required to pull off this type of blues shuffle, even experienced pros relax this rule a bit, and tend to favor two-string power chords. If you find it too difficult to hold down a barre while reaching with your pinky for the sixth and flat-seventh notes of these shuffle chords, go ahead and let go of the barre, stand your first and third fingers up on their tips, and just play it as a power chord.

Common keys for playing this type of blues shuffle include E, A, G, B♭, B, C, D, and E♭—with the flat keys favored by horn-based groups. You can use the chord method just shown to play in all 12 chromatic keys. Here is a chart showing where to play

PART **2** SECTION 4

the I, IV, and V chords in each key, using an E shape (root on the sixth string) as the I chord:

Finding the frets in all keys: E shaped I chord

Key (I chord)	(E shape)	IV chord	(A shape)	V chord	(A shape)
E	open	A	open	B	2nd fret
F	1st fret	A♯/B♭	1st fret	C	3rd fret
F♯/G♭	2nd fret	B	2nd fret	C♯/D♭	4th fret
G	3rd fret	C	3rd fret	D	5th fret
G♯/A♭	4th fret	C♯/D♭	4th fret	D♯/E♭	6th fret
A	5th fret	D	5th fret	E	7th fret
A♯/B♭	6th fret	D♯/E♭	6th fret	F	8th fret
B	7th fret	E	7th fret	F♯/G♭	9th fret
C	8th fret	F	8th fret	G	10th fret
C♯/D♭	9th fret	F♯/G♭	9th fret	G♯/A♭	11th fret
D	10th fret	G	10th fret	A	12th fret
D♯/E♭	11th fret	G♯/A♭	11th fret	A♯/B♭	13th fret
E	12th fret	A	12th fret	B	14th fret

Alternately, you might find it advantageous to use a barre or power chord based on the A shape chord (root on the fifth string) to play the same progression. In this case your I chord will be on the fifth string, and your IV and V chords will be on the sixth string. Here is a chart which shows where to play each chord in all 12 chromatic keys using the fifth-string I chord:

Finding the frets in all keys: A shaped I chord

Key (I chord)	(A shape)	IV chord	(E shape)	V chord	(E shape)
A	open	D	5th fret*	E	open
A♯/B♭	1st fret	D♯/E♭	6th fret**	F	1st fret
B	2nd fret	E	open	F♯/G♭	2nd fret
C	3rd fret	F	1st fret	G	3rd fret
C♯/D♭	4th fret	F♯/G♭	2nd fret	G♯/A♭	4th fret
D	5th fret	G	3rd fret	A	5th fret
D♯/E♭	6th fret	G♯/A♭	4th fret	A♯/B♭	6th fret
E	7th fret	A	5th fret	B	7th fret
F	8th fret	A♯/B♭	6th fret	C	8th fret
F♯/G♭	9th fret	B	7th fret	C♯/D♭	9th fret
G	10th fret	C	8th fret	D	10th fret
G♯/A♭	11th fret	C♯/D♭	9th fret	D♯/E♭	11th fret
A	12th fret	D	10th fret	E	12th fret

* Use 5th fret A shape chord for D

** Use 6th fret A shape chord for D♯/E♭

S E C T I O N 4   PART **2**

The boogie-woogie roll

There is one more common shuffle technique a blues player must know. I call this technique the boogie-woogie roll, because its rolling musical movement was borrowed—initially by Delta blues pioneers such as Robert Johnson and later by whole generations of blues greats—from early 20th-century boogie-woogie blues piano players such as Albert Ammons, Pinetop Smith, Jimmy Yancey, and Meade Lux Lewis. Though you are a guitarist, these early blues piano greats definitely deserve a listen—it's really fun music.

Just like the basic sixth and flat-seventh shuffle patterns shown above, the boogie-woogie roll can be quickly transposed from one chord to another—or one key to another—simply by changing strings, or sliding a power chord up or down the neck and repeating the fingering in a new location.

Using the basic A (or A5 chord) as our starting point, we will use our second finger to play the third fret on the fifth string, followed by our third finger on the fourth fret of the fifth string. The note C at the third fret is the minor or flat third and the note C♯ at the fourth fret is the major third of the A scale. Also, when utilizing this technique, in some songs we pick both notes; while in others we hammer-on the third finger. When necessary throughout this book I'll tell you which technique to use. Go ahead and pick the notes for these initial examples, rather than using a hammer-on technique.

This rolling rhythm can prove tricky to master in the beginning, but eventually will become second nature to most guitarists, which is good because this technique is used in thousands of classic blues, rock, country, and jazz songs. The easiest version of this pattern can be understood using a single string and a straight eighths rock rhythm, rather than the shuffle rhythm you'll eventually want to use.

CD TRACK 10

Example 4.38

In the second measure we'll play the open A note as a chord to thicken up the sound a bit:

The most basic "boogie roll"

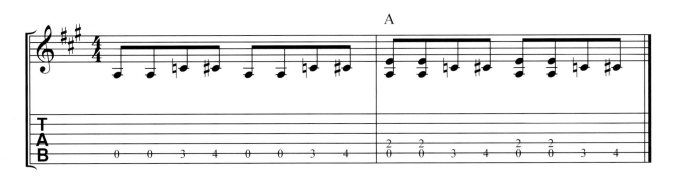

Many times the boogie-woogie roll alternates with sixth and/or the flat-seventh notes from the shuffle techniques you learned above. Following are two different musical examples illustrating how the boogie-woogie roll alternates with sixth and flat-seventh notes. Notice how the roll is played on beat two in the first measure of example one, sort of kicking the rhythm off, and in beat four in the second measure, wrapping up the two-measure riff, so to speak.

CD TRACK 10
Example 4.39

The "boogie roll" with added notes

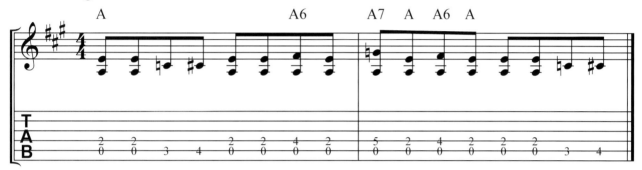

The boogie roll is regularly used in a musical phrase which requires reaching over two strings to play the octave root note, as in the A note at the second fret on the third string for a boogie roll on the A chord. For this reason you should barre across the second fret with your first finger, with your first finger holding down both the E at the second fret on the fourth string, and the A at the second fret on the third string.

CD TRACK 11
Example 4.40

The "boogie roll" with added notes, played with a first finger barre

This same barre technique works and is routinely used on the E chord.

The "boogie roll" with a first finger barre, on the E chord

CD TRACK 11

Example 4.41

Unfortunately, due to the tuning of the second string, the barre doesn't work with the open position D chord. If the song calls for that octave D note (at the third fret on the second string), reach your second finger over to play that note.

The "boogie roll" on the D chord. Use the second finger to play the octave D on the second string

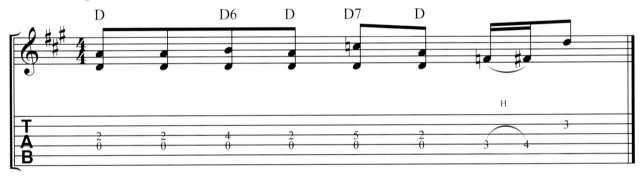

CD TRACK 11

Example 4.42

PART **2** S E C T I O N 4

Now that you've mastered playing the boogie-woogie roll using a straight eighths rock groove, it's time to apply the shuffle feel. We'll play all the same notes as in the examples above, but with the lurching shuffle feel, instead of the straight eighths rock groove.

CD TRACK **12**

Example 4.43

A complete song featuring the "boogie roll" in A

Shuffle

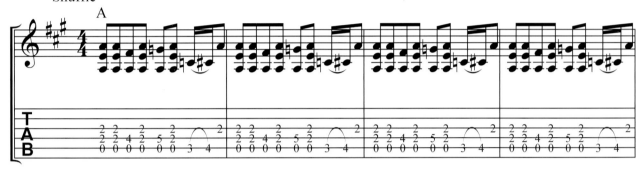

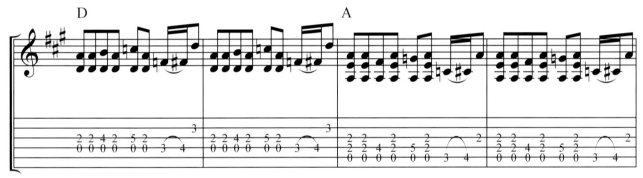

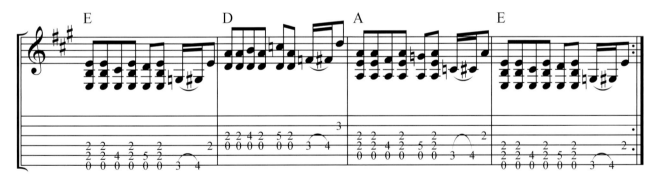

S E C T I O N 4   PART **2**

CD TRACK **13**

Example 4.44

Another common feel for this technique involves playing the roll using a galloping triplet groove. This pattern calls for a slightly quicker rolling of the flat third/major third notes than in the previous examples, in which they were played as eighth-notes. The count on this basic version of the boogie roll would be "1-and, 2-triplet, 3-and, 4-triplet," with the flat third note played on 2, the major third on "trip," and the chord played on "let." Use alternate picking to best accomplish this rhythm.

The "boogie roll" played with a faster, triplet feel

CD TRACK **13**

Example 4.45

This rhythm pattern, which I'll demonstrate in E, was famously used by Led Zeppelin on their 1969 blues-based recording 'Bring It On Home,' which borrowed liberally from the Willie Dixon song of the same name, initially made famous by Sonny Boy Williamson (II) in 1963. It's a very familiar pattern to most guitar players, whether they come from a blues or a rock background.

The "boogie roll" in E, 'Bring It On Home' style

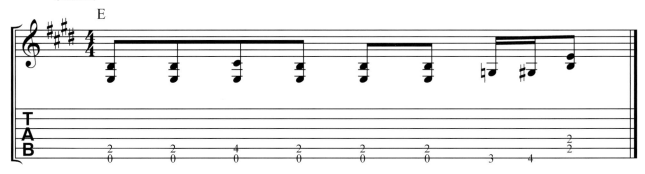

PART **2**   S E C T I O N   4

Jump blues rhythm patterns

Uptempo blues songs are often categorized as jump blues, a style that initially grew out of the piano-based boogie-woogie prevalent in the 30s and 40s. Early practitioners of jump blues included T-Bone Walker and B.B. King (when they weren't playing slow blues songs), as well as jazzier artists such as Lionel Hampton and Louis Jordan. Many blues and jazz artists straddled the line in the 40s, playing either genre as the occasion required. And the jump blues groove has long been a mainstay of both blues and mainstream jazz performers, primarily because it gets people dancing.

A really hot jump blues song can be a lot of fun to play. Because the tempo on a jump tune can be very fast, the old axiom "less is more" definitely comes into play, and works to the guitarist's advantage.

One of the most common jump blues guitar figures involves nothing more than a two-string barre and a hammer-on. In this example, demonstrated as the I chord in the key of A, we simply barre the fifth fret of the third and fourth strings with the first finger, then hammer-on the second finger at the sixth fret of the third string.

When playing this "riff" use a quick slashing strum of the two strings, hammer-on the second finger, then make another quick slash at the two strings. The timing is a bit "syncopated," with the second hit coming on the "and" of beat two. It's just like riding a bike: Once you've got it, you'll have it forever.

CD TRACK 14

Example 4.46

A cornerstone of jump blues rhythm riffs

Because this "chord" is played in the same basic position where you would play a full six-string barre chord, albeit barring only two strings, it is easy to transpose to any chord. In a 12-bar blues in A, we will simply slide this fingering up to the tenth fret for the D (IV) chord. This is right where we would play a full D barre chord. Then move the figure up two more frets, to the 12th fret, to play our V chord, E.

Once you've got the hang of sliding this pattern up and down the neck, apply it to the complete 12-bar tune.

S E C T I O N 4   PART **2**

A full jump blues 12-bar in A

A more advanced version of this jump blues technique (Example 4.48, opposite) involves adding a quick third-finger barre to the pattern. The third finger comes in on beat four; all other beats remain the same as in the previous examples.

When using this pattern, we sometimes jump ahead to the next chord position on beat four of the final measure of each chord in our 12-bar pattern (Example 4.49). For example, at the beginning of the song, in the fourth and final measure of the I chord, we'll jump our hand up into position to play the IV chord on beat four, playing the third finger barre that launches us into the complete IV chord jump technique in measure five.

On beat four of measure six, just before returning to the I chord in measure seven, we'll slide back to the I chord position, in anticipation of that seventh-measure downbeat.

PART **2**   S E C T I O N 4

A common variation on a basic jump blues rhythm riff

This anticipatory move continues throughout the 12-bar song when using this popular jump blues figure.

CD TRACK 16
Example 4.48

CD TRACK 17
Example 4.49

A full jump blues 12-bar in A

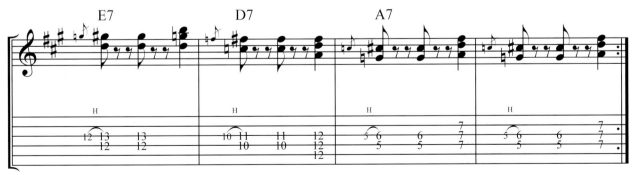

SECTION 4 PART **2**

CD TRACK **18**

Example 4.50

This more advanced jump pattern can also be given additional forward motion by hitting that third-finger barre two times in quick succession, rather than just once per measure as shown above.

A more aggressive variation of the basic jump blues rhythm riff

CD TRACK **19**

Example 4.51

The basic jump blues figure shown above is sometimes enhanced with additional riffs, creating endless variations on the theme. Here are two more common versions:

Two more variations of the basic jump blues rhythm riff

PART **2**   S E C T I O N   4

I could go on and on with inventive ways of adding on to the basic jump rhythm, some of which begin to lean toward lead guitar playing. I'll cover some fun methods of combining this basic jump blues pattern with lead guitar playing in the Lead Guitar section of *The Blues Guitar Handbook*, and with riff-based rhythm playing later in this section.

Common blues seventh chord shapes

Regardless of the tempo, or whether the song is a jump blues, a slow blues, or something in between, seventh chords are very common in blues guitar playing. In fact, they are far more common than a straight major or minor chord. If you need a reminder of what makes a major or minor chord, or a seventh chord, revisit Section Three of this book, in which I explain how chords are built, particularly the entries on "How Chords Are Built" and "Special chord rules."

In this section I'll examine a variety of seventh chord fingerings and show how these chord shapes might be used in blues rhythm guitar playing. There are two basic types of seventh chords blues players typically use: dominant seventh chords, built off a major chord (these are so common, we usually just refer to them as seventh chords), and minor seventh chords, built off a minor chord. I'll explore the dominant seventh chords first.

Different fingerings of the dominant seventh chord can be created using any of the five "CAGED" chord shapes. Here are diagrams of the most basic of these shapes, and examples of their common use in the blues:

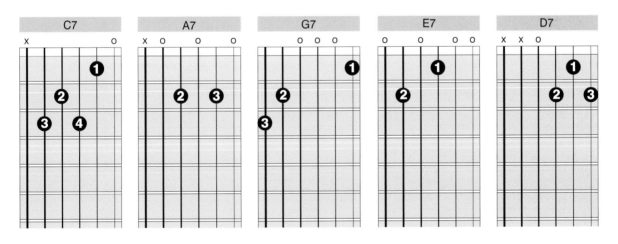

C-shape seventh chords

Using barre chords, or otherwise sliding these basic shapes up the neck of the guitar, we find additional forms of the seventh chord. For example, a C-shape seventh chord, slid up the neck—as an eighth-fret F7 in this illustration—can be played two different ways:

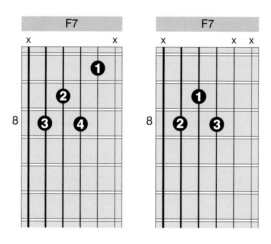

Using that C-shape seventh chord, we often find blues rhythms such as the vamp in measure one. Another cool and common move with the C7 shape involves sliding the chord up to the IV chord chromatically, hitting every fret on the way, as in measure two:

CD TRACK 20

Example 4.52

A common vamp and chromatic climb featuring the C-shape 7th chord

The C7 shape (some might think of this fingering as a B7 shape, since it is so often used as B7 in many blues songs in the key of E) is often slid down chromatically during a turnaround:

A common turnaround move in E featuring the bottom three notes of the C-shape 7th chord

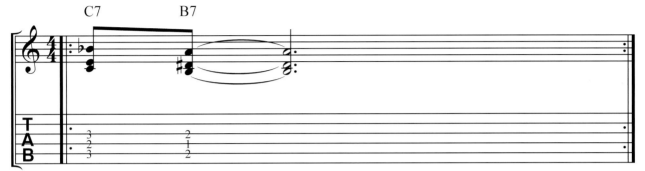

A-shape seventh chords

An A-shape chord, slid up to the third fret and played as a C7 in this example, offers us these three common seventh chords:

CD TRACK **20**

Example **4.53**

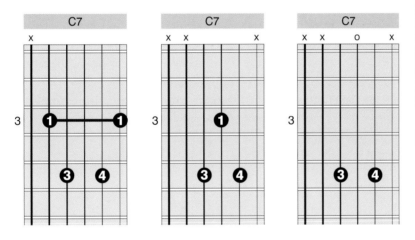

The A-shape seventh chord can be used for general comping, meaning to play simple accompaniments. Often this is done using the following rhythmic pattern:

CD TRACK **21**

Example **4.54**

A common vamp featuring the A-shape 7th chord

SECTION 4 PART **2**

CD TRACK 21

Example 4.55

Another great use of the A-shape seventh chord is in the turnaround of a blues chord progression. A very common fingering, shown here in the key of E, would look like this:

A common turnaround in E featuring the A-shape 7th chord

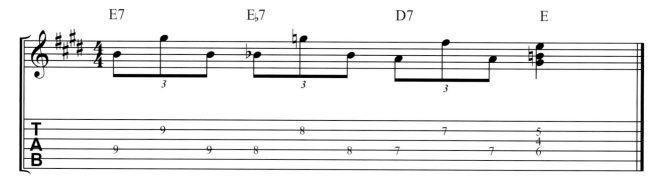

G-shape seventh chords

A G-shape seventh chord is easily played as either a three-finger voicing on the low strings, or as a partial barre chord on the high strings:

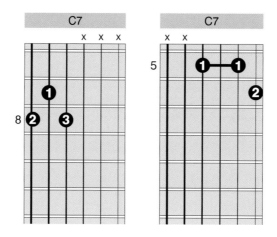

The lower pitched voicing was a favorite of Albert King, and can be easily slid from the I chord directly to the IV and V chords (Fig. 1) and it can also be moved chromatically (Fig. 2.):

PART **2** SECTION 4

This thick-sounding version of the G-shape 7th chord was a favorite of Albert King

The higher-pitched chord shape offers a sparkly high seventh chord tone that works well for comping:

CD TRACK 22

Example 4.56

A common vamp featuring a higher-voiced G-shape 7th chord

E-shape seventh chords

An E-shape seventh chord, slid up the neck and played as a barre chord—as an eighth-fret C7 in this illustration—is often played with one of these three fingerings:

CD TRACK 22

Example 4.57

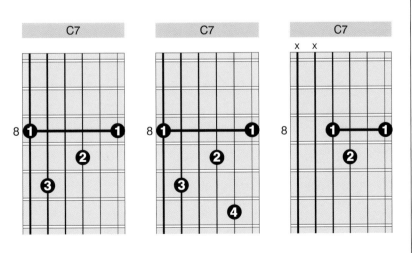

CD TRACK **23**
Example **4.58**

The barred E-shape seventh chords work great for simple blues comping. Here is a commonly found comping pattern:

A common comping pattern featuring the E-shape 7th chord, played as an eighth-fret C7

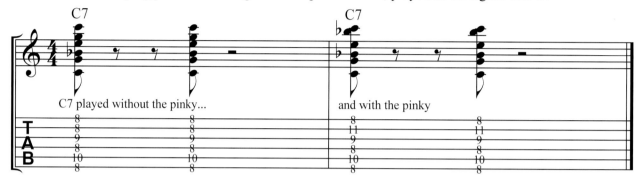

This version of the barred E-shape seventh chord, with the seventh played by the pinky on the fifth string—which is a bit of a stretch and may take some practice—works well and is commonly used for a blues shuffle away from open position:

Power chord style E-shape chord, with the pinky adding notes to make a C6 and C7 chord

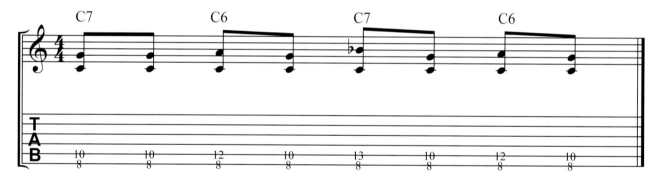

CD TRACK **23**
Example **4.59**

PART **2**   S E C T I O N 4

Here are a few bonus seventh chord shapes derived from the E-shape barre chord. The first two are a mainstay of both jazz and blues guitarists, and the third shape is one we covered in the jump blues discussion above.

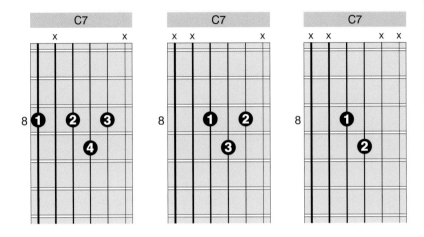

Any of these three chord shapes work well with a simple comping pattern, or with a more active strumming pattern. Notice how you slide into the chords from one fret behind in this example:

CD TRACK 23

Example 4.60

This version of the E-shape 7th chord is easily slid and works well with 16th-note rhythmic patterns

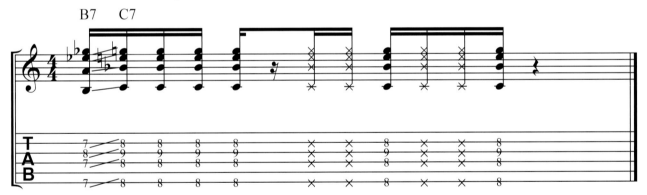

D-shape seventh chords

Of course, a D-shape seventh chord can also be played up and down the neck and is often used in blues turnarounds. The fourth-string root note is optional, and fingering can be adjusted to either include this note, or play the chord with just three notes. This chord shape is shown here as a G7 chord, in both three- and four-note varieties:

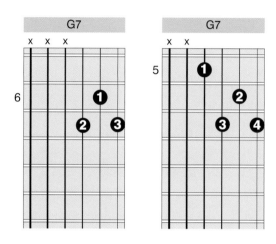

CD TRACK 24

Example 4.61

Here is a great comping rhythm using this D-shape seventh chord for our I chord, and the G-shape seventh chord for the IV and V chords. In this example G7 is our I chord, with C7 and D7 as our IV and V chords.

A turnaround in G featuring G-shape 7th chords on D and C, and a D-shape 7th chord on G

PART **2**   S E C T I O N 4

And of course that D-shape seventh chord is regularly used in blues turnarounds. Try this one for size:

CD TRACK **24**

Example 4.62

A common turnaround end phrase in G featuring the D-shape 7th chord

As a recap, all the above seventh chords are those we regularly refer to simply as seventh chords, but which technically should be called dominant seventh chords, to distinguish them from other types of seventh chords. Blues guitarists also have a need to know a variety of minor seventh chords. Let's take a look at the common fingerings of minor seventh chords, and some ways in which they are typically used in blues.

There are no particularly common minor seventh chords based on the C or G chord shapes, but the E-, A-, and D-shape chords do provide us with minor seventh chords often used in blues rhythm guitar playing.

E-shape minor seventh chords

The E-shape barre chord, played as a minor chord, provides us with three common alternatives, shown here as a seventh-fret B minor seventh (Bm7) chord:

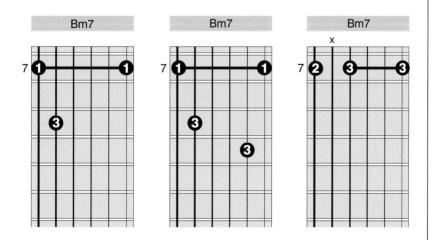

CD TRACK 25

Example 4.63

Using the full barre shape of this chord, and a strumming pattern reminiscent of B.B. King's 'The Thrill Is Gone,' we find a common minor blues groove:

An E-shape minor 7th chord played as Bm7

CD TRACK 25

Example 4.64

Adding the pinky to the second string and sliding it from the sixth to the flat-seventh of the chord provides a nice alternative to the rhythm above.

Another variation on an E-shape minor 7th chord comping pattern

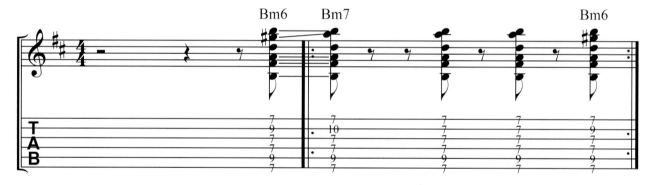

CD TRACK 25

Example 4.65

A heavier minor blues sound can be achieved using the third variety of the E-shape minor seventh chord. Here is a rhythm pattern straight out of the Billy Gibbons/Z.Z. Top blues songbook:

A thicker-toned E-shape minor 7th chord, played as Gm in the style of Billy Gibbons of Z.Z. Top

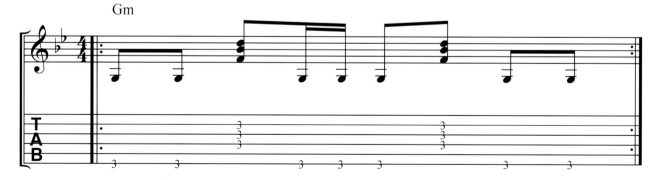

PART **2**   S E C T I O N 4

A-shape minor seventh chords

The A-shape barre chord, played as minor, also includes three common alternatives, shown here as a third fret Cm7 chord:

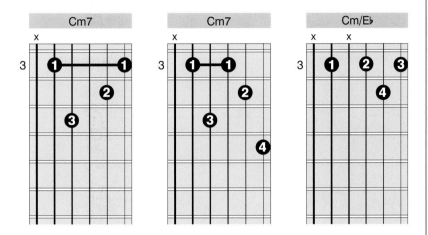

This A-shape barre minor seventh chord, played in this example as a third fret Cm7 chord, can provide us with a slightly jazzy blues groove, in the style of some West Side Chicago blues players such as Otis Rush—or even a blues/rock groove such as Santana might play:

CD TRACK 26

Example 4.66

The A-shape minor 7th chord, played as C minor in the style of 'Black Magic Woman'

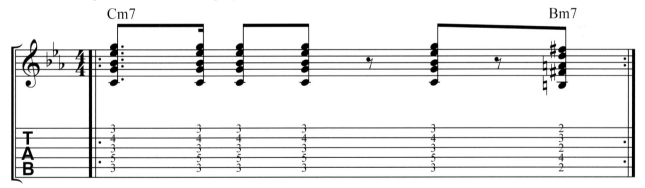

CD TRACK 26

Example 4.67

This same type of groove can be spiced up by simply adding the pinky to the first string. In this example we'll again slide from the sixth to the flat-seventh:

Use your pinky on the first string to create higher-voiced Cm6 and Cm7 chords

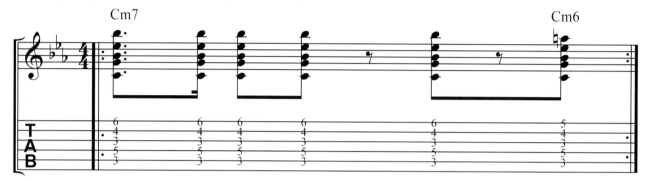

CD TRACK 27

Example 4.68

The lighter sound of this A-shape minor seventh chord is due to the fact that we have left off the fifth of the chord, which would have fallen on the fourth string. The openness of such chords provides a nice change-up to a power-chord or barre-chord heavy set-list.

Eliminating the 5th from the A-shape minor 7th chord provides a more open, jazzy tone

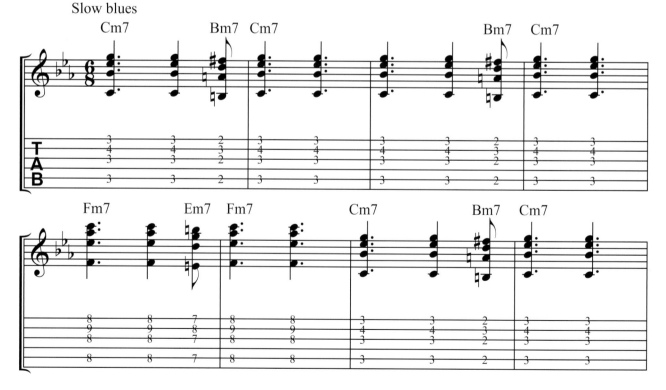

PART **2**   S E C T I O N   4

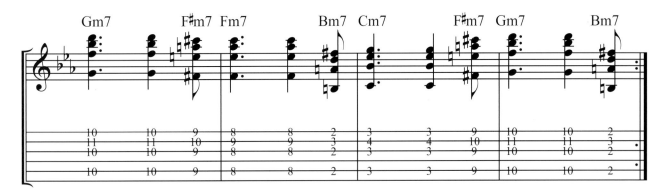

D-shape minor seventh chords

And the D-shape chord provides us with a sweet-sounding minor seventh fingering, shown here as a Gm7:

CD TRACK **27**

Example **4.68**

(continued)

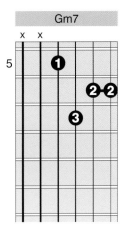

We might find this chord voicing used in a minor blues in 6/8 time:

CD TRACK **28**

Example **4.69**

A slow blues utilizing the melodious D-shape minor 7th chord

Slow blues

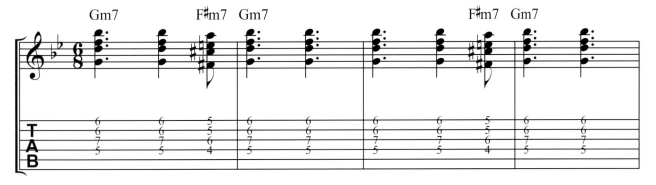

S E C T I O N 4   PART **2**

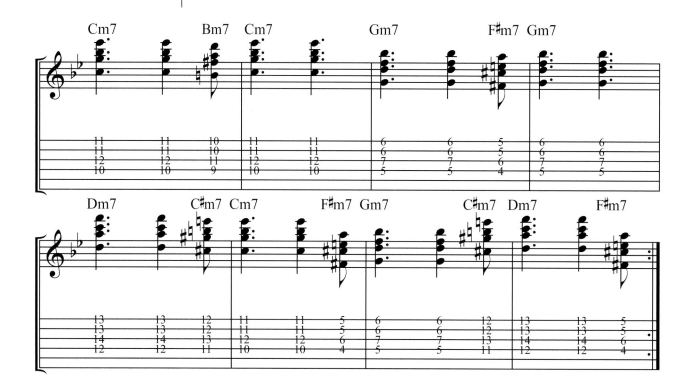

CD TRACK 28

Example 4.69

(continued)

Common blues ninth chord shapes

Blues guitar players love the sound of a good ninth chord. The most common blues use of ninth chord specifically involves a major chord, with a ninth and usually a flat-seventh added. But don't worry too much about the theory behind it all, just learn the shapes and start having fun.

The ninth chord shapes we most often see in the blues are based on the C and E shape chords. There are ninth chords based on the other CAGED system shapes—A, G, and D—but they are not commonly used by blues players.

C-shape ninth chords

There are two basic fingerings of the C-shape ninth chord, shown here as an F9 chord at the eighth fret.

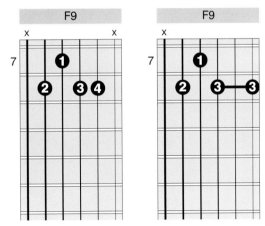

CD TRACK **29**

Example 4.70

Using that C-shape ninth chord, we often find blues rhythms such as this:

The C-shape 9th chord, played as F9 in this example, is a mainstay of funk-blues

That same basic shape of ninth chord is often found in a blues turnaround:

The C-shape 9th chord as commonly used in a turnaround

CD TRACK **29**

Example 4.71

SECTION 4 PART **2**

There is another, closely related variety of this chord shape which is commonly found in blues music, and especially in blues-based rock. Jimi Hendrix and The Allman Brothers, as well as modern blues-rockers such as Kenny Wayne Shepherd, have regularly used this "altered" chord, in which we raise the ninth a half-step and call that note a sharp-ninth, and the resulting chord a seven sharp-ninth chord. Though this chord can be slid to any fret—its root note is on the fifth string—here it is shown as an E7♯9:

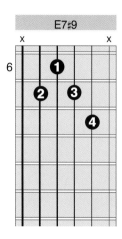

CD TRACK 30

Example 4.72

The E7♯9 chord might be put to use with a rhythm in which we alternate the chord with a low, open E-string bass note:

The "Jimi Hendrix" chord, the 7♯9, played in E

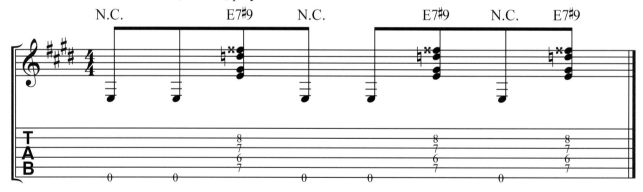

E-shape ninth chords

There are four fingerings of ninth chord based on—or closely positioned to—the E-shape barre chord. All four of these shapes are regularly used by blues guitarists. I've shown them here as a C9 chord, at or near the eighth fret.

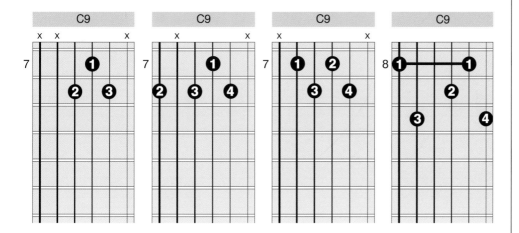

The easiest of these chords, shown in the first measure, involves just three fingers, and is often slid to from one fret above or below in a blues comping pattern. Strum only the three strings fingered. In the second measure, by placing the first finger on the sixth string, we add the low bass root note to that same chord shape.

CD TRACK 31

Example 4.73

Two variations on an E-shape 9th chord played over a jump blues groove

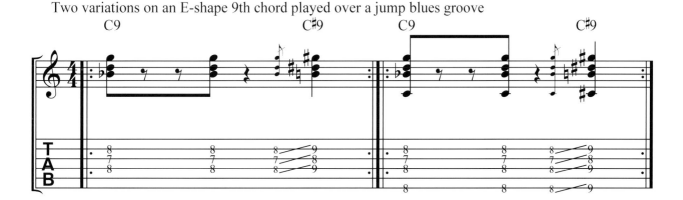

CD TRACK 32

Example 4.74

A favorite ninth-chord voicing of veteran blues guitarists—albeit a slightly more complicated fingering—involves moving that low bass root note to the major third of the chord. B.B. King used this shape to achieve the classic climb from the I to the IV chord in the intro of his *Live At The Regal* recording of 'Every Day I Have the Blues.'

The E-shape 9th chord of choice for many blues pros, as in B.B. King's 'Every Day I Have The Blues'

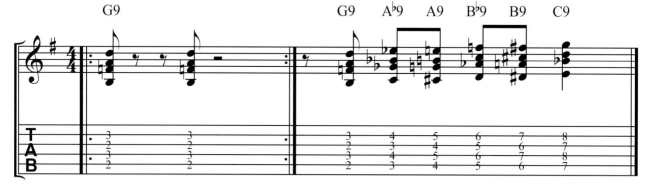

CD TRACK 33

Example 4.75

This final rhythm uses an E-shape ninth chord which actually *looks* like a barre E-shape chord. Hold a regular E-shape barre chord, and simply play the ninth of the chord on the first string with the pinky. Here we'll treat the ninth as a passing tone, giving the chord a sense of movement, and leading us to the IV chord.

A true barre E-shape 9th chord with the 9th on the first string

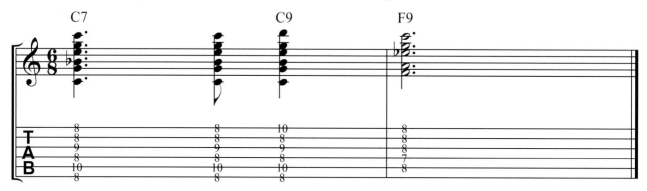

Minor ninth chords

Minor ninth chords have a decidedly jazzy flavor. The use of either the C-shape minor ninth or the E-shape minor ninth chords I'll show here will add a very uptown feel to a minor blues.

PART **2**   S E C T I O N 4

C-shape minor ninth chords

There is just one voicing of the C-shape minor ninth chord you need to know, shown here as a Cm9 chord at the third fret—and the same chord with a raised or sharp ninth.

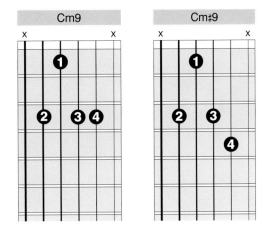

Either of these chord voicings works well in a minor blues setting.

CD TRACK **34**

Example **4.76**

The C-shape minor 9th chord and the same chord with a raised 9th

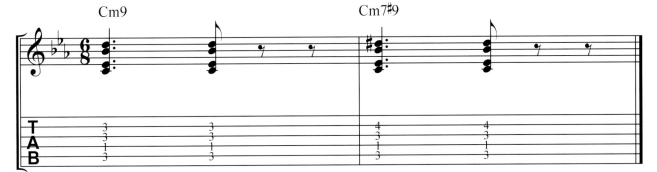

SECTION 4   PART **2**

E-shape minor ninth chords

We can easily play the ninth or the raised ninth using the pinky with the E-shape barre.

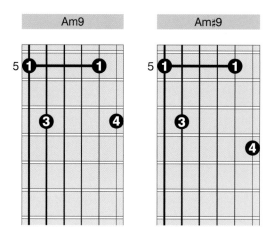

CD TRACK **35**

Example 4.77

A minor blues featuring the ninth sound often moves back and forth between the E-shape minor ninth and the C-shape minor ninth. In this scenario, the E-shape chord performs as the I chord, with the C-shape chord acting as our IV chord.

The E-shape A minor 9 chord serves as i in this example, while the C-shape D minor 9 is the iv chord

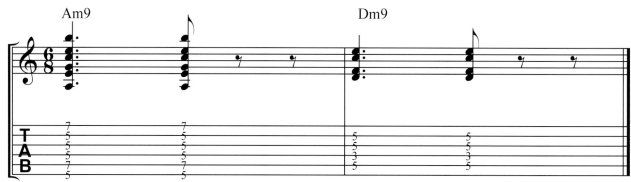

Blues riffs

Solid blues guitar playing involves much more than just a few cool chords. In this section of *The Blues Guitar Handbook*, we'll explore how single-note riffs—based on the pentatonic scale patterns—are used as rhythm-guitar parts, often mimicking or complementing the bass guitar. These riffs, which are sometimes combined with chords, are the building blocks of many classic blues songs.

Common blues riffs and basslines

Blues rhythm guitar playing often requires the guitarist to play single note lines, or riffs, rather than chords. Often these riffs mimic a bass guitarist's part, or a figure played with the left hand on the keyboards; at other times the guitar and bassist or keyboardist play complementary figures which are not identical. Also, there are plenty of blues songs in which the guitarist will alternate between a single-line rhythm riff and one or more chords. In this section I'll show you the basic patterns used to play common blues rhythm riffs, and then illustrate with examples.

The most common riffs are drawn from the pentatonic scale patterns—the same patterns you'll use to play blues lead guitar. It can't be said strongly enough: master the pentatonic scale patterns and you'll be well on your way to mastering blues guitar.

There are five pentatonic scale patterns you should learn, but just two of these give us most of the blues riffs used in rhythm guitar playing. The diagrams show these two pentatonic scale patterns in the relative keys of A minor and C major.

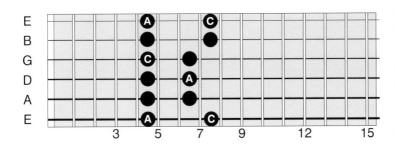

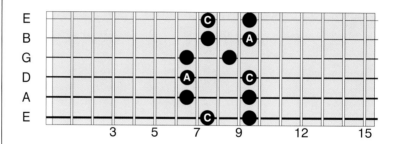

And in addition, one pattern based on the pentatonic scale, known as the blues scale, is an obvious must-know pattern:

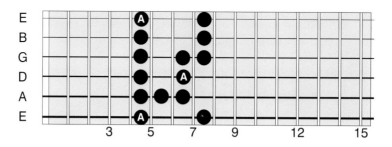

All of these scale patterns are "sliding," which means you can slide them up and down the fretboard to use them in different keys.

Riffs using the main pentatonic pattern—minor keys

While there are five pentatonic scale patterns that work together to cover the length of the fretboard in any one key (I'll show you the rest in the section titled Blues Lead Guitar), there is one pattern which is simply more widely used than any of the rest, both in rhythm and lead guitar playing. I call this pattern the "main" pentatonic pattern. Many blues songs are based on rhythm riffs that come straight out of this pattern, or its matching blues scale. Work hard on this pattern, and playing riff-based songs such as Sonny Boy Williamson's 'Good Morning Little Schoolgirl' or Albert King's 'Born Under a Bad Sign' will come easy to you.

Also, many people think of this pattern as a "minor" pentatonic scale pattern. It can actually be played as minor or major, depending on which note in the pattern you treat as the root note of the scale, because every minor scale is related to a major scale and shares the same notes. If you are puzzled by this, re-read the entry on relative major and minor keys in the Music Theory section of this book. I'll cover that more in the lead guitar section of *The Blues Guitar Handbook*.

Here is a very common blues rhythm riff using the main pentatonic. Notice we need only play on the three lowest strings.

CD TRACK **36**

Example 5.1

A common pentatonic-based blues bass and guitar riff
Shuffle

Using these same notes, the blues greats came up with countless variations of main pentatonic blues riffing. Here is another riff which simply switches a couple notes around:

CD TRACK **36**

Example 5.2

Another variation on the pentatonic-based blues bass and guitar riff
Shuffle

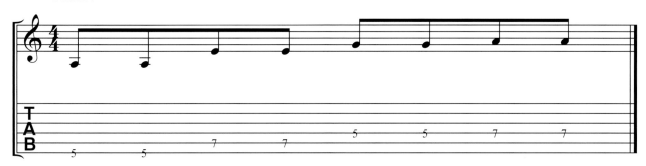

Here is another, with a slightly more active rhythmic figure:

CD TRACK **36**

Example 5.3

Shuffle

SECTION 5   PART **2**

I could go on and on with patterns such as these, taken directly from the main pentatonic scale pattern. Typically, in a riff-based song, we will play the identical riff over the I, IV, and V chords. One way we can accomplish this is by simply sliding the pattern to the appropriate fret for each "chord." In this example, written in A, we play at the fifth fret for the I "chord" (A), then at the tenth fret for the IV chord (D), and at the 12th fret for the V chord (E).

CD TRACK 37

Example 5.4

A pentatonic-based riff over the I, IV, and V chords in A

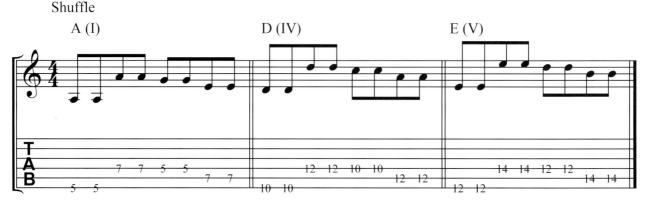

Sometimes, however, it makes more sense to keep our hand in one place on the fretboard, rather than sliding up and down so many frets. To play this exact same song without jumping around the fretboard so much, we can play this pattern starting on the sixth string for the I chord, then simply move the pattern over one string—beginning each riff of the IV and V chord on the fifth string. In this way, we never have to move more than two frets from our starting position.

For example, in the key of A, our D riff would be played at the fifth fret of the fifth string, and our E riff would be played at the seventh fret on the fifth string.

Example 5.5

A pentatonic-based riff over the I, IV, and V chords all within two frets of our starting point

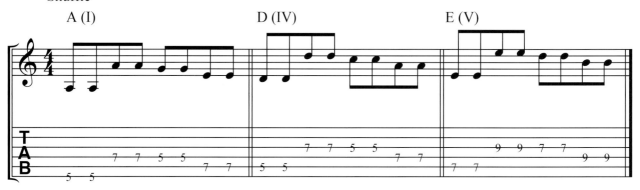

PART **2**   S E C T I O N   5

This kind of movement, from a I chord root note on the sixth string to IV and V chord root notes on the fifth string, is very common. It can go the other way too. In a song in the key of E, we can start with our I chord (E) riff at the seventh fret on the fifth string, then play our IV chord (A) riff at the fifth fret on the sixth string, and the V chord (B) riff at the seventh fret on the sixth string.

CD TRACK 38

Example 5.6

A pentatonic-based riff over the I, IV, and V chords with the I chord on the fifth string

Shuffle

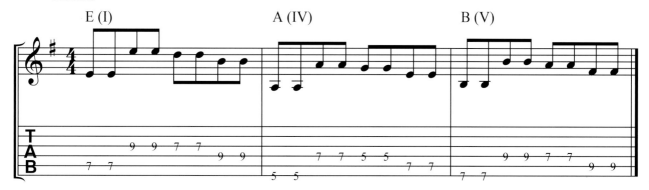

Riffs using the second pentatonic pattern—major keys

Not all blues songs rely on a minor-based riff, as played in the examples above. Many blues songs lean toward major keys. One of the most common ways to play one of these major key, riff-based blues tunes is to use the "second" pentatonic scale pattern. This is the same scale pattern in which lead guitarists find the notes for the aptly named "B.B.'s Box." This popular guitar position is so named because B.B. King (and every other blues guitarist who has ever lived) uses this pattern extensively in their soloing.

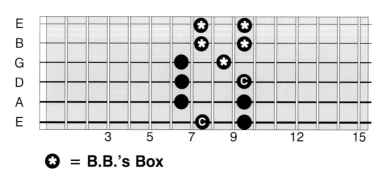

✪ = B.B.'s Box

S E C T I O N 5   PART **2**

For the rhythm guitar work on which we are focusing, we won't need those high string notes which B.B. King uses to such great effect in his soloing. Instead we'll stick with the three low strings, just as we did in the main pentatonic pattern. In this example, in the key of C major, we'll position our second finger on the eighth fret of the sixth string to start this very familiar major blues riff:

Example 5.7

A common major pentatonic-based blues riff
Shuffle

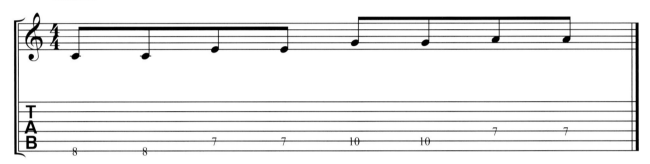

CD TRACK 39

Example 5.8

Once again, we can slide this pattern up and down the neck—keeping the root note for each of our riffs on the sixth string. In this particular key we'll end up with some open strings on our IV chord riff (F), then find the V chord (G) at the third fret.

A major pentatonic-based riff over the I, IV, and V chords
Shuffle

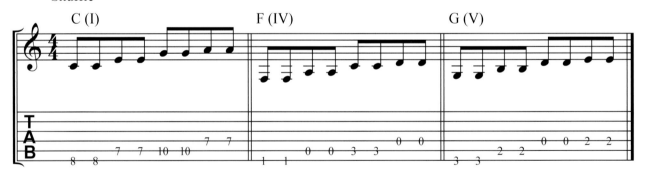

PART **2**   S E C T I O N 5

But just as with the main pentatonic blues riffs, it is often preferable to simply move the pattern—and our root notes—across one string, to eliminate the need to slide so far up and down the neck. Here we'll simply move to the eighth fret, fifth string for our IV chord (F) riff, and then the tenth fret, fifth string for the V chord (G) riff.

Example 5.9

A major pentatonic-based riff over the I, IV, and V chords all within two frets of our starting point

In many blues songs we vary this basic riff slightly to include the flat-seventh of each chord.

A common variation on the major pentatonic-based riff

CD TRACK 39

Example 5.10

S E C T I O N 5

PART **2**

Notice how we will use that flat-seventh to push us from one chord to the next:

A complete 12-bar blues featuring the common major pentatonic-based riff

Shuffle

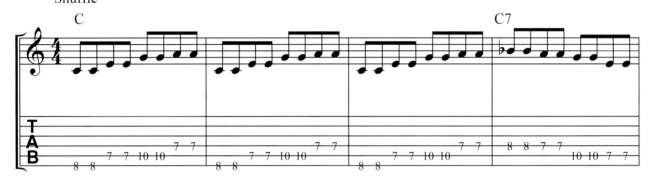

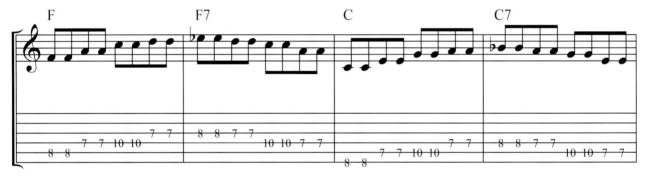

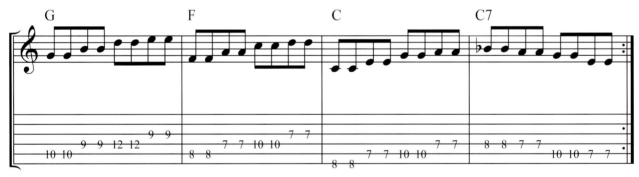

CD TRACK 40

Example 5.11

An alternative major blues riff

When we use the second pentatonic pattern to play major-based blues riffs, the first two notes in the riff are the root note and the major third of the scale. This is what gives us the major sound. There is another common method of playing this major style of blues riff, one in which we start on the same root note in the second pentatonic pattern, but slide up into the third pentatonic scale pattern to finish the riff.

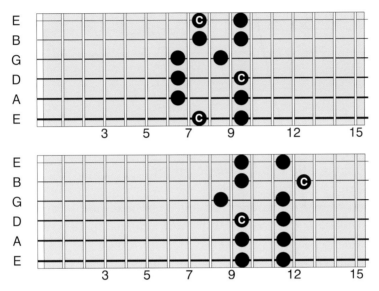

The notes we'll play in this version of the major blues riff are the same as we played in the riffs based on the second pentatonic scale, shown above. In the following example, however, rather than reaching to the fifth string for the second note in the pattern, we perform a quick slide to play that same note on the sixth string. This slide is very definitive and will probably sound very familiar to you. Early rock artists such as Carl Perkins and Elvis Presley recorded songs with this feel, and it is a staple of many blues songs as well. I often think of Presley's 'Hound Dog' when I hear this riff.

CD TRACK **41**

Example 5.12

Slide into the E in this variation on the major pentatonic-based riff

And just as we can jump the other blues riffs over to the fifth string to complete our I-IV-V chord progression, we can do the same with this alternative major blues riff:

Slide into the third note on each "chord" in this I-IV-V progression

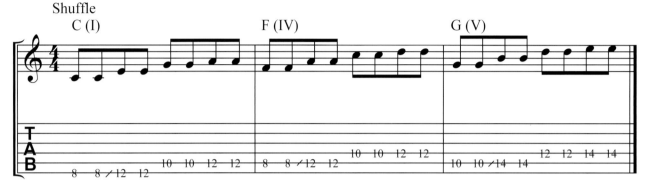

Playing riffs and chords together

We can combine these blues riffs with chords, partial chords, and chord-like movements to create something bigger than just a simple riff. Once again, the possibilities are endless, but we've got limited space, so I'll show just a couple of examples illustrating the concept. Once you get the hang of this you can let your imagination—and your fingers—run wild.

In this first example I'll use the main pentatonic riff with some simple seventh chord voicings. Notice the additional chording in the final measure of this 12-bar blues:

CD TRACK 42

Example 5.14

A I-IV-V 12-bar blues mixing riffs and chords
Shuffle

CD TRACK 43
Example 5.15

I'll jazz it up a bit more in this example. Notice that I completely replace the riff with a chord on the IV chord in measure ten.

Another variation on a I-IV-V 12-bar blues mixing riffs and chords

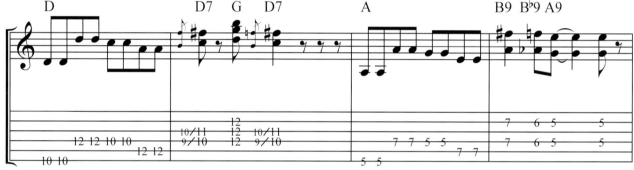

PART **2**   S E C T I O N 5

This same kind of mix of riffs and chords works with the major riffs as well. In this example I'm playing a riff low on the frets—with open strings—for the IV chord (F), but combining that fingering with a higher positioned F9 chord. Again, the possibilities are endless.

CD TRACK 44

Example 5.16

A major 12-bar blues demonstrating a mix of riffs and chords
Shuffle

PART 2

This riff-chord gumbo works with the sliding major blues riff as well:

Another variation on the major 12-bar blues featuring riffs and chords

CD TRACK 45

Example 5.17

Other must-know blues rhythm figures

There are a handful of blues rhythm figures every blues player simply must know which don't fall so neatly into the chord patterns and pentatonic patterns shown above. Some straddle the border between riff and chord, others use patterns other than those illustrated previously in this chapter.

One of the most basic of these must-know blues rhythm patterns is a simple four-note bass guitar riff often copied by guitarists. This up-tempo blues rhythm sets the foundation for many a blues classic, and shows up routinely at blues jams around the globe. In this example, shown in the key of G, our root note is on the tenth fret of the fifth string.

CD TRACK 46

Example 5.18

Another classic blues bass and guitar riff

CD TRACK **47**

Example 5.19

To move this pattern to the IV and V chord, simply slide it up or down the neck, positioning your root note as necessary on the fifth string.

Notice the slight change in the riff when changing from chord to chord

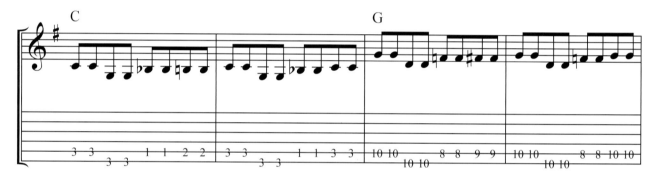

This next pattern is straight out of the John Lee Hooker school of thought, as in simple, simple, simple. It eventually went beyond blues to become a staple of rockabilly players too.

PART **2**   SECTION 5

CD TRACK 48

Example 5.20

Shuffle

Here is that pattern as it might be played over a I-IV-V progression.

A complete low-down boogie in the style of John Lee Hooker

CD TRACK 49

Example 5.21

Shuffle

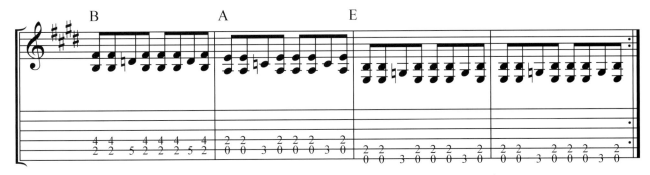

S E C T I O N 5   PART **2**

CD TRACK 50

Example 5.22

One more essential riff-based blues pattern is also perhaps one of the most familiar blues riffs of all. Channel Muddy Waters when performing this stop-time riff.

In the style of Muddy Waters

Slow blues

CD TRACK 51

Example 5.23

And one more riff, very common and absolutely essential to know, is the walk-up from the I chord to the IV chord, which guitarists often do in sync with the bassist or a left-hand figure on the piano or keyboards.

The classic climb from I to IV

Shuffle

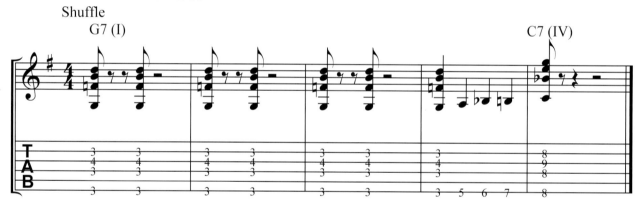

Becoming a blues rhythm master

The study of blues rhythm guitar can be as rewarding and inspiring as any lead guitar playing. The rhythm examples shown in this section and throughout this book are truly the tip of the iceberg. Dedicated blues guitarists continue to learn new tricks for a lifetime, and becoming a true blues rhythm master sometimes takes that long.

Challenge yourself to go beyond the simple riffs or chords you may have played until now and become truly creative with your comping skills. Continue to seek out new riff-based patterns, untried chord voicings, increasingly inventive turnarounds—and new ways to put them all together—and your blues guitar playing will take on a whole new meaning.

Blues lead guitar

Blues lead guitar playing ranges from simple, sustained single notes to explosive, cascading flurries of shredded scale patterns—and everything in between. Whatever your preferred approach, I'll help you make more sense of it with this primer on essential fretboard patterns, some basic scale concepts, a few show-stopping tricks, and the foundations of solid blues improvisation.

Regardless of your current abilities on guitar, I want to assure you that there is no reason to feel stressed, discouraged, or embarrassed over what you don't yet know, or what you can't yet do. Mastering any musical instrument, or gaining the ability to improvise freely on a musical instrument, takes time, and at least some degree of dedication (as in practice, practice, practice). But fortunately, with blues music, you can play the most basic of musical phrases and still sound like a life-long pro.

Many of the early blues guitar greats were not schooled in music in any way whatsoever. They simply picked up the instrument and practiced. They had friends and mentors show them a few things here and there, much the way you are doing simply by scanning through this book. If they put in the time, they got results. Some took it much further than others; how far you choose to take your playing is a personal choice.

But the blues is—at its heart—a folk music, accessible and easy to learn. Take it one lick at a time, one pattern at a time. Know that repetition is key. Don't forget to use your ears. Listen to your heroes; listen to yourself. You're going to get frustrated along the way. When you do, set the guitar down and walk around the block if you need to—or better yet, listen to or watch some inspiring musical performances—but then get back in there and try that tricky guitar part over and over until you nail it. Let's get started.

The secret of great improvisation

The definition of the word improvisation is to "perform on the spur of the moment, without previous preparation." To make it up on the fly. To wing it. Playing lead guitar—improvising—is truly a whole lot of fun, and I want to help you really master it.

There is a secret to great blues improvisation, and here it is: just like every blues guitarist before you, you have to learn to copy the improvisation of others before you can master improvisation yourself.

SECTION 6

PART **2**

Robert Johnson did it. So did B.B. King. Same with Eric Clapton, and Stevie Ray Vaughan, and Jimi Hendrix. They all copied the licks of those who came before them—as closely as possible, sometimes through painstaking effort—until they were able to take off on their own incredible flights of improvisation.

For the most part, all the blues guitar greats learned a few basic, classic blues lead guitar lines, and then they mixed and matched those licks in a different order from song to song, to create their next solo, and their next. And you can too, especially if you really dig into the information and killer blues licks I'm about to share with you.

You'll be needing these

Whether they know it or not, lead guitar players are using scales for everything they do. It goes without saying that you'll play better—and learn faster—if you know the scales forwards and backwards. Fortunately, there are only a few essential patterns. You'll pick them up in minutes, memorize them in a week or two, and really be flying through them with just a few hours of work. Afterwards, you'll enjoy a lifetime of fun with your guitar.

The most important scale patterns in the blues are the pentatonic scale patterns. A pentatonic scale takes its name from the Greek word "penta," which means five. The scale is so named because there are five different notes in one octave of the pentatonic scale, making it a very easy scale to finger, and to memorize. You probably already know this pentatonic scale pattern:

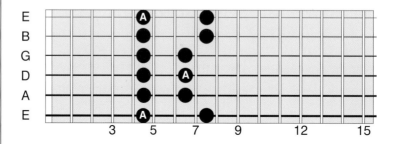

A good blues lead guitarist uses that "main" pentatonic pattern extensively, but it quickly gets old playing in just one place on the neck. Of course you can simply slide that same pattern up 12 frets (on an electric guitar) to play one octave higher:

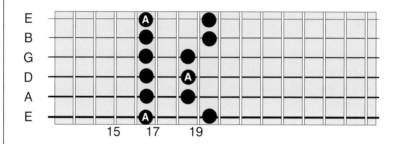

But what about all the frets in between? Let's not let those go to waste, they're full of awesome blues licks! And they're also full of other pentatonic scale patterns that work in conjunction with our "main" pentatonic. In fact, in any one key there are five pentatonic scale patterns that cover the entire fretboard.

Five notes in the pentatonic scale, five different pentatonic patterns ... Do you

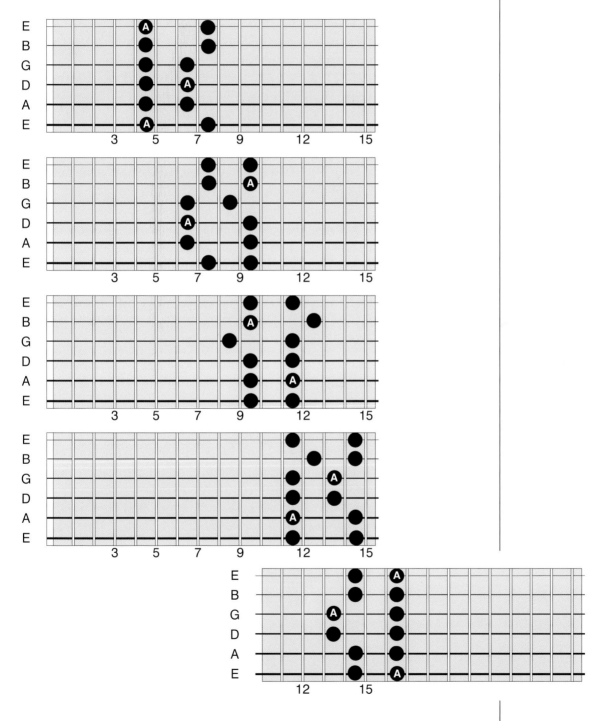

think there might be a (*ahem*) pattern here? There is. Each of the five different pentatonic scale patterns begins on a different note taken from the pentatonic scale.

Notice the starting notes in the five patterns shown on the previous page—A at the fifth fret, C at the eighth fret, D at the tenth fret, E at the 12th fret, and G at the 15th fret. These notes—A, C, D, E, and G—are the same notes that make up the A minor pentatonic scale in the first place. And these same five notes are repeated over and over again across the strings and up and down the fretboard, within the five pentatonic scale patterns, in that key of A minor.

If we choose a different key, the five note names (and the frets at which we start each pattern) would change—but the fingering patterns would remain exactly the same. They simply slide up and down the neck of the guitar, maintaining both their shape and their positioning relative to each other. Learn to play these five patterns in one key, and you'll know how to play them in every key.

Just to prove that point, on the opposite page we can see how those same five patterns line up in the key of G minor.

Each of these five pentatonic scale patterns contains certain classic blues guitar licks that every blues guitarist should know. And in many cases, those same licks can't comfortably be played in any other pattern. Each pattern has its unique licks.

This is why you want to learn each and every individual pattern inside and out, memorizing the fingerings and positions of the notes, and then eventually become comfortable improvising in and playing the classic blues licks found in each individual pattern. Before I show you some classic licks pulled from these patterns, I'll show you a few simple exercises you can apply to each pattern to help you master them.

And then you'll want to put the five patterns together. When playing in any one key, or over one chord, the lead guitarist can simply slide from one pattern to another, pulling off one classic lick after another, while moving up or down the fretboard, working through the five patterns in that key.

But to do that, these five patterns must remain precisely in the same position relative to each other. In the A minor example shown previously, the main pentatonic pattern begins on the fifth fret of the sixth string, the note A. The second pattern begins on the eighth fret of the sixth string, the note C—and so on.

Learning to lock these five pentatonic patterns into position relative to each other is an essential skill for any lead guitarist. In this section of *The Blues Guitar Handbook*, I'll show you a couple of ways to practice moving between the patterns—locking them together in your muscle memory.

Once you are able to do that, you can then move the whole batch of five patterns up or down the fretboard to change key or play over a different chord. We can even use these same five pentatonic scale patterns to play in major keys—it's very unlikely you'll play every song you know in the key of A minor. Using these five pentatonic scale patterns to solo in the key of E minor, or G major, or B♭

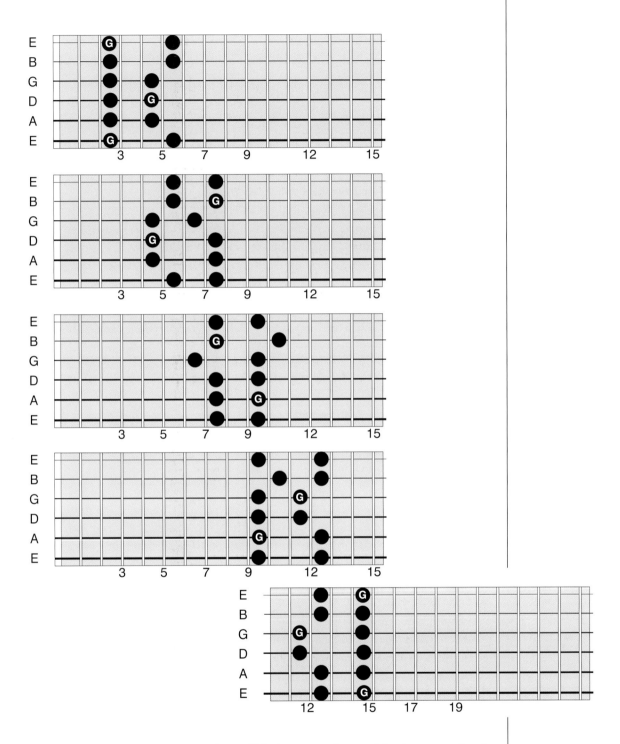

major—or any key—is also something I'll help you understand in the pages ahead.

When you become fluent playing within these five patterns, and after learning some classic blues licks as well, you'll be able to play blues lead breaks which will really turn some heads at your next jam.

SECTION 6 | PART **2**

Essential pentatonic exercises

Mastering each individual pentatonic scale pattern is the first important step. You can begin to do so by first playing each scale pattern from lowest note to highest note and back again. Don't do anything tricky, just play the notes in order up the scale, and then back down the scale. You'll need to do this with every pattern, and do so playing that pattern at every fret, sliding up one fret at a time until you've covered the entire fretboard with that one pattern. Then do it again with the next pentatonic pattern.

In this exercise I've placed the main pentatonic pattern at the first fret, played from lowest note (on the sixth string) to highest note (on the first string) and back again. Then I slide that pattern to the second fret and repeat. Remember to use alternate (down-up, down-up) picking whenever playing any single-note lines, scales, or exercises.

CD TRACK **52**

Exercise 1: Play each pentatonic scale across the strings and back, at every fret on the guitar

PRO TIP: It may take many repetitions of the above exercise with each of the five pentatonic scale patterns before they become completely natural to you. It can be helpful to focus on one a day, or one a week, depending on how much time you have to practice each day.

You don't need to master that initial exercise with all five pentatonic scale patterns before putting the next exercise into play. Chances are you have been playing the main pentatonic pattern for years, and are already fluent with it, but not so much with the second or third pentatonic patterns. If that's the case, stick with Exercise 1 for the second and third patterns (and fourth and fifth), and get going with Exercise 2 with the main pentatonic scale pattern. Gradually work your way through all the exercises with each of the patterns.

Again, this may seem like a mountain of only semi-musical homework—sure, it's more fun to just jam—but the effort will pay off with a lifetime of pure enjoyment, allowing you to fly up and down the fretboard in any key, on any song, soloing and improvising like you could do it in your sleep. Believe me, it's really fun to have the fretboard mastered in this way.

With Exercise 2 we'll play the pattern in groups of three notes. Go slowly until you get it right, then gradually increase the tempo. I call this exercise "up one, back one," because I start on the first note of the scale, play up one note, and then go back to my starting note to complete the group. Then start on the second note of the scale and play up one, back one from there, and so on through the whole scale.

CD TRACK **53**

Exercise 2: Play in groups of three, ascending the scale in each pentatonic pattern

Going back down the scale, Exercise 2 looks like this:

CD TRACK **53**

Exercise 2 continued: Descending the scale in groups of three completes the exercise

In Exercise 3 we're also playing groups of three notes, but this time three different notes. I think of this exercise as "up two, back one," because I start on a note and play that note and the next two notes—three altogether—then I go back one note and start the next group of three there. Up two, back one.

CD TRACK **54**

Exercise 3: Ascend the scale playing groups of three notes in an "up two, back one" sequence

Going back down the scale, Exercise 3 looks like this:

CD TRACK **54**

Exercise 3 continued: Descend the scale playing the same three note sequences in reverse

Here is a fun alternative to the descent on Exercise 3—and this one actually sounds musical! Try using pull-offs when descending from the highest notes to the lowest notes on Exercise 3, and you'll actually be playing a real lead guitar riff used by countless blues and rock guitarists on many a classic recording. If you aren't sure how to do a pull-off, read the next section in this book: "Left Hand Techniques And Articulations."

We could go on and on with exercises patterned after those above. Try playing four notes at a time. Use four notes including your starting note, and go up three, back one. Try up three, back two. Try five-note sequences, six-note sequences—whatever you can dream up will help you become more fluent with the patterns and move you toward exceptional lead guitar skills.

Repeating exercises such as these with every scale pattern you ever learn will not only completely burn those patterns into your brain and your fret-hand muscle memory, they will also give you an invaluable dose of ear-training, which will help you in learning solos from your favorite guitar heroes down the road. They'll also provide finger exercise which will make your fret-hand fingers much more agile, flexible, quick, and accurate, and will help you build strength and stamina for all the great extended guitar solos yet in your future.

But wait, there's more. In addition to all the benefits described above, the work you do with these exercises will serve to synchronize your fret-hand and pick-hand to the point where you will rarely ever pick the wrong string again, and will help bring you to the point where your pick is simply on autopilot, and rarely ever needs any of your concentration at all. And that's a great place to be, free to focus completely on what your fret-hand is doing—and eventually, once that hand is also on autopilot, wherever your improvisational muse takes you!

Locking the patterns together

Now let's work on a few exercises to get the five pentatonic scale patterns locked together, so that you can learn to slide effortlessly up and down the fretboard, kicking out classic licks from each of the five pentatonic scale patterns as you pass through them, just like the legends.

With Exercise 4 we'll play just the four lowest notes of the main pentatonic pattern—going up the scale using just the notes on the sixth and fifth string—then slide up into the second pentatonic scale pattern. At that point we'll descend the scale, ending back on the starting note from the main pentatonic pattern. With this exercise you'll learn to start in one pattern, slide up into the next pattern up the fretboard, and then slide back to your starting pattern—just like you'll often do when soloing.

CD TRACK **55**

Exercise 4: Slide from one pentatonic pattern into the next, then back again

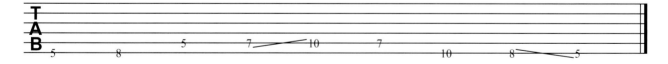

Now let's do the same exercise using the first six notes of the main scale pattern, starting on the sixth string and playing up to the fourth string before sliding into the second pentatonic scale pattern, and back.

Exercise 5: Play the first six notes of the first pattern before sliding up   CD TRACK **55**

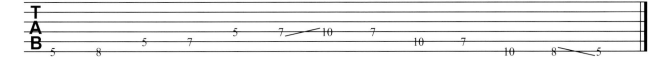

It's very helpful to be able to see the starting points on the sixth string, and often on the fifth string, of various chords and scale patterns. Exercises 4 and 5 will help you with this. It is also helpful to be able to find your way up and down the fretboard—moving through the five pentatonic scale patterns—finding and using the starting points for each pattern on the first and second string. Much of the time, when soloing and improvising, you'll be playing only on the higher strings. Exercise 6 duplicates Exercise 4, except on the two highest strings, rather than the lowest strings. By doing both exercises you learn both ends of the scale inside and out.

Exercise 6: Slide between pentatonic patterns on the high strings   CD TRACK **55**

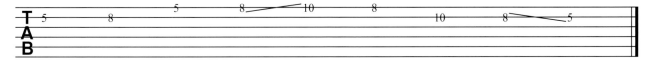

The previous exercises, in which you practice sliding between two adjacent scale patterns, will help you become accustomed to moving smoothly up and down the fretboard the way you've heard all the blues greats do time and again. Repeat these same exercises using the second and third pentatonic patterns, the third and fourth patterns, the fourth and fifth patterns, and finally the fifth pattern sliding into the main pattern.

We can take this a step further too. If you really want to become fluent moving between these all-essential pentatonic scale patterns, try skipping patterns, ie, move from the main pentatonic pattern directly to the third pattern, or directly to the fourth pattern, and back again. The more repetitions you put in, the smoother your transitions will become—and the easier it will become for you to copy the great blues soloists, or take off on your own incendiary improvisations.

Once you've put time into these exercises, mastering the movement between scale patterns by sliding up and down the neck, the distance from one pattern to another will become automatic. Eventually you won't even need to look at your fret hand to be able to move from one pattern to the next and the next. Once you've gotten to this point, you'll be able to do it in any key. Simply by changing your starting position, the fret at which you initially place the main pentatonic pattern, for example, the other pentatonic patterns will simply fall into place. Guitar playing becomes really inspiring once you've reached this point.

The fretboard repeats itself

You may realize that the fretboard repeats itself after 12 frets, or one octave. In the key of A minor, as shown above, the main pentatonic pattern is played at both the fifth fret, and one octave higher, at the 17th fret. If that pattern can repeat, all the other patterns can repeat as well, if there is room on the fretboard. In the earlier diagrams of the five pentatonic patterns shown in A minor, I didn't show you any patterns below the fifth fret. Let's fill in those frets now so you can see how the fretboard repeats itself.

Let's start with the main pentatonic pattern up at the 17th fret. Look at the pattern right behind it, the fifth pentatonic pattern beginning at the 15th fret:

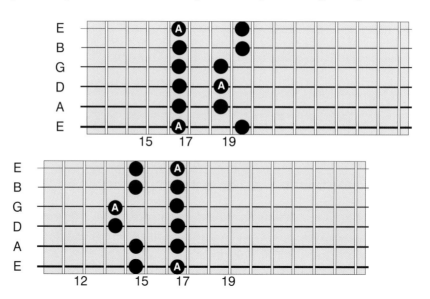

To play in A minor pentatonic below the fifth fret, simply move this fifth pattern down one octave, to the third fret, placing it right in position behind the fifth fret main pentatonic, just like it was one octave higher on the neck. There are some classic blues and rock lead guitar patterns and rhythm riffs which begin in this fifth pattern at the third fret, then slide up into the main pentatonic at the fifth fret, and sometimes beyond.

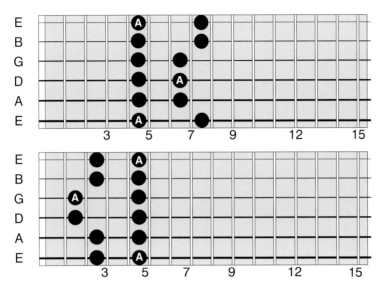

We still have some unused fretboard below that pattern, and one more pentatonic pattern we can fit in that space. In this key we'll end up using some open strings, but we can play the fourth pentatonic pattern starting with the open E-string. Take a look at how the fourth, fifth, and main pentatonic patterns fill in those first few frets.

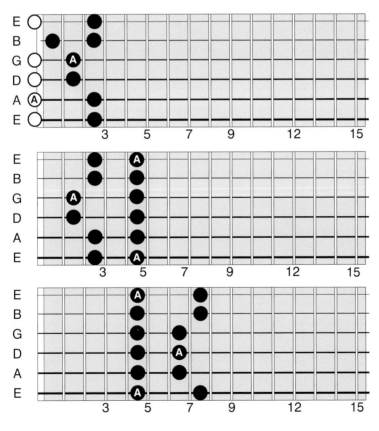

So the pentatonic scale patterns wrap around, if you will, and repeat every 12 frets, and always in the same order. In some keys—such as C or D—the main pentatonic pattern may only be found in a truly comfortable position once on the neck. In other keys, as we've seen in the key of A minor, it can be comfortably played in two different octaves (at least on the electric guitar). In the key of E minor, the main pentatonic pattern is played in the open position, using open strings, and again one octave higher, at the 12th fret. Stevie Ray Vaughan is one blues player who frequently soloed using the open string position of the E minor pentatonic scale.

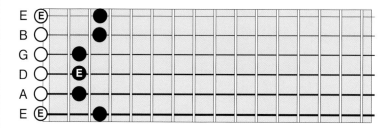

Once you've got the five patterns memorized, and have worked to lock them into position relative to each other, you should be able to move them up and down the fretboard to play in any key, without too much trouble. But just to help you out, here is a chart showing the starting position for each pentatonic scale pattern, in all 12 keys. This chart shows each of the 12 notes on the fretboard as a minor key. Later we'll look at how to use these same patterns to play in a major key.

Frets for pentatonic scale patterns in all keys

Key	Pattern 1*	Pattern 2**	Pattern 3	Pattern 4	Pattern 5
A	5	8	10	12 or open	3 or 15
A♯/B♭	6	9	11	1 or 13	4 or 16
B	7	10	12	2 or 14	5 or 17
C	8	11	1 or 13	3 or 15	6
C♯/D♭	9	12	2 or 14	4 or 16	7
D	10	1 or 13	3 or 15	5 or 17	8
D♯/E♭	11	2 or 14	4 or 16	6	9
E	12 or open	3 or 15	5 or 17	7	10
F	1 or 13	4 or 16	6	8	11
F♯/G♭	2 or 14	5 or 17	7	9	12
G	3 or 15	6	8	10	1 or 13
G♯/A♭	4 or 16	7	9	11	2 or 14
A	5 or 17	8	10	12	3 or 15

* The "main" pentatonic pattern

** The "B.B.'s Box" pentatonic pattern

Classic blues riffs in each pentatonic pattern

Now that you know the five pentatonic scale patterns, I want to show you some classic riffs found in each pattern. Some lead guitar licks can be played in more than one pattern, but many are unique to just one pattern.

Beginning with the main pentatonic pattern—the most widely used pattern for soloing and improvisation—we have licks like these:

CD TRACK 56

Example 6.1

Examples of lead guitar licks in the main pentatonic pattern

CD TRACK **57**

Example 6.2

In the second pentatonic pattern—the pattern that includes the area known as B.B.'s Box—blues guitarists regularly play licks like these:

Examples of lead guitar licks in the "B.B.'s Box" area of the second pentatonic pattern

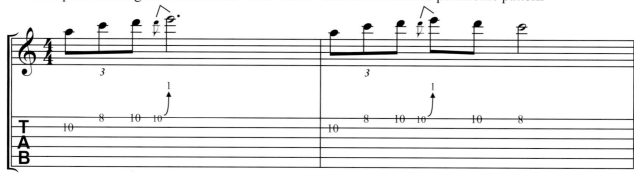

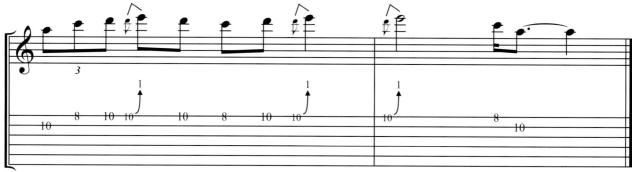

The third pentatonic pattern was a favorite hangout for Albert King, and the spot where he played some of his monstrous two-step bends:

Examples of lead guitar licks in the third pentatonic pattern

CD TRACK **58**

Example 6.3

PART **2**   SECTION 6

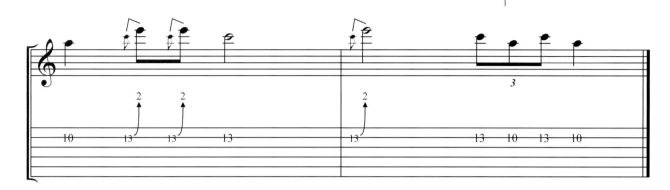

Eric Clapton has long favored licks pulled from the fourth pentatonic pattern, as have many other blues greats. The fourth pentatonic pattern is, in a sense, a "root-five" (meaning root note on the fifth string, instead of the sixth) repeat of the main pentatonic pattern, and is thus very finger-friendly for soloing. The fourth pentatonic pattern gives us licks like these:

CD TRACK **58**

Example 6.3

(continued)

Examples of lead guitar licks in the fourth pentatonic pattern

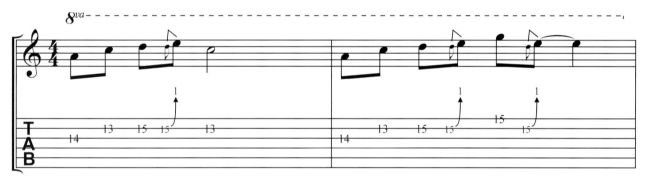

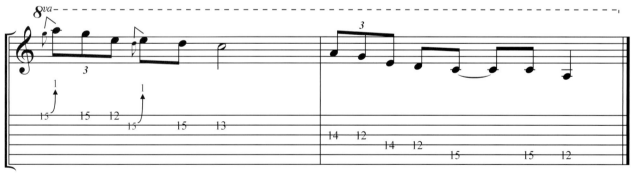

CD TRACK **59**

Example 6.4

SECTION 6 PART **2**

CD TRACK 60

Example 6.5

Often overlooked by lead guitar players, the fifth pentatonic pattern yields some tasty licks:

Examples of lead guitar licks in the fifth pentatonic pattern

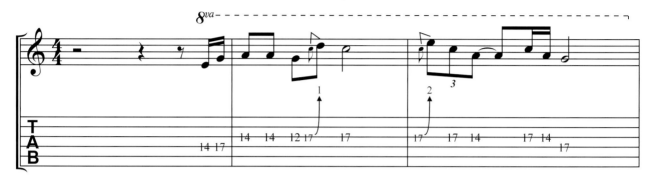

CD TRACK 61

Example 6.6

Here is a short solo piecing together blues lead guitar licks from each pattern, progressing up the fretboard from the main pentatonic pattern at the fifth fret, until it repeats at the 17th fret:

Examples of lead guitar licks progressing through each of the five pentatonic patterns

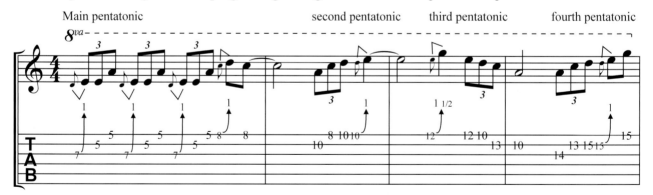

PART **2**   S E C T I O N   6

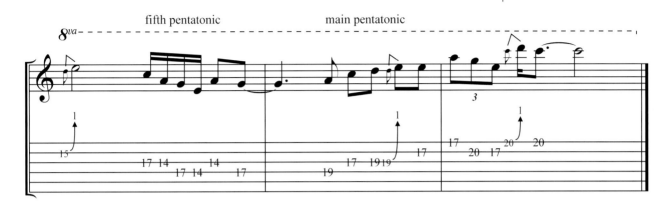

Once you understand how to move from pattern to pattern, up and down the fretboard, playing classic blues licks from each pattern, it is easy to follow a similar model in any key. Here is the same solo, played in G minor. Understand that I am simply playing over one chord here: the "I" chord of the I-IV-V chord progression. I do this as an example of how you can move from scale pattern to scale pattern over one chord. But to play a real solo over a real blues tune, you'll need to be able to play over not just the I chord, but the IV and V chords too.

CD TRACK 61

Example 6.6

(continued)

CD TRACK 62

Example 6.7

Slide all the patterns up or down the fretboard to play the same progression of licks in a different key

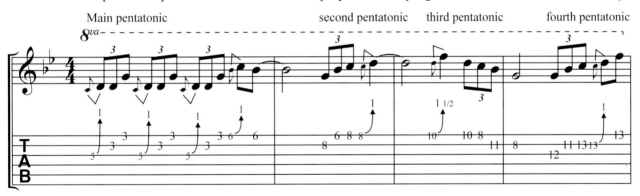

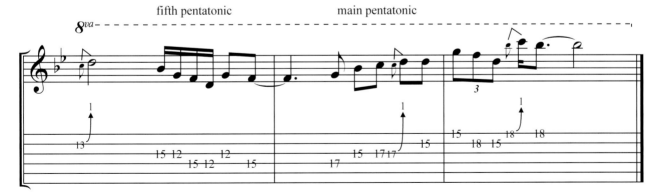

Methods for playing over the I-IV-V chord progression

The licks and riffs I've shown you thus far work great over the I chord, or the A chord in most of the examples shown above. But blues guitar soloing requires that we also be able to play over the IV and V chords as well. How do we handle that?

There are three basic methods I'll show you here: easy, intermediate, and more advanced. Let's walk through each of them step by step.

The easy solo method

The easy method of soloing involves staying in one position—such as the main pentatonic scale pattern—and finding the notes that sound right over each chord. Typically a lead guitarist finds the right notes by finding the "chord tones," or the notes that make up that chord. For example, over the A chord, we might want to play an A (the root of the A chord), a C (the minor or flat third of the A chord), or an E (the fifth of the A chord). The chord tones are the arpeggio tones of that chord, and each of these chord tones is found in the A minor pentatonic scale.

A riff in the main pentatonic scale pattern which works over the I chord in A minor might look like this:

CD TRACK **63**

Example 6.8

Focus on the chord tones: An easy solo highlighting the root (A), third (C), and fifth (E) of the I chord (A minor) as found in the main pentatonic scale pattern

The IV chord, in this case, D, is made up of the notes D, F, and A for D minor, or D, F♯, and A for D major. In our main pentatonic pattern in the key of A we don't have an F or an F♯, but we do have the notes D and A. By playing a riff that focuses on those notes, we can play a suitable lick over the D or IV chord in A minor.

CD TRACK 63

Example 6.9

More chord tones: Easy licks highlighting the root (D), and fifth (A) of the IV chord (D) as found in the main pentatonic scale pattern

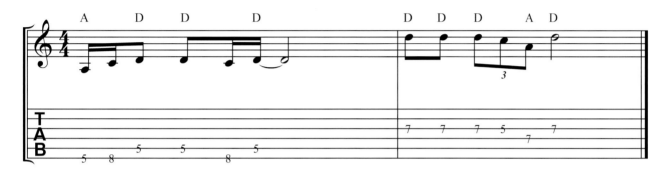

And the V chord, E, is made up of the notes E, G, and B for E minor, or E, G♯, and B for E major. Once again, we don't have all those notes in the main pentatonic in A. We do have an E and a G though, so let's focus on those.

CD TRACK 63

Example 6.10

Still more chord tones: An easy lick highlighting the root (E) and third (G) of the V chord (E) as found in the main pentatonic scale pattern

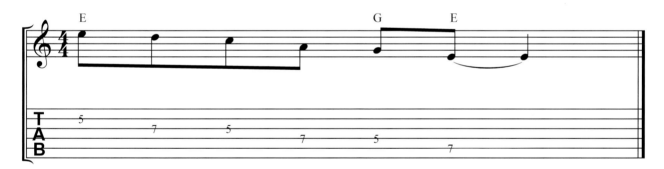

SECTION 6 | PART **2**

Putting that all together, in a 12-bar pattern, we might come up with something like this:

Keep the focus on the chord tones: This easy solo highlights the appropriate chord tones for each chord in the 12-bar progression as found in the main pentatonic scale pattern

CD TRACK 64

Example 6.11

It may not sound like much, but at least we have played appropriate notes over each chord in the progression, including the IV and V chords (D and E), even though we're playing an A minor scale. We accomplished this by focusing—at the appropriate time—on the chord tones for the IV and V chord found within the main pentatonic of the I chord. Pretty cool, huh?

This very simple method of improvising over a I-IV-V chord progression can be used in any key. Simply slide that main pentatonic scale pattern into position wherever the E-shape barre chord for your I chord would be located (ie, at the eighth fret for a C barre chord), and you're good to go.

Also, by finding the root notes or chord tones for the I, IV, and V chords in each of the five pentatonic scale patterns, you can repeat this process up and down the fretboard in each scale pattern, which is a great exercise all by itself. Take it one pattern at a time, and learn to play simple licks involving the appropriate chord tones for the I, the IV, and the V chord in each scale pattern.

For example, an easy solo highlighting the A, D, and E chord tones found in the second pentatonic pattern might look like this:

CD TRACK 65
Example 6.12

Find the chord tones in each pentatonic pattern: This solo highlights the appropriate chord tones for each chord in the 12-bar progression as found in the second pentatonic scale pattern

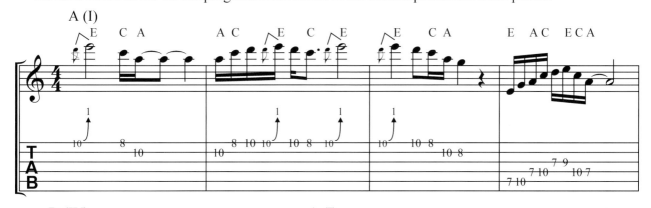

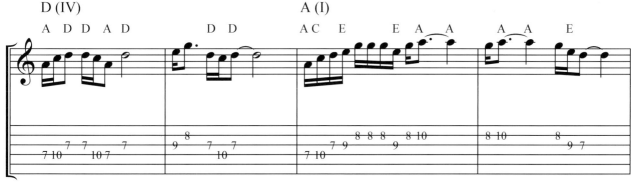

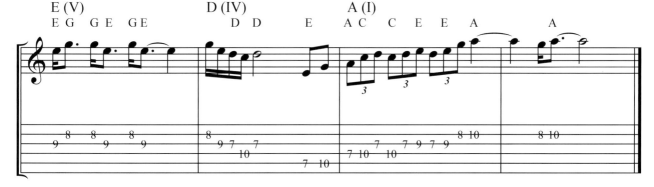

SECTION 6 | PART 2

And just to get you started, here are diagrams of all five pentatonic scale patterns with the I, IV, and V chord tones noted, again, in a minor key:

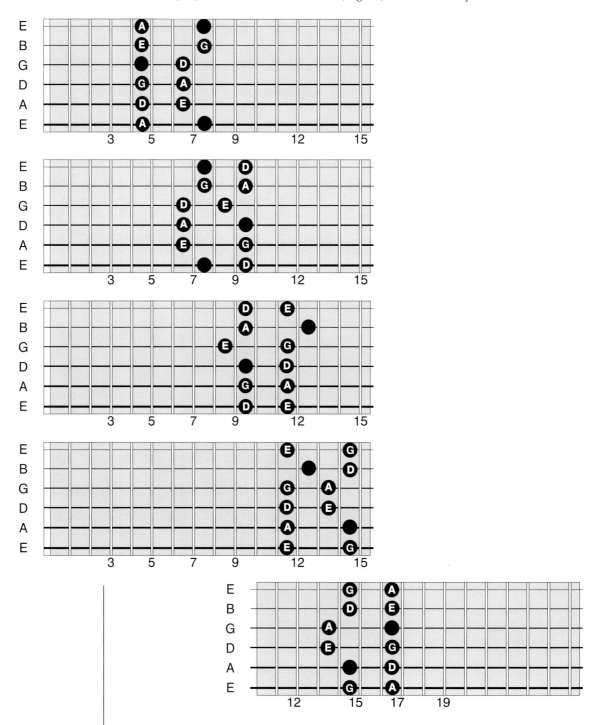

An intermediate solo method

The second, and slightly more intermediate method of soloing over a I-IV-V chord progression is to use a technique you might think of as "following the chords." In this case, we'll simply slide our main pentatonic scale pattern up and down the fretboard to position it where the E-shaped barre chord would land for each of our primary chords.

In the key of A, we will place the main pentatonic pattern at the fifth fret for A, the 10th fret for D, and the 12th fret for E, just as we would do with the barre chords. As an exercise let's play the same riff over each chord, simply changing frets with the chords.

CD TRACK **66**

Example 6.13

Intermediate solo method: Follow the chords by moving the pentatonic scale pattern with each chord

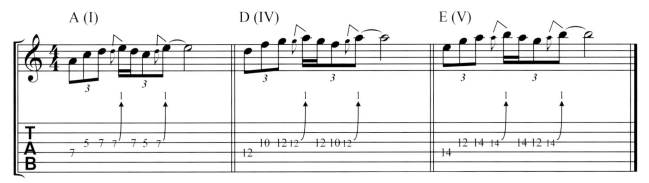

This is a technique often used by the likes of B.B. King, Stevie Ray Vaughan, and countless other blues greats. The same method of sliding an identical or nearly identical riff up and down the fretboard to play over the I, IV, and V chords, can be done with licks taken from any pentatonic scale pattern. Here is an example using licks played in the B.B.'s Box section of the second pentatonic pattern:

CD TRACK **67**

Example 6.14

Intermediate solo method continued: Practice following the chords with each pentatonic scale pattern

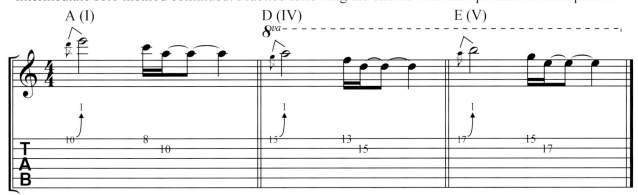

S E C T I O N 6 | PART **2**

Practice this same technique using each of the licks in the section titled "Classic blues riffs in each pentatonic pattern," shown earlier in this section. Even just practicing this technique sounds very musical, very bluesy, and is a whole lot of fun!

An advanced solo method

A more advanced way to look at soloing over the I, IV, and V chords is to change scale patterns for each chord. But more than just changing scale patterns, we're actually going to change key for each chord, albeit temporarily, and only during that chord. We actually did exactly that in the previous exercises, where we slid the identical riffs up and down the fretboard to cover the I, IV, and V chords. But this time we're going to be staying closer to our starting point by using a couple of different scale patterns, reducing left-hand movement.

This is actually a more common way to solo over chord changes than the sliding technique, which is very useful, but gets old fast. Fortunately it's not as difficult as it sounds, but it does require a pretty solid knowledge of the five pentatonic scale patterns, and an understanding of how to play each of those patterns in different keys.

In this example, we're going to use the main pentatonic pattern at the fifth fret over the I chord (A minor). When we switch to the IV chord (D minor), we're going to use the fourth pentatonic pattern at the fifth fret. This would actually put us into the key of D minor, but that's only temporary, because when we get to the V chord (E minor), we're going to take that same fourth pentatonic pattern and slide it up two frets, to the seventh fret. This essentially puts us into the key of E minor but, again, it's only temporary.

To pull off this method of changing scales/keys with each chord, we'll use the scale patterns as shown in this diagram:

Use over I chord (A minor)

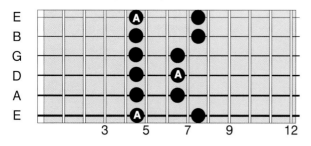

Use over IV chord (D minor)

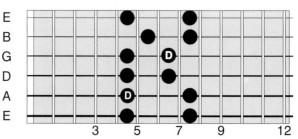

Use over V chord (E minor)

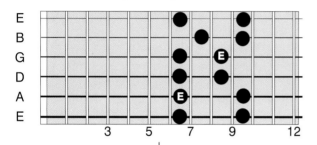

PART **2**   SECTION 6

Here is a simple solo, in A minor, with D minor and E minor chords and lead licks:

An advanced soloist might opt to change keys and scale patterns over each chord

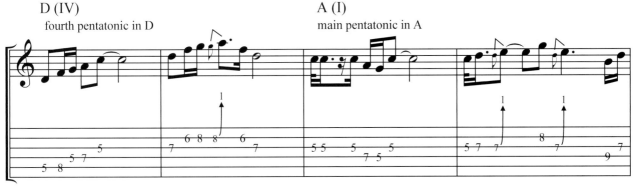

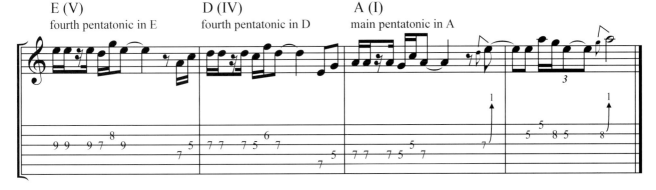

Again, practice using all five different pentatonic scale patterns to cover each of our primary chords, alternating on each chord between the various scale patterns. Use the repertoire of classic licks I've previously shown you from each pattern as a starting point in those patterns. It'll take time to try all the combinations, but the journey of discovery is a really fun voyage.

CD TRACK 68

Example 6.15

PRO TIP: Try putting on your favorite blues jam track or song, and focus on one or two scale patterns at a pass, while you solo throughout the entire song—even while the vocalist is singing. This will give you a good four or five minutes of highly focused lead guitar practice per song, and will really solidify your understanding of how to put all the pentatonic patterns into play.

The blues scale

This is a great point for us to add the famous blues scale to our arsenal of blues tools.

The blues scale is almost identical to the pentatonic scale, with the addition of one extra note per octave, making it a six-note scale. The note we will add to the pentatonic scale is called the flat-fifth, diminished fifth, or blue note, and it falls right between the fourth and fifth scale steps of the minor scale. While we could add this note to any one of the five pentatonic scale patterns, for most players it appears primarily in the main pentatonic pattern.

But to show how we might use it along with the technique of changing to the fourth pentatonic pattern for our IV and V chords, let's compare these diagrams of the main and fourth pentatonic patterns with their related blues scales:

A pentatonic scale

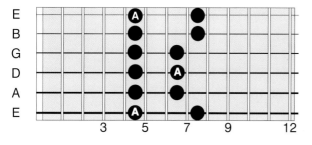

A blues scale

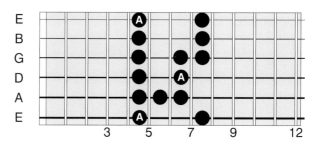

D pentatonic scale

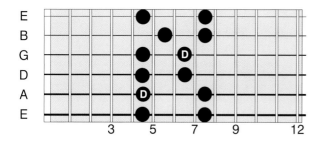

D blues scale

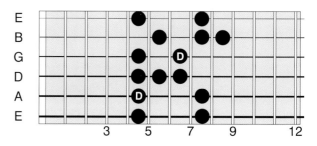

PART **2**   SECTION 6

Now let's play a blues solo in A minor in which we use the blues scale over our I, IV, and V chords—adding the blue note to the main pentatonic pattern for the I chord and the fourth pentatonic pattern for the IV and V chords.

Add the "blue note" to pentatonic scale patterns for a bit of extra flavor

CD TRACK **69**

Example 6.16

SECTION 6 PART **2**

Beyond the pentatonic and blues scales

Now I want to introduce an even more advanced soloing concept, namely, adding notes outside the pentatonic pattern (other than the blue note). To go in this direction it will be helpful for you to understand that pentatonic scales and blues scales are not the only scales guitarists must eventually learn.

This next step involves scale patterns which include seven notes per octave, called "diatonic" scales. These are really just our basic "do-re-mi" major and minor scales. Since there are seven notes per octave in a diatonic scale, it stands to reason that we could come up with seven different scale patterns, one starting on each note of the scale, just as we did with the five-note pentatonic scale and the five pentatonic scale patterns.

If you have already memorized your five pentatonic scale patterns, you have already done most of the work of learning your diatonic patterns, because they include all the pentatonic notes. In fact, the pentatonic scale patterns form the framework, or skeleton, of five of the seven diatonic scale patterns. Compare the five pentatonic patterns with their corresponding diatonic scale patterns:

Pentatonic

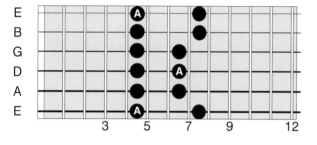

Diatonic

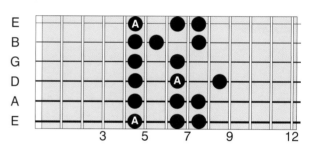

Pentatonic

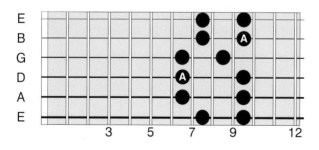

Diatonic

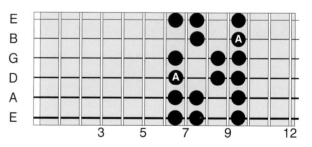

Pentatonic

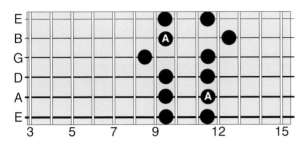

Diatonic

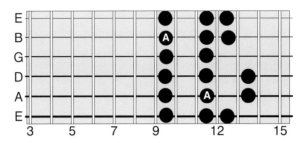

Pentatonic

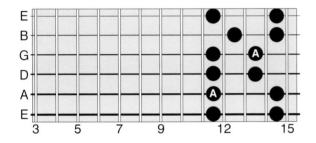

Diatonic

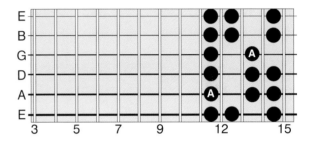

Pentatonic

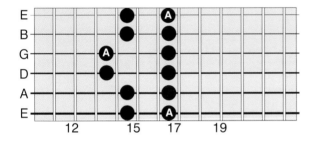

Diatonic

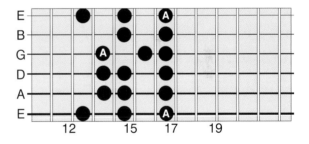

Now let's take another look at that A minor blues solo. This time we'll use the main pentatonic pattern at the fifth fret, plus the A blues scale at the fifth fret, and the A minor diatonic scale pattern at the fifth fret—all interchangeably over the I chord.

When we move to the IV chord, the D minor, we'll use all three varieties of scale there as well: the fourth pentatonic pattern at the fifth fret, that same pattern with the blue note added, and the diatonic D minor scale. We'll repeat these same patterns two frets higher for our V chord, E minor (Example 6.17, over page).

Once again, we can repeat this learning process and practice routine using all five pentatonic scale patterns, any version of the blues scale we can fit over those pentatonic patterns, and any related diatonic scale pattern as well. In fact, a truly advanced soloist knows how to do just this using any and all scale patterns.

S E C T I O N 6   PART **2**

Combining natural minor riffs with pentatonic and blues scale patterns

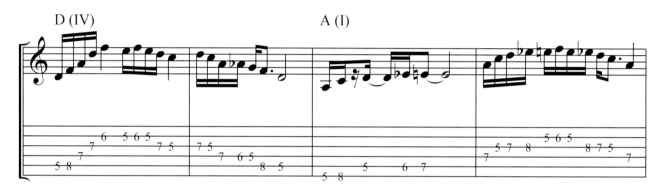

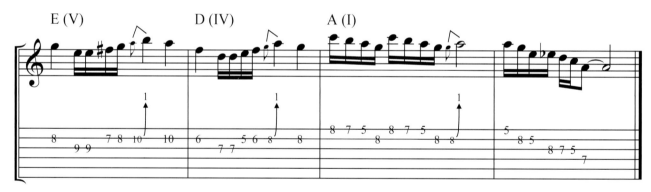

CD TRACK **70**

Example 6.17

PRO TIP: To become completely fluent with the fretboard, focus on one pentatonic pattern (plus its related blues and diatonic scales) per day, or per week—and really, *deeply* learn how to use each related set of patterns. Try, at first, the sliding technique I showed you in the Intermediate section earlier, staying with just one pentatonic/blues/diatonic pattern group over each of the I, IV, and V chords in the progression.

Try mixing and matching various patterns when you're doing your fretboard exercises. Once you've gotten to this level of understanding and skill, just simply practicing in this manner is really fun, and pretty much consists of just jamming, albeit in a highly focused, goal-oriented manner—your goal being to conquer each and every pattern so that in a real blues jam or band situation, you can turn heads with your complete mastery of the fretboard!

What about the major keys?

Every step I've walked you through so far involved playing in minor keys and, as an example, primarily the key of A minor. I've done this because it is usually easier for guitarists to learn to solo starting with the minor keys, especially focusing on that "main" pentatonic scale pattern most of us learn in our first few guitar lessons. That pattern just seems to fall so naturally under our fingers, and the notes all seem to sound so *correct*, no matter how or when we use them.

Ironically, though the very term "blues" conjures up images of despair and misery—for which minor keys are perfect—most blues is actually not minor blues. You may have noticed how down-and-out a true minor blues chord progression— as in the chords Am, Dm, and Em—really sounds. Do you want to run everybody out of your local live music venue? Well, just play two or three minor blues songs in a row, and you're sure to have the place emptied out and all to yourself real quick. Nobody wants to be that sad, at least not for more than one or two songs per night.

Remember that in its public performance, from its earliest days in the juke joints on the Delta to the bandstand in any blues club in the world today, most blues is upbeat and danceable. It always was and still is, primarily, a party music, meant to help people leave behind the troubles and the grind of their daily life and get rid of the blues.

When it comes to the sound of a minor key vs a major key, one basic emotion rules: Minor equals sad, major equals happy. As such, the lead guitarist needs to know how to solo over chord progressions that are primarily major in nature. And I say "primarily major in nature" because the major blues isn't truly major, or played with a true major scale. A true major scale, in the key of A, looks like this:

Example 6.18

The A major scale, with a "major 7th"

A major scale

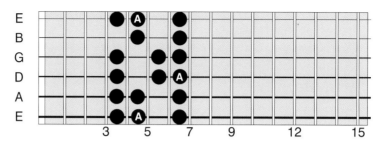

This major scale pattern has a major third, rather than a minor third (C♯ instead of C-natural, in this key), and a "major" seventh (G♯ in this key), one half-step below the root note of the scale. The major third can be a pretty sweet sounding note in the blues, but that major seventh just sounds wrong. Save the major sevenths for pretty rock or country ballads, or for your jazz excursions.

Blues simply does not use a major seventh at all. It's like that note just doesn't exist. Instead, we replace that note with something called a minor, flat, or dominant seventh, a whole-step (two frets) below the root note of the scale. In the key of A, that would be the note G.

If we simply change that one note from major to flat seventh, we get a scale pattern that looks like this:

Example 6.19

Lowering the 7th a half-step turns the A major scale into the A Mixolydian mode

A Mixolydian scale

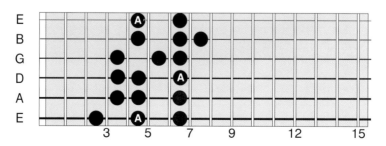

And there is a special name for this grouping of notes and this formula of half-steps and whole-steps: Mixolydian. Yes, most blues music—and plenty of the rock music it inspired—is played in what we call the Mixolydian mode, which is primarily a major mode because it has a major third. Blues played with a major third rather than a minor third still sounds like blues, but regardless of whether we use a major or minor scale pattern, blues music exclusively uses the flat seventh. And a major scale with a flat seventh is known as the Mixolydian mode.

Now I could go off on a whole book worth of information about modes, and how to use the various modes, of which Mixolydian is just one of seven, but in the context of the blues—and the parameters of this book—I can fortunately keep it much more simple. In fact, I'm not even going to burden you with all the scale patterns or even much of the music theory of the Mixolydian mode.

Instead, I'm going to simply show you some easy methods of tweaking the scale patterns we've already mastered—namely the pentatonic scales—to change them into this all important Mixolydian mode or, actually, a hybrid of that mode and the basic blues/pentatonic scale I like to call the "Mixo-blues scale."

The Mixo-blues scale
To visualize this hybrid called Mixo-blues, understand that we're simply going to put the blues scale and the Mixolydian finger patterns together. It is easiest to start with the main pentatonic scale pattern or the main blues pattern.

A blues scale

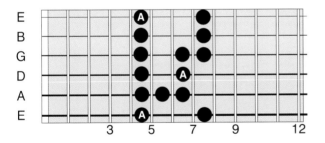

A Mixolydian scale

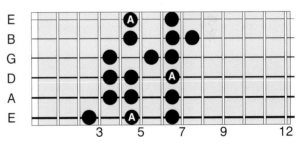

A Mixo-blues scale

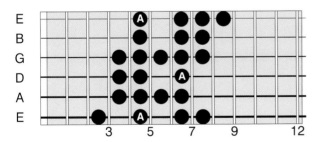

SECTION 6   PART **2**

Notice that in this hybrid scale we have the following notes:

■ Root note (A)

■ Second or ninth (B)

■ Minor third (C at the eighth fret on the sixth string, at the fifth fret on the third string, and at the eighth fret on the first string)

■ Major third (C♯ at the fourth fret on the fifth string and at the sixth fret on the third string)

■ Fourth (D)

■ Flat fifth (E♭)

■ Fifth (E)

■ Major sixth (F♯)

■ Flat seventh (G)

CD TRACK **71**

Example **6.20**

Using that tasty little gumbo of, basically, major and minor, we come up with some truly classic blues licks, such as these, shown over an A chord:

Two classic Mixo-blues licks

There are some loosely-defined rules regarding how we treat the thirds in this hybrid scale, and in most major blues playing. In this type of playing, which works well over a jump blues rhythm, we often use the minor third when a lick is ascending the scale, or even a quick hammer-on from the minor third to the major third, as in the first phrase above.

We will also often end a musical phrase on the major third, which we can either arrive at from one fret above—as in the second phrase above—or again from the minor third. We do not, however, play these thirds in reverse order, moving from the major third to the minor third. In a major blues setting you can either hit the major third directly, or play it quickly after the minor third.

The major sixth and flat seventh are also important notes in major blues playing, and the ninth can be fun to fool around with as well. Notice the use of the sixth, flat seventh, and ninth—which is often bent up to a major third—in this example:

CD TRACK **71**

Example 6.21

Mixo-blues lick in the style of Chuck Berry

PRO TIP: When playing a major or jump blues, position your hand—and your brain—to play the main pentatonic scale, and simply add the major thirds, the blue notes, and the major sixths as needed.

Now let's put some of these great licks together over a I-IV-V progression. For this example, let's use the "follow the chords" technique you learned earlier in this section, so that we can focus on playing identical or similar Mixo-blues licks, using our main pentatonic as a sort of home base.

CD TRACK **72**

Example 6.22

An "up-town" Mixo-blues solo

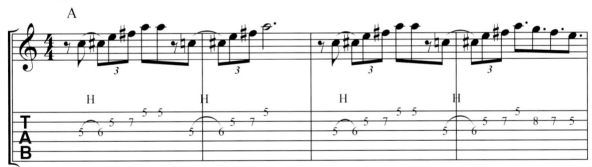

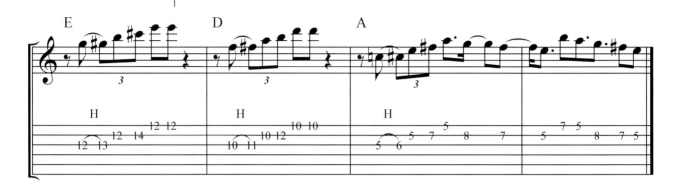

CD TRACK **72**

Example 6.22

(continued)

Pretty cool licks, aren't they? Using this Mixo-blues hybrid is the key to playing truly advanced blues lead guitar. We can also find some classic Mixo-blues licks in two patterns other than the main pentatonic. But first we'll have to explore another essential skill: that of using the pentatonic patterns in their major configuration.

The major pentatonic scale patterns

Until now we've been looking at the five pentatonic scale patterns as minor scales. But remember that every minor key has its relative major key—the key with which it shares all the same notes. In the key of A minor, the relative major is C. If we want to understand how to use the pentatonic scales in their major configuration, we have to be able to find that relative major note and treat it as our I.

Here are the five pentatonic scale patterns with their relative major root notes highlighted. In this case, the root note is C:

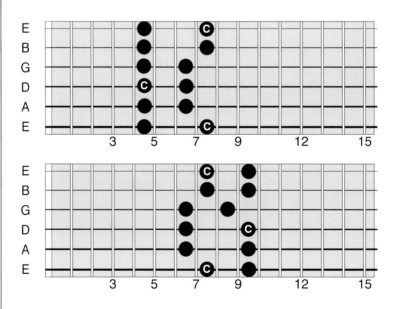

S E C T I O N 6

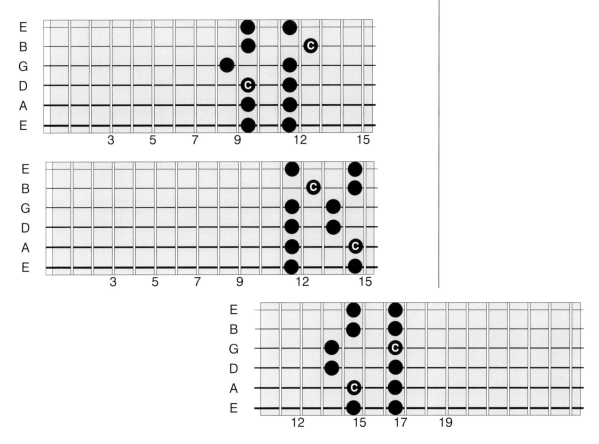

Using that major root note as the "home base" of our musical phrases, there are some classic *major* blues riffs to be found among these patterns. In the licks to follow, I'll also add some mixo-blues notes—including the flat third and the flat seventh—to the basic pentatonic shapes, as is often done.

In the main pentatonic, played as major, we might have riffs such as these:

CD TRACK 73

Example 6.23

A combination of common major pentatonic and Mixo-blues licks

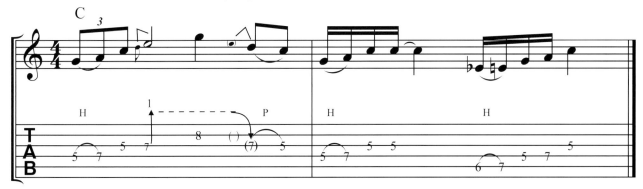

CD TRACK **74**
Example 6.24

In the second pentatonic, played as major, we find these riffs:

Common major pentatonic and Mixo-blues licks in the second pentatonic position

CD TRACK **75**
Example 6.25

The third pentatonic can be played as major with licks like these:

Common major pentatonic and Mixo-blues licks in the third pentatonic position

CD TRACK **76**
Example 6.26

In the fourth pentatonic pattern, played as major, we might have riffs such as these:

Major pentatonic and Mixo-blues licks in the fourth pentatonic position

PART **2** SECTION 6

CD TRACK **77**

Example 6.27

And in the fifth pentatonic pattern, we find licks like these:

Major pentatonic and Mixo-blues licks in the fifth pentatonic position

One easy trick a lot of guitarists use to find the major key is to move the main pentatonic shape down three frets, and then play it as major—focusing on the major root notes instead of the minor root notes. Using the main pentatonic version of A minor as a starting point—in which the minor root note is our first finger, fifth fret starting note—simply slide that pattern down three frets. The first finger now lands on the second fret (F♯), but the pinky is now on A, and is now our major root note.

A minor pentatonic scale

A major pentatonic scale

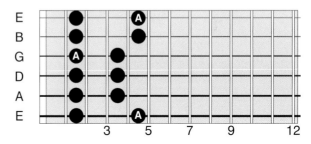

PRO TIP: Simply move the main pentatonic—or any pentatonic scale pattern—down three frets and then focus on the major root notes to play the major pentatonic of any minor key.

A classic blues or blues rock solo over the I chord in A might look like this:

A typical major pentatonic/Mixo-blues inspired lick in A

CD TRACK 78

Example 6.28

CD TRACK 79

Example 6.29

Playing a major I-IV-V solo

To put all these major pentatonic or Mixo-blues riffs into play over a I-IV-V chord progression, we commonly use the "follow the chords" routine, in which we simply slide one major pentatonic shape up and down the fretboard to land on each of our primary chords. Earlier in this section we did just that using the main pentatonic played in minor position, but tweaked with our Mixo-blues notes to make it major. In this example, let's use the main pentatonic pattern slid down three frets and played as major.

Follow the chords with the main pentatonic/G-shape pattern played as major

Another, perhaps more common—though slightly more complicated—method of soloing over a major I-IV-V progression, and using the major pentatonic patterns (liberally sprinkled with Mixo-blues notes, of course) involves less fretboard movement, but necessitates the use of different scale patterns to cover each chord. We did this previously in a minor configuration. Now let's try it in major.

To become comfortable playing this way, it may help to recognize that the main pentatonic pattern, slid down three frets and played as major, basically outlines a G-shape chord. We'll use this for our I chord, in this case, A. The chord A includes the root note (A), the third (C♯), and the fifth (E).

A major chord tones

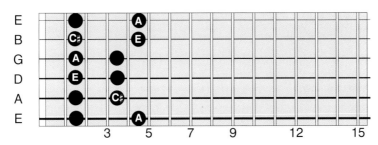

For our IV chord, we'll use a different pentatonic pattern—the fourth pattern played as major. In this format, notice the major root note is part of a C-shape chord. The IV chord in A is D. The D chord includes the root note (D), the third (F♯), and the fifth (A).

D major chord tones

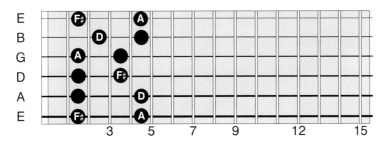

CD TRACK **79**
Example 6.29
(continued)

SECTION 6 PART **2**

We'll simply slide this pattern up two frets to play our V chord, E. The E chord includes the root note (E), the third (G♯), and the fifth (B).

E major chord tones

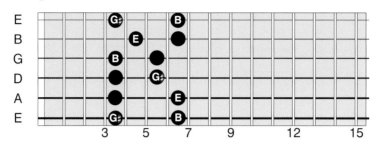

Put these major pentatonic patterns together—with some tasty Mixo-blues notes added—and we come up with a major blues solo such as the example opposite.

Putting it all together

Blues lead guitar playing and purely improvised solos over a blues chord progression (or any other chord progression) are often a mixture of many of the techniques, patterns, cliché riffs, and more advanced concepts I've touched on in this section of *The Blues Guitar Handbook*. Putting it all together requires a good dose of study, a growing understanding of the patterns, and of course going with the tried and true licks played by all the greats. Oh, and a lot of repetition!

Pick any one of the techniques or patterns shown in this section and play them over and over and over again and you will eventually master that technique, or that fingering, or that riff. Then choose a new riff or technique or pattern and repeat the process. Understand that blues (and rock) musicians often throw the rules out the window as far as mixing major and minor, notes outside the scale, etc. Don't be afraid to experiment, and just let your ear tell you whether something sounds good or not. Most of all, be patient, be diligent, and be persistent, and the skills will come.

In this solo, the IV and V chord licks are played over the fourth pentatonic/C-shape pattern

Example 6.30

Special techniques and articulations

The special techniques which turn simple notes into emotion-packed melodic statements are known as articulations. Study this section of *The Blues Guitar Handbook* and we will learn to master vibrato, hammer-ons, pull-offs, bending, and much more!

The essential articulations

Listen to B.B. King play any of his classic solos and you'll hear him wiggling and shaking and sliding all over his fretboard. This is where your melodic phrases truly come to life, where the human element enters the equation, almost as though the soul of the player were speaking through the guitar strings. This is where Cs and Ds turn into "oohs" and "aahs." This is where you really grab your listener, and pull them in to your emotions, your feelings, your woes, and your passions. And of course there is a name for this kind of musical magic, or—in a more down-to-earth way of looking at it—for this element of guitar study: articulation.

Artic-u-what? Articulation: the things you do to the notes to make them so much more than mere notes. We're talking about wiggling and bending and shaking and sliding and all manner of special effects, if you will, which a guitarist uses to infuse life into his melodies.

There are six important techniques all guitarists must know: the bend, the slide, vibrato, hammer-ons, pull-offs, and muting. Some of these techniques can be broken down into further skills as well. Consider spending time practicing each technique until that skill is perfected and can be added to a melodic line without conscious thought.

A veteran lead guitarist does not have to think about adding vibrato to a note; it usually just happens—because that player has simply used that technique so many times before that it has become involuntary. We'll kick-start your involuntary use of these seven deadly skills by mastering one at a time, starting with the bend.

The bend
Easy enough to understand, the bend simply means to bend a string—to push or pull it out of its original straight alignment. By bending a string we raise its pitch.

We might bend a note at the fifth fret to make it sound like the note normally fretted at the sixth fret, or perhaps the seventh fret.

How far we bend a note—how far we raise its pitch—is referred to by the number of half-steps or whole-steps we raise the pitch of the bent note. Remember, a half-step is one fret; a whole-step two frets. In blues we might bend as much as two whole-steps—as Albert King did routinely—or as little as a quarter-step, not even one fret.

Don't be shy about bending a string. To execute a proper bend you need to grab the string firmly and push fairly hard—remember, unless you're playing a nylon-stringed classical guitar, your strings are made of metal. You'll probably have to practice the bending technique quite a bit to build up the strength and the stamina to routinely and competently use this essential skill.

Also, a basic rule of thumb says that we push the first, second, or third strings toward the ceiling (and away from the edge of the fretboard), and pull the fourth, fifth, and sixth strings toward the floor.

PRO TIP: When bending, use all available fingers to help bend the string. For example, if you bend a note using your third finger, place the first and second fingers on the same string, behind the third finger, to help push.

In learning to bend, it is also helpful to learn to read the notation either in tablature and/or sheet music that indicates that we are to bend a note, and also to understand how much to bend the note. The following sheet music and tablature shows a series of bends, from a half-step to two whole-steps. Typically the tablature for a bend includes an arrow and a number above the arrow indicating how far to bend. Occasionally the word "full" is substituted for the number "1." Either "full" or "1" indicates a whole-step (two-fret) bend. Traditional sheet music typically shows a bend by connecting two note heads with a pointed line.

Example 7.1

Common bends, ranging from one-half step to two whole-steps

Example 7.2

On occasion we find it useful to play a slight or "micro-tone" bend, a bend of less than a half-step. This type of bend requires just the slightest push or pull on the string, and is usually notated as a quarter-step bend.

A series of slight or microtone bends indicate bends of less than a half-step

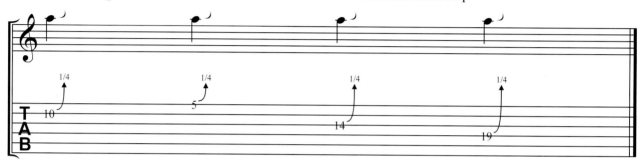

Example 7.3

Also, we sometimes see a series of consecutive bends in which the amount of bend gradually increases with each note played. An example of this series of bends might start with a quarter-step bend, followed by a half-step bend, a three-quarter-step bend, and a whole-step bend. This can be a very catchy solo technique in itself.

Common blues bends, ranging from one-quarter step to two whole steps, including quarter-tones

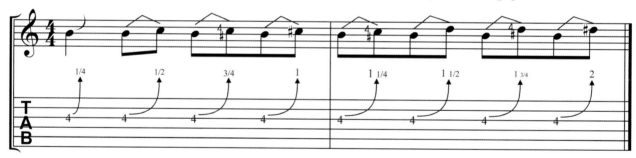

Usually a bend happens slowly enough that we hear the changing pitch of the bent string. Sometimes however, we bend the note so quickly, the only thing we hear is the destination note, not the note on which we started the bend nor the pitch changing before the arrival at the destination note. This is referred to as a grace note bend. A grace note bend is usually indicated in sheet music by a note-head with no stem, or a mini note with a slash through it. The original note, the grace note, does not take up any time.

A regular bend, and two different notations for grace-note bends

Example 7.4

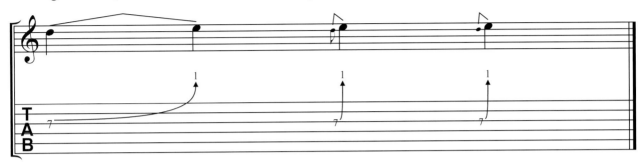

Similar to a grace note bend is a pre-bend, in which we actually bend the note before striking the string with our pick.

Example 7.5

Compare two types of grace-note bend with a pre-bend, in which the note is not struck until after the string is bent to the desired pitch

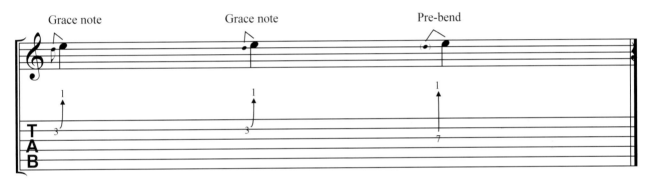

A very common bend technique is called bend and release. In this technique we bend a note, then release it back to its original pitch without picking the string again, and without letting the sound of the note die off. In the following tablature, notice the fret number shown in parentheses, indicating that we are not to pick that note.

Example 7.6

Bend and release: Strike the note, bend it, then release it to the original pitch without striking again

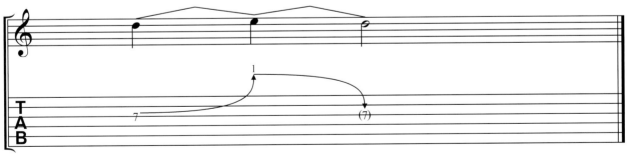

Example 7.7

The bend and release can also be used effectively with a pre-bend.

Bend and release works with pre-bends as well

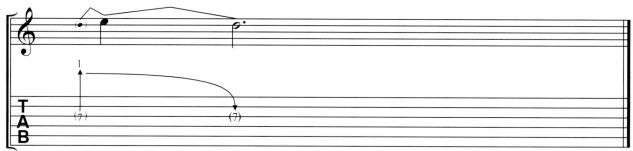

Blues, rock, and country guitarists often use a bending technique involving two strings. There are several classic riffs using this technique. One is known as a unison bend. The other is sometimes referred to as a country or "train" bend.

The unison bend is commonly heard in blues and blues rock and involves playing two notes together and bending one of those notes up to the same unison pitch as the other note. This is most often done with two notes on the third and second strings, with the note on the third string bent up a whole-step to come into unison with the note on the second string.

Example 7.8

Unison bend: Strike two notes simultaneously and bend the lower-pitched note into unison

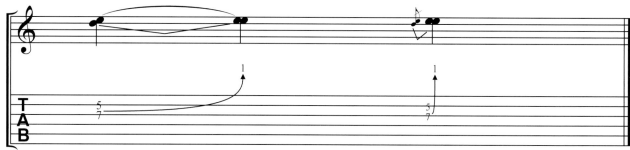

Another common unison bend takes place on the first and second strings, and again involves a whole-step bend.

Example 7.9

Unison bend shown on the first and second strings, notice three fret separation

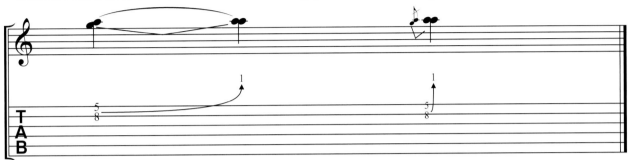

The country or "train" bend—so called because it is very common in country music and can easily be made to sound like a train horn—is typically played in the main pentatonic scale pattern.

The very popular "train bend," played here on the second and third strings

Example 7.10

The train bend can also be played on the top two strings.

The "train bend" played on the first and second strings

Example 7.11

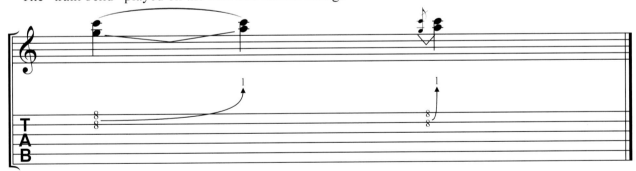

All of the bend techniques shown above are essential to the lead guitarist, blues or otherwise. Spend time practicing each variety of bend over and over until you perfect the sound.

The slide

The slide is probably the easiest of the articulation techniques. It is exactly as it sounds, a sliding of the fret-hand fingers from one note to another. Slides can be one or two frets, or the whole length of the fretboard, and can go from low pitch to high pitch, or from high to low. The slide is often used to move from one scale pattern to another.

There are two basic types of slides, the legato slide, and the shift slide. In the legato slide, we pick the first note, then slide to the second note without picking it, giving us a smooth "legato" sound. It is notated with both the angled slide line and a curved line running between both notes. With the shift slide, we pick both the beginning and the ending note. There is no curved line on a shift slide, only the angled line indicating a slide.

Example 7.12

Two types of slide: Shift and Legato

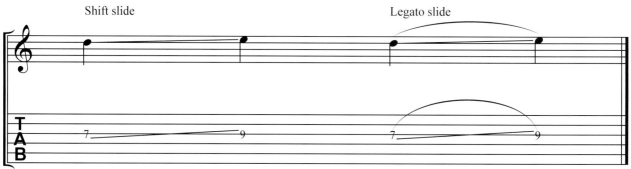

Vibrato

Vibrato may be the most talked about articulation of all, because everyone seems to have an opinion on what makes for good or bad vibrato, who has the best vibrato, and how best to mimic them. It really needn't inspire such controversy, and besides, who has or what constitutes the "best" vibrato is really a personal choice—an opinion, not necessarily a fact. Regardless of opinions, it is a fact that vibrato is almost always added to notes at the end of a melodic phrase, or any time a note is sustained.

There are two basic schools of thought on how to achieve vibrato. One school says the string should be slightly bent back and forth. The other says the string should remain stationary while the finger wiggles back and forth. Either technique is fine. Do what works for you.

The easier vibrato technique is to simply bend the string slightly up and down—not quite enough to be considered a bend though, or at most, a quarter-tone micro-bend. Some players like to exaggerate their bends and make them a little wider, bending the string as much as a half-step. You may, at times, decide to use a wider or more subtle vibrato in your playing.

It is slightly trickier to master the wiggle (not-bent) vibrato. This is a technique you might see someone such as B.B. King use on occasion (he uses the bending style of vibrato as well). Some say this technique resembles the motion of your hand turning a door knob, or shaking off water. When using this technique, let go of the neck of the guitar with your thumb, so that only the fingertip on the string is touching the guitar, and wiggle or twist your wrist rapidly. It can take quite a bit of practice to master this type of vibrato, and it can also be very subtle. Start by wiggling slowly, then gradually build up speed—but keep it consistent.

PRO TIP: It can help to use a metronome while working on the wiggle style vibrato technique. At first, wiggle in time with quarter-notes at a slow tempo, then gradually increase the speed while you perfect the technique.

Either way you play it, vibrato is usually noted in either tablature or sheet music with a wavy line above the note. In some songbooks, a thicker wavy line indicates a wide vibrato.

Example 7.13

Vibrato is achieved with a slight wiggling of the string

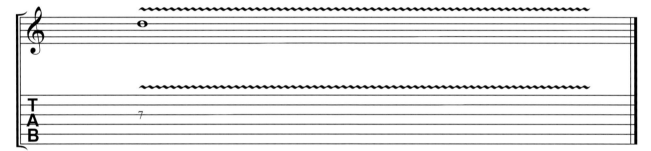

Hammer-ons

A hammer-on may seem easy, but can take some practice to master. With a hammer-on, we slam a finger down on a string hard enough to make a note sound without having to pick the note. Typically we hammer-on after picking another note. For example, we might place the first finger on the third string at the fifth fret, pick that note, then slam the second finger down at the sixth fret on the same string, making that note sound without an additional pick stroke.

Practice hammer-ons with every combination of fingers: first and second, first and third, first and fourth, second and third, second and fourth, and—gasp—third and fourth. You might also want to work on playing one note, then hammering on two notes after that—such as playing a note fretted with the first finger, then hammering on the second and fourth fingers in quick succession. Try also hammering the third and fourth fingers after playing a note with the first, and work on playing the first finger and hammering the second and third fingers. Every combination of fingers comes into play sooner or later.

A hammer-on is indicated in both tablature and sheet music by a curved line connecting two notes, the second note higher than the other. Multiple note

Example 7.14

hammer-ons are indicated by consecutive notes connected by curved lines, each note higher in pitch and higher on the fretboard than the note before.

Common markings indicating a hammer-on or series of hammer-ons

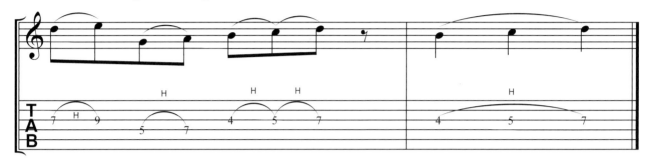

Pull-offs

A pull-off is the opposite of a hammer-on, but unfortunately is not nearly as easy to perform. When we pull off from one note to another, we are first picking the higher of two notes on one string, then pulling that finger off the string to make the lower note sound. It's not as simple as just lifting the finger off the string though—that won't make the second note sound.

A pull-off actually requires a bit of a plucking motion. The finger you are pulling off cannot simply lift off the string, but instead must actually pluck the string on its way off. To accomplish this, you'll need to apply additional downward pressure on the string at the same instant you are removing the finger. The finger pulling off does not simply lift away from the string, but instead moves in a more lateral direction across the fretboard, basically toward the floor.

A pull off is indicated in tablature and sheet music by a curved line between two notes, the second note lower than the other. Again, multiple pull offs are indicated by consecutive notes connected by curved lines, each note lower in pitch and higher on the fretboard than the note before.

Example 7.15

Common markings indicating a pull-off or series of pull-offs

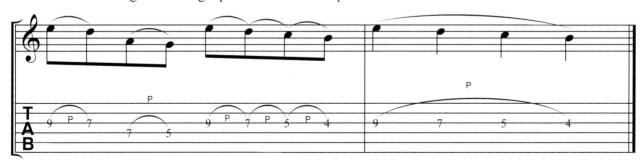

Muting

If we don't apply some sort of muting to our strings, the sound of the guitar quickly gets out of control, with open strings resonating, notes we don't want ringing, and possibly even ear-shattering feedback. We can and should use both hands to keep all this extraneous noise under control. We can refer to muting applied to the strings as either fret-hand muting or palm muting.

Fret-hand muting should be self-explanatory, referring to muting done with the fretting hand on the guitar. Palm muting refers to muting done with our pick-holding or finger-picking hand. Both techniques require some degree of practice.

With fret-hand muting, we are largely referring to the slight release of pressure on the strings between strums of a chord. To give certain rhythms the right feel, we often hold a chord shape, but only press down on the strings at the instant that we strum, and we release that pressure immediately after the strum, but keep our hand on the strings holding the chord shape and deadening the strings. This type of muting gives us a short, controlled, staccato feel. Jump blues tunes, in particular, rely on this staccato type of rhythm.

Practice this technique using a simple quarter-note rhythm, but don't let the quarter-notes ring—legato style—into each other. Instead, chop them off immediately upon playing them, as if they were written as eighth- or 16th-notes with rests between them. Remember to hang on to the chord shape, and keep your fingers on the strings to deaden, damp, or dampen them. Keeping your fingers right in place allows you to quickly press them back down for the next chord strike.

Songbooks don't often make any special notation of this technique or this type of muting, though they could—a small dot appearing above the written note indicates the notes or chords are to be played staccato, or shorter than their actual written value. Nevertheless, a little experience in the blues realm will help you know when to use this muting technique. In this example, play the first measure, written as quarter-notes, as if it were written with 16th-notes and rests, as in the second measure.

Example 7.16

Fret-hand muting can be used to play staccato, as indicated by the dots in the first measure

Occasionally we will see sheet music or tablature notation which does indicate a more serious style of fret-hand muting, typically written with an "x" replacing a notehead (in sheet music) or a fret number (in tab). This is a type of fret-hand muting in which we may not even finger a chord shape at all, but simply hold our fret-hand flat across one or as many as six strings to mute or muffle them while we strum. Think of the intro Jimi Hendrix played on 'Voodoo Child,' in which he strummed the muted strings before finally launching into the single note line that kicks the song into gear.

Example 7.17

Fret-hand muting is often indicated by an x, meaning to strike the string while muting with the fret hand

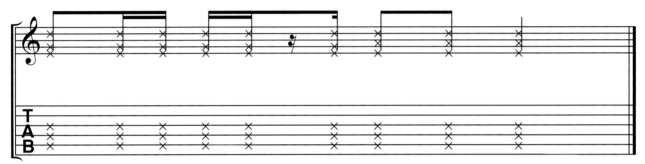

As important as fret-hand muting is, palm muting—muting the strings with our pick hand—is actually more important. Palm muting keeps an electric guitar from feeding back at high volumes, it keeps unwanted strings from ringing, and it adds a very desirable percussive texture to our guitar tone, whether on acoustic or electric. Even before the age of electrics, players such as Robert Johnson were using palm muting to define their guitar tone.

Again, this technique may take some practice to perfect, but once you have it, palm muting becomes completely automatic and you rarely ever have to think about it again. The hard part is getting used to the angle you'll need to assume with your pick hand to begin with. If you are the type of player who usually has your pick hand floating free in the air, you'll need to pay special attention to this lesson.

Begin by clamping the pinky-side edge of your pick hand (called the "heel" of your hand) firmly down on the guitar, on the bridge, or just slightly forward of the bridge. Keep it pressed down there while you strum, and experiment with different amounts of pressure and by moving the hand toward and away from the bridge, listening for how these variables affect your guitar tone.

Especially on an acoustic guitar, too much pressure, and moving too far forward of the bridge can essentially cut off all melodic sound from your guitar, leaving only the percussive strike of the pick (or your thumb, if you are playing fingerstyle) against the string.

This is called palm muting, and in sheet music and tablature it is sometimes notated with the letters "P.M." and a dotted line indicating which notes or measures on which to apply palm muting. Palm muting is actually used almost all the time by pro players, however, and the notation of palm muting in sheet music is only done when a more extreme level of palm muting is called for.

Example 7.18

Pick-hand, or palm muting, is indicated when a more noticeable amount of muting is desired

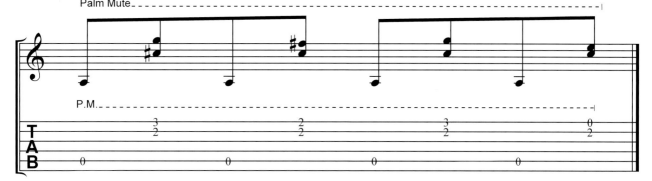

Once you've figured out how much palm muting is too much, back off a little—using less pressure and/or moving your hand back toward or even onto the bridge of the guitar. Just like vibrato, the right amount of palm muting is a personal choice. Also, you will find that you'll want to apply more or less palm muting during different songs, or in different parts of the same song. And there will be times when you lift the heel of your hand off the strings and don't apply any muting at all—though your default position should be with your heel down on the strings.

Advanced players often alternate between pressing the heel of their hand down on the bridge and slightly rocking their hand off the bridge using the pinky of their pick or fingerpicking hand as a sort of stand. This too takes practice, but using your pinky (and possibly even more fingers) to keep the pick hand from unnecessary or erratic movement will really improve the speed and accuracy of your picking.

Other fun articulations

The techniques discussed in the preceding pages are essential to all guitar players. There are other articulations which may or may not be prevalent in the style of music you play, but you may want to know about them. These include harmonics, trills, tapping, rakes, pick scrapes, and tremolo picking.

Harmonics
A harmonic is a bell-like chime and can be played numerous ways.

A "natural" harmonic can be easily played at the fifth, seventh, and 12th frets (and not quite as easily played in a few other positions) by striking the string while lightly touching the string, without pressing down.

A "pinch" harmonic—a favorite of Billy Gibbons of ZZ Top (listen for pinch harmonics on the outro solo of 'La Grange') is accomplished by fretting a note normally, and adding the edge of the thumb to the normal strike of the pick.

A "harp" harmonic is played by fretting the note normally, and lightly touching the string above the octave 12 frets higher (right over the fret), while picking the string.

Example 7.19

Three common varieties of harmonic: Natural, pinch (with pick), and harp harmonic

Trills

A trill is a rapid series of hammer-ons and pull-offs. Usually you pick the first note and afterwards rely on the strength of your hammer-ons and pull-offs to keep the note(s) ringing. Occasionally, a longer trill might require an additional pick strike. Typically the first note of the trill is written normally, while the second note is in parentheses. The abbreviation "tr," followed by a wavy line indicating the length of the trill, is shown above both the tablature and sheet music.

Example 7.20

A trill is a rapid hammer-on/pull-off combination between two notes

Tapping

Tapping, or finger tapping—made truly famous by hard rock legend Edward Van Halen—is not often heard in blues music, though ZZ Top's Billy Gibbons threw in a couple in his early recordings (and long before Van Halen became known). It can be an effective and catchy technique, adding variety to your improvisation.

Tapping is usually accomplished by fretting a note with the index or middle finger of the pick hand, and often pulling off from that note to a lower fretted note, or an open string. You may want to "palm" your pick—that is, quickly hold your pick in your palm with your non-tapping fingers—when attempting this technique. Tapping is indicated by a "+" sign (sheet music) or a "T" (tablature).

Example 7.21

Finger tapping is the technique of hammering-on with a pick-hand finger, indicated by a + or T

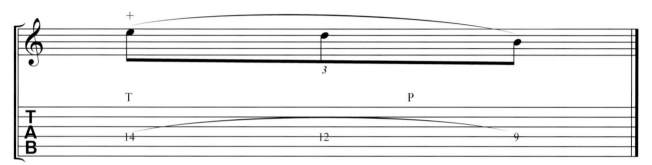

The rake

B.B. King is famous for using the rake technique, in which several non-fretted strings are strummed (as muted strings) immediately before a fretted note on a higher string. In this example, lay your first finger across the first four strings at the seventh fret, but do not press down. Strum quickly across those muted strings, then immediately play the eighth fret on the first string with your second finger.

Example 7.22

The rake, a technique often used by B.B. King, indicates sweeping the pick across muted strings before before finally playing a fretted note on a higher string

Pick scrapes

Example 7.23

Slide the edge of the pick up or down the strings, making a scratchy sound.

The pick scrape: Slide the edge of the pick down the strings, creating a scraping sound

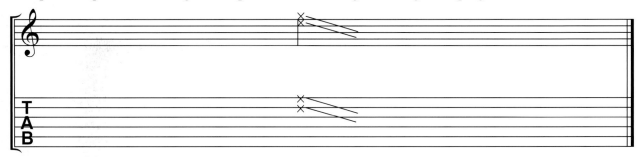

Tremolo picking

Example 7.24

Tremolo picking is rapid up/down strumming of a note or chord. Strum as fast and continuously as possible. Stevie Ray Vaughan used this technique on the chords to his slow blues song 'Dirty Pool.'

Tremolo is the rapid strumming of a chord or single note

Becoming articulate

It's all about soul, right? You can play all the right notes, but without adding articulations, your playing will simply sound lifeless. Together with a solid familiarity with the common scales and licks blues players use to build their solos, the articulations you've learned in this section of *The Blues Guitar Handbook* will help you achieve a truly living, breathing sound—a soulful sound. Throw in a little vibrato here, a hammer-on there, and a cool bend-and-release and you'll be playing like a pro in no time.

Tutorial
PART 3
BLUES STYLES THROUGH THE AGES

Acoustic blues

It all started with the acoustic blues. Generations before electric guitars and amps were even dreamt of, guitarists were playing the blues on acoustic guitars, singing and playing on Southern plantations and at Saturday night juke-joint dances, making a little extra cash and a name for themselves. The blues was born in the South, often on mail-order acoustic guitars purchased in the hope of busting out of the world of manual labor. In this section of *The Blues Guitar Handbook* we'll take a look at the playing styles of two classic acoustic blues artists.

Before they plugged in

Before lightbulbs, before radios, before electricity, acoustic guitars were already common in the American South. As far back as the mid 1800s, acoustic guitars, often of the small "parlor guitar" build, were to be found in many homes. On the plantations, black musicians, still enslaved at the time, were sometimes requested to perform by their white owners. These musical patrons served, in some cases, as benefactors in a relationship not unlike that between European royalty and the great composers centuries before—albeit in more invidious circumstances.

After slavery was brought to an end by the American Civil War (1861–1865) and President Abraham Lincoln's Emancipation Proclamation (1863), large stores such as Sears, Roebuck, and Co. and Montgomery Ward began to offer acoustic guitars in their mail order catalogs. The instruments soon became widely distributed in the South. Saving just a handful of dollars would reward a would-be musician with a decent acoustic guitar, delivered to locales where no music store exists even today.

The history of the blues is sadly incomplete before the turn of the 20th century, but many scholars believe that by the late 1800s the blues was already an established musical idiom. That it was born in poverty and in the far corners of rural territories has kept its early history murky. Once the new century arrived, however, bringing such new-fangled gadgets as the record player and later the radio—and savvy businessmen eager to make money from unsophisticated rural musicians—everything changed.

The recorded canon of early acoustic blues, beginning in the late 20s, is rich with musical heritage, bringing us the powerful voices and impressive instrumental skills of those who left this world generations ago. There are many styles of acoustic blues, including Delta, country, Piedmont and pre-war fingerstyle, but in this section of *The Blues Guitar Handbook*, I'll teach and explain the musical styles of a player who allegedly sold his soul to achieve guitar greatness, and another who became a highly popular acoustic guitarist in the 60s blues revival.

King of the Delta blues

Legend has it that Robert Johnson (1911–1938) met the Devil at the crossroads at midnight and sold his soul in return for amazing guitar skills and fame. He got the skills, found some measure of fame, then died an agonizing death by poisoning at a young age, after messing with another man's woman. Could the legend be true?

Superstitions aside, Robert Leroy Johnson is easily the most influential and well known of the Delta bluesmen. His style has had profound impact on players over many generations—Eric Clapton called him the most important blues singer who ever lived—and the legend of his crossroads meeting with Satan only makes for more intrigue.

Johnson was born in rural Mississippi, and by his teens was infatuated with the local blues guitarists whose stages he often crashed, much to their dismay. Son House and Willie Brown were often the recipients of Johnson's attention and musical bravado, and considered him a decent harmonica player but a terrible guitarist. Somehow that all changed around 1930 or '31, when Robert would have been 19 or 20, and that's when the legend was born—though few blues historians ever seem to appreciate that Robert might simply have practiced a lot that year.

Nevertheless, after "magically" acquiring incredible guitar proficiency, and after a couple of failed marriages, Robert Johnson took to the life of an itinerant blues musician, walking the rural countryside from town to town, busking on street corners for change, and playing Saturday night dances at the local juke joints. He eventually sought out a recording contract through the legendary talent scout H.C. Speir, but sadly recorded a scant 27 songs before his death, and he earned little from those recordings in his lifetime.

In the fall of 1938 Johnson was scheduled to appear at Carnegie Hall in New York City, at the invitation of blues impresario John Hammond—an event which might have had a profound impact on his career—but he died before making the trip. It was decades after his death, on the 1961 Columbia Records release *King Of The Delta Blues Singers*, that Robert Johnson finally achieved worldwide recognition as anointed royalty of the pre-war acoustic blues.

On the *Blues Guitar Handbook* CD (track 80) I've recorded a track reminiscent of Johnson's 'Kindhearted Woman Blues' and other classic Johnson acoustic blues tracks. This song, in the key of A, includes trademark Delta blues riffs common not only to Johnson, but to players such as Charley Patton, Blind Lemon Jefferson, and countless others.

The track maintains a driving single-note thumb bassline throughout, but more complex chordings than would be used by a player like Lightnin' Hopkins. Use right-hand muting to give the bass line an almost staccato sound, rather than letting the notes ring. This creates a more percussive guitar tone and allows the melody notes to cut through.

Also, this classic Delta style tune includes three different shapes of A7 chord, as shown in these diagrams:

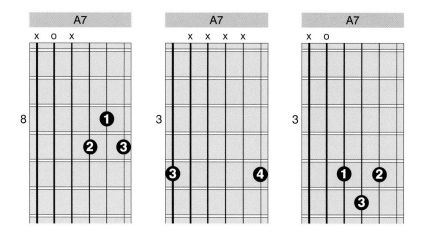

Notice (opposite) how the chord shapes are slid chromatically down the fretboard in measures one and two on the triplet-based intro, and also later in the song. Measure three gives us chord shape two and another great turnaround lick—demonstrating two classic acoustic blues turnarounds in just the intro of the song. Practice each of these until they are second nature. They can be used individually in almost any blues song, acoustic or electric.

Once the 12-bar pattern kicks in, with measure five, we find the third A7 shape, and again we slide this chord shape chromatically to create movement and tension against the four measures of the I chord. Use thumb and fingers to play this chord, then brush your thumb across all the strings in measure six to set up the cool A diminished seventh chord so common in Delta blues.

Notice the approach to the IV chord (D7) in measure nine, with a walking bass line that begins on the open E-string before landing on F♯ on the second fret of the sixth string—the third of the chord, creating a tasty D7/F♯ chord. This move is another common Johnson and Delta blues move, and a fairly sophisticated musical technique.

In the second chorus we replace the A7 chord on the middle strings with a similar chord on the high strings, again moving chromatically to add tension to the line. Catch the bent third string to wrap up the I chord on the walkdown, then head back into the D7/F♯. Later in the tune, on the turnaround of the second chorus, notice that the bass line approaches that same D7/F♯ from above, playing G at the third fret on the sixth string rather than walking up from the open E-string.

In the style of Robert Johnson

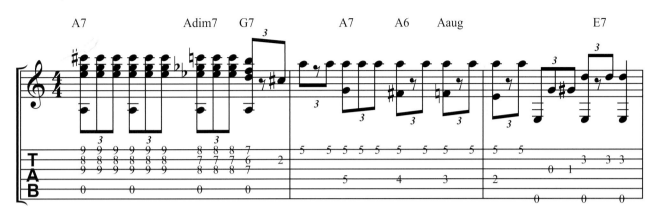

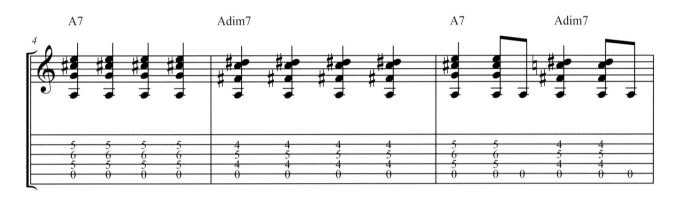

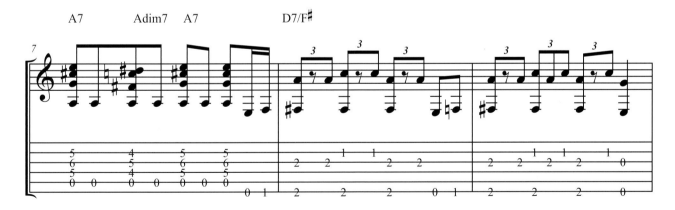

CD TRACK 80
Example 8.1
(continued over)

SECTION 8 | PART 3

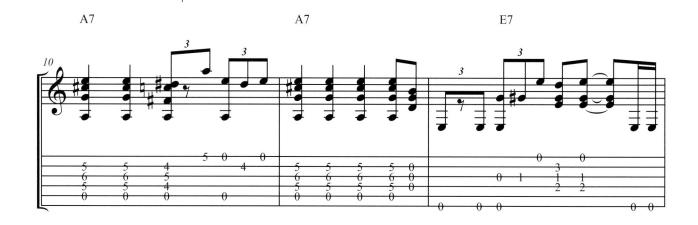

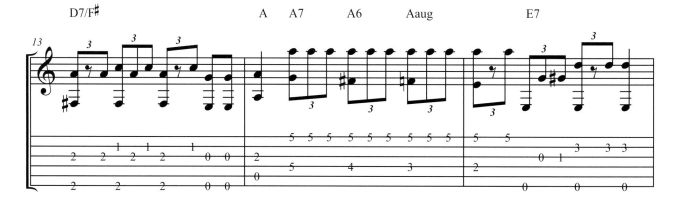

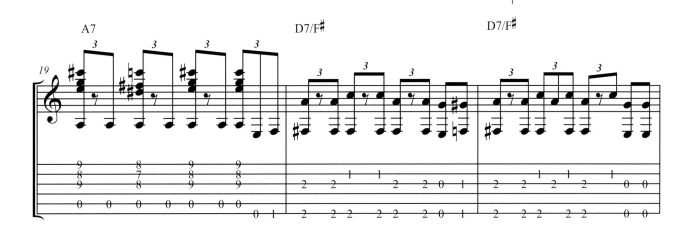

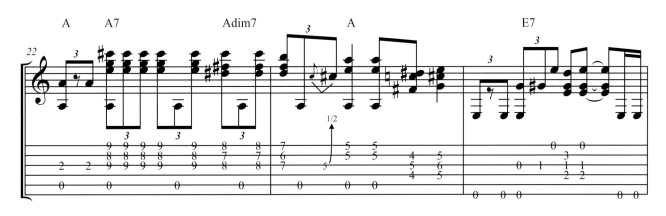

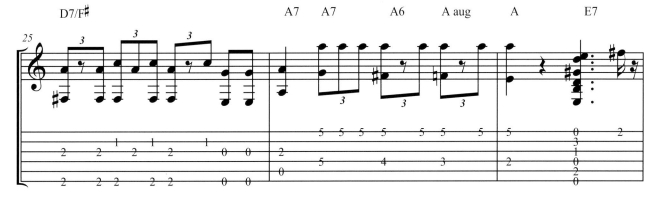

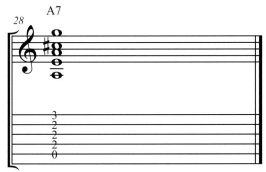

You can strum the blues too

The great Walter "Brownie" McGhee (1915–1996) proved that not all acoustic blues guitar requires painstaking hours of fingerstyle practice. He was certainly adept at fingerpicking the blues in either the Delta or Piedmont styles; as a young man he was a protégé of Piedmont blues great Blind Boy Fuller and was often called "Blind Boy Fuller No. 2." But he often performed and recorded in a looser, strumming style. That style has been imitated far and wide.

McGhee was born in Tennessee and found music early in his life, hitting the road by his early twenties playing guitar and singing gospel and performing in minstrel shows. He landed a recording contract with Columbia and began recording for the label's subsidiary, Okeh Records, by 1941. It was a year later, however, that McGhee joined forces with a harmonica player who would become his musical partner for decades. McGhee had met Sonny Terry when Terry was playing harmonica for Blind Boy Fuller, and the eventual pairing of Sonny Terry and Brownie McGhee would last nearly 40 years, until 1980.

The duo, who recorded dozens of albums together, were hugely popular during the folk and blues revival of the 60s, and toured worldwide—as much as 11 months each year—earning much adulation and critical acclaim. McGhee's simple yet elegant acoustic playing inspired countless musicians to follow.

For the *Blues Guitar Handbook* CD, I've created a track (CD track 81) reminiscent of a Sonny Terry and Brownie McGhee version of 'Key To The Highway,' in the key of E. This eight-bar blues tune moves quickly from the I chord to the V chord, rather than the typical I-IV move of a 12-bar blues (for more on eight-bar blues song formats, see Section Four).

The song begins with a standard turnaround before digging into a blues shuffle groove. But notice the fancied-up chord work on the I chord, E, in measure three, and even more so in measure seven. This "uptown" method of spicing up a simple I chord is a trademark of McGhee and other artists who strum acoustic blues tunes. The first chorus finishes with a classic acoustic blues turnaround not demonstrated elsewhere on this CD.

In the second chorus, the IV chord is played with a melodic highlight on the high E-string, in a move that McGhee and others would have learned from as far back as the Delta blues of Charley Patton and Robert Johnson. In the final turnaround notice a different riff off the E chord, and a final slide into a seventh-fret E9 chord, another classic ending move for blues players throughout the ages.

In the style of Brownie McGhee

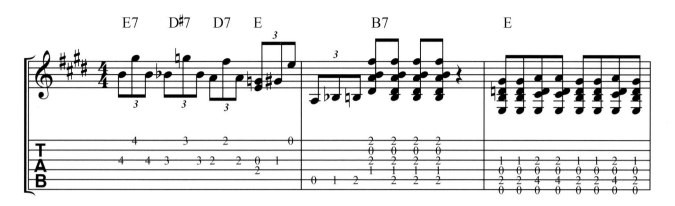

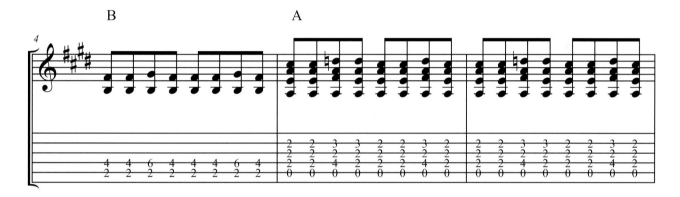

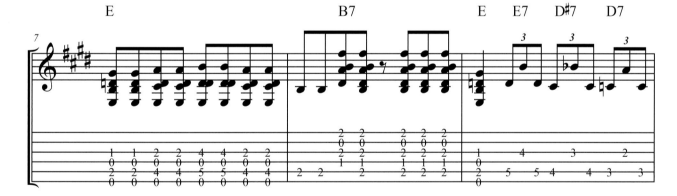

CD TRACK 81
Example 8.2
(continued over)

SECTION 8

PART **3**

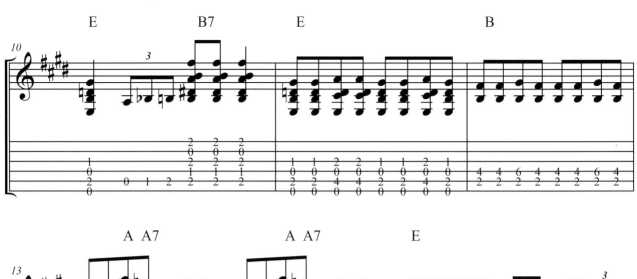

Slide blues

The magical sound of the slide guitar has been at or near the forefront of blues guitar playing since before the dawn of the 20th century. By 1903, when the oft-proclaimed "Father Of The Blues," W.C. Handy, first heard the blues played with a slide in a Mississippi train station, the art form had already long been practiced in the deep South. Where slide playing truly began—whether among rural musicians in the Mississippi Delta in the late 1800s, or long before that in Africa—is uncertain. But slide guitar and blues are a natural fit. In this section of *The Blues Guitar Handbook*, we'll look at the slide-guitar styles of two legendary blues musicians.

Bottleneck blues

There is no sound quite like the eerie tone of a slide guitar. That moaning, near-vocal quality evokes something deep inside the listener that cannot be ignored. Blues players picked up on that facet of the sound early on, and slide guitar became a staple of the blues genre from the start.

The technique of sliding some sort of resonator up and down a string to create a musical pitch may have originated in Africa and been imported hundreds of years ago with the slave trade, or it may have developed on its own in America. No one knows for sure.

What is known is that many a young Southerner enjoyed sliding a pocket knife, a piece of pipe, or even a stone up and down a metal wire connected to the side of a house, barn, or shed. The diddley-bow, as this contraption is known, was a common plaything for many kids in the Delta. Many legends of the blues, including Chicago blues master Buddy Guy, recalled playing diddley-bow in rural Mississippi during the early decades of the last century. Transferring from diddley-bow to slide guitar would not have been a big leap. And guitarists of that era were a resourceful lot, using anything that resonated to play slide guitar. Pocket knives, wrenches, and cigarette lighters were favorite tools for slide playing, but perhaps the most common of all was a glass slide made from the sanded-down neck of a bottle, hence the common term "bottleneck."

In this section of *The Blues Guitar Handbook*, I'll demonstrate and examine the styles of two slide legends from the electric blues era.

King of Chicago

McKinley Morganfield, aka Muddy Waters, (1913–1983) is among the most influential blues musicians of all time, and was sometimes referred to as the King of Chicago blues. Perhaps even more important than his blues legacy, he is often credited as having created the format for the modern rock band: two guitars, bass, and drums (which he augmented with harmonica and keyboards).

The Rolling Stones, among many other famous classic rockers, were huge fans of Waters—they took their name from the title of one of his songs. His songs have been covered or remade by a Who's Who of rock stars, including the Stones, Eric Clapton, Foghat, and Led Zeppelin, to name just a few.

Waters started out on harmonica, but by age 17 was playing guitar as well, emulating the styles of Son House and Robert Johnson. He performed as a solo acoustic act in the Delta blues tradition throughout the 30s while working area farms and plantations. Muddy recorded his first tracks for Alan and John Lomax and the Library of Congress in 1941, on the porch of the small juke joint he ran at the Stovall Plantation. Muddy performed there on Saturday nights, and was particularly proud to have his Library of Congress recordings on the juke box.

Eventually the lure of the big industrial cities to the north became too much to resist. Muddy relocated permanently to Chicago in 1943, hoping to become a full-time musician. A hard worker, he landed a day job almost immediately while he found his musical footing in the fast-paced city.

It wasn't long before Waters had found his groove—and his band—and the rest is history. He became the most successful artist at the most important blues record label in existence, Chess Records; he kept a heavy touring schedule; received radio airplay just about everywhere; and enjoyed boatloads of cash and eventually world-wide fame.

On the *Blues Guitar Handbook* CD I've laid down a track reminiscent of Muddy Waters' first commercially successful single, 'I Can't Be Satisfied,' in the key of G. The repeating single-note melody in the opening bars is true Muddy Waters—sparse and wobbly. Waters would play simple riffs leading into the IV (C7) and V (D7) chords, then return to his opening line. Count the measures and listen out for the quick return from the IV chord back to the I chord in the sixth bar of each chorus.

Muddy's original recording of 'I Can't Be Satisfied' features minimal instrumentation, so I've followed suit with the minimal rhythm section arrangement on the CD. The chart opposite shows you the chords. The rhythm guitar plays simple seventh chord shapes on the "and" of each beat. Watch out for the sixth measure of each chorus, where I've cut the bar off after the second beat—a half measure, in the style of Muddy and many other Delta blues players. Incomplete or extra measures are common on the blues recordings of old, so be ready for either a sudden or delayed chord change at any time when playing along with the old masters.

Rhythm track in the style of Muddy Waters

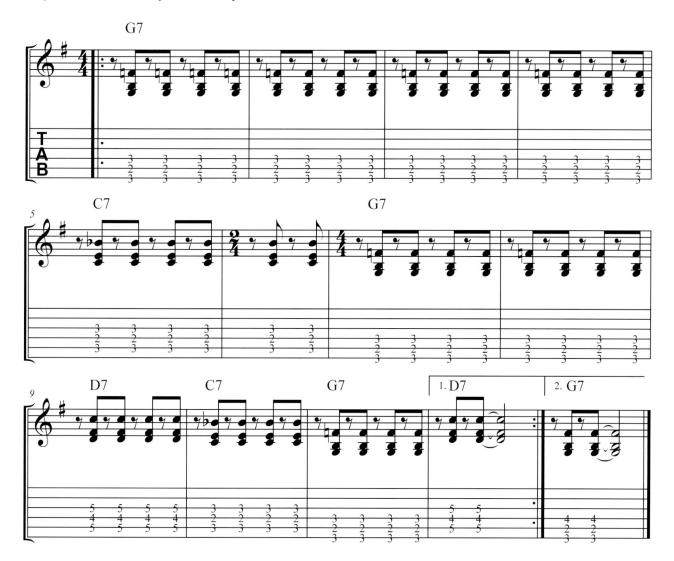

CD TRACK 82

Example 8.3

S E C T I O N   9

PART **3**

King of the slide guitar

There is a lot of royalty in the blues, and here's another blue-blood: the King of the Slide Guitar, Elmore James (1918–1963). Like so many other great bluesmen, James was born in rural Mississippi to field-hand parents. He took up playing the one-stringed diddley-bow as a boy; by his teens he was performing at local dances. He eventually played with blues harp legend Sonny Boy Williamson II, and may also have played with Robert Johnson—there is some debate as to whether Johnson or James actually wrote the blues classic 'Dust My Broom.'

After a stint in the U.S. Army during World War II, in which he took part in the invasion of Guam against the Japanese, Elmore returned to Mississippi, moved in with his adopted brother Robert, and began tinkering in his electronics shop. Guitarists are always looking for better tone, but Elmore actually created his own, hot-wiring his own amps, and, some say, his pickups too.

Elmore James was in the studio with Sonny Boy Williamson II in 1952 when he laid down a track that was to become a surprise hit. Ever after, the song 'Dust My Broom' would be his signature tune, and provided his band name, The Broomdusters. After the success of this single, and with the help of Ike Turner, James would record out of Memphis for the Bihari Brothers' Modern, Meteor, and Flair record labels—and later many others, including Chess in Chicago.

He scored numerous hit songs through the years, many of which have been covered by rock legends, including Eric Clapton, The Allman Brothers, The Black Crowes, and Stevie Ray Vaughan, among others. Unfortunately Elmore James had a serious drinking problem—it would lead to his early demise—and in his later years he became less and less reliable as a performer, as a bandleader, or as a contracted recording artist.

On the *Blues Guitar Handbook* CD, I've recorded a song reminiscent of the Elmore James classic 'Dust My Broom.' The song is played in E, in open E tuning (E-B-E-G♯-B-E, low to high). The trademark riff at the start of the song is easily the most commonly copied slide blues lick of all. Stick close to the IV (A7) and V (B7) chord positions when they come up: the licks leading into these changes are never more than a fret or two away from the chord shape.

The rhythm-guitar part for this track (opposite) is a straight 12-bar I-IV-V shuffle, played in E, in standard tuning. The turnaround lick, similar to the Broomdusters version of 'Dust My Broom,' or many another classic blues song, requires hybrid picking—using the pick to play the descending bass line on the fifth string and a finger to play the repeated E note at the fifth fret on the second string. This is just one of a thousand turnarounds you'll eventually want to have in your bag of blues tricks.

Rhythm track in the style of Elmore James

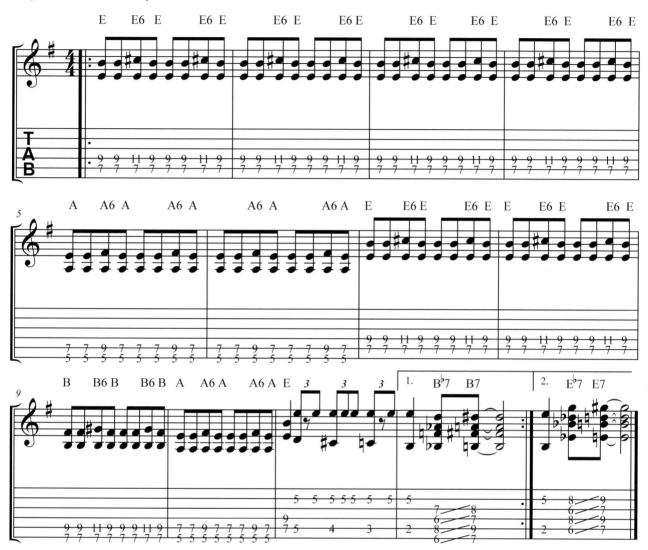

CD TRACK 83

Example 8.4

Classic electric blues

The electric, post-war, and classic Chicago blues style evolved from acoustic blues as players from the Delta moved to the big cities of the North around the time of World War II. The faster pace of city life, combined with a need to be heard in a crowded nightclub, had many a guitarist plugging in for the first time. Future legends such as Howlin' Wolf, Muddy Waters, B.B. King, Albert King, Albert Collins, Freddie King, Otis Rush, and Buddy Guy launched their careers in this era. In this section of *The Blues Guitar Handbook*, we'll look at the musical styles of two hugely influential electric blues guitarists.

The blues goes electric

Musicologists refer to the female vocalist-dominated blues music of the 20s as the classic blues era. But to most guitar-playing blues fans, the true classic blues is either the music of the Delta and acoustic blues guitarists of the pre-war 30s or the classic tunes of the post-war era, from the late 40s to the 60s.

This electrified blues, often known as Chicago blues—though not all of the music originated in Chicago—saw many former solo acoustic players pick up an electric guitar and put together a band. Typically consisted of a lead vocalist, one or two guitarists, a bassist, a drummer, and possibly a harmonica or keyboard player, these electric blues bands became the blueprint for practically all rock bands to follow.

In this section of *The Blues Guitar Handbook*, I'll demonstrate and examine the styles of a boogie master and the world's most famous living bluesman.

King of the boogie

Let's start with the boogie master, John Lee Hooker (1917–2001). Hooker was a unique character, who—after scoring his first big hit in 1948 with 'Boogie Chillen'—often recorded the same songs over and over, under a litany of pseudonyms and for a variety of record labels, even when he was under exclusive contract to record for a label such as Modern Records. Hooker's recorded work can be found under the names Texas Slim, Johnny Williams, Birmingham Sam, Johnny Lee, The Boogie Man, Delta John, and even John Lee Booker or John Lee Cooker. After his success with Modern, other label-owners would offer him large chunks of cash to record material for them. John Lee liked this cash-in-hand method of compensation, and didn't turn down too many offers.

It was also easy for Hooker to slip into a studio and lay down tracks quickly because he worked alone for much of his early career, playing as an acoustic solo act—and many of his early recordings reflect that. As such Hooker got away not only with skirting the exclusivity clause in a legal recording contract but also with a major quirk as a musician: he rarely paid much attention to the number of bars in a song, or from verse to verse—and he often stayed on the I chord throughout the entire song. Later in his career, when he was put into the studio with a backup band, the listener can often hear the band moving through the chord changes almost against Hooker's will, with him reluctantly following them—or not at all.

One of Hooker's most well-known songs is 'Boom, Boom,' a hit for him in 1962, which was eventually covered by The Yardbirds, The Animals, modern rockers Big Head Todd & The Monsters, and even country music's Oak Ridge Boys.

This classic electric blues tune begins with a sinewy, yet simple lead guitar solo part alternating with a stop-time rhythm section. I've captured the spirit of John Lee Hooker's style and the song 'Boom, Boom' on the CD.

Count off the measures and you will hear that in the first 12 measures the lead guitar is featured *a cappella*, if you will, between meaty bursts of the band. This call-and-response style is very popular in blues music. Notice that the choice of notes—while all derive from the E minor blues scale—changes with the chord. Hooker skillfully found the chord tones for the I, IV, and V chords during this section of the tune. At least for this one hit, he followed—for the most part—a 12-bar, I-IV-V pattern.

Once the band kicks in, the lead guitar riffs actually lay back a bit, as was Hooker's style. In the second half of this example, we stick very close to the E minor pentatonic scale in the open position. One exception to this is the D♯ used as a leading tone, heard at the start of the second 12 measures and throughout the solo. Hooker would bend this note slightly, then release it to the root note.

The rhythm part for this Hooker-style groove (over the page) is reminiscent of his minimalist playing on recordings throughout his lengthy career. The rhythm on the track features little more than a duplication of the bass line in the first 12 measures, and quick stabs at the E, A7, and B7 chords once the band kicks in.

Rhythm track in the style of John Lee Hooker

PART **3**   S E C T I O N I O

King of the blues

The world's most famous bluesman is, of course, B.B. King (born 1925). He started life as Riley B. King and took his stage name from early days busking on Memphis street corners, where he became known as the "Beale Street Blues Boy," which he shortened to B.B.

B.B. King's early style was largely influenced by T-Bone Walker, and many of his initial hits reflected T-Bone's swinging, jazzy tone and phrasing. B.B. effectively launched his career in 1952 with 'Three O'Clock Blues,' which spent five weeks at Number One on the American R&B charts. He followed that up with numerous R&B hits in the years to come. The example of B.B. King's style demonstrated on the CD that comes with this book is reminiscent of his 1955 hit 'Every Day I Have The Blues,' which was also featured on his 1965 concert masterpiece, the *Live At The Regal* album.

To this day, King tours with a large band, including a horn section. Horn players typically play in the keys of B♭ or E♭, among other keys not so often chosen by guitarists—hence B.B.'s choice of B♭ as the key of 'Every Day.'

The solo in this jazzy 12-bar tune begins hesitantly. Count the measures and you will hear the guitar burst out in measure three with a riff very reminiscent of T-Bone Walker's playing. This same basic lick has been repeated by King on countless recordings, and is used throughout this recorded example. Also notice, beginning in measures five and six and throughout the piece—particularly over the IV chord—the very raucous "tritone" or flat fifth, slightly bent and repeated in a syncopated fashion before resolving into the chord tones of the I chord in measure seven. This tritone figure is a mainstay of blues guitarists today.

The rhythm part for this slightly jazzy B.B. King-style song (over the page) features the classic and very thick-sounding ninth chord shape that blues players love to utilize. Notice in particular the chromatic climb from the I to IV chord in the second chorus.

Rhythm track in the style of B.B. King

Blues rock

The legends of classic rock spent their formative teenage years listening to and copying the legends of the electric blues. How and when rock'n'roll was actually born is up for debate, but that it is the direct offspring of electric blues is both unmistakable and unarguable. Rock legends such as Eric Clapton, Keith Richards, Jeff Beck, Jimmy Page, George Harrison, Jimi Hendrix, and Stevie Ray Vaughan never failed to credit the masters of the electric blues era as their main source of inspiration. In this section of *The Blues Guitar Handbook*, I'll examine the link between blues and rock while taking a close look at the playing of two of rock'n'roll's most respected guitarists.

The blues had a baby ...

Some say the 1951 hit 'Rocket 88' by sax-player-turned-vocalist Jackie Brenston—produced by and featuring Ike Turner on keyboards—was the first true rock'n'roll song. Others may credit the likes of Elvis Presley or perhaps Carl Perkins as the originators of the rock'n'roll sound.

Regardless, by the early to mid 60s it was clear that a new sound was becoming the dominant musical force, replacing crooners, big-bands, country, rhythm & blues, and, yes, even blues music as the most popular genre for listeners worldwide—a dominance that continues to this day.

But rock'n'roll might not—probably would not—exist were it not for the influence of the blues, and particularly the electric blues of the 50s and 60s. While some were rockin' 'round the clock at their local high-school sock hops, teenagers such as Eric Clapton, Jimmy Page, and Jeff Beck, not to mention the future members of The Beatles and The Rolling Stones, to name just a few, were wearing out vinyl records by guys named Muddy and Wolf, trying to copy the hot guitar licks found on their records.

They took those licks and reworked them, gradually at first, then more radically. And beginning in the early to mid 60s, those young men, now with bands and recording contracts of their own, fused the blues licks they had studied with a more impassioned beat, and became rock'n'roll legends.

In this section of *The Blues Guitar Handbook*, I'll demonstrate and examine the styles of two blues-rock greats—an Englishman and a Yank—and the sound that continually thrills new generations of listeners.

SECTION II PART 3

Slowhand style

The reigning king of the original generation of blues rockers, and perhaps the most influential elder statesman of the rock world today, Eric Clapton (born 1945) has enjoyed a seemingly blessed career. Through many years and through many changes, he has retained the approval of fans worldwide, crafting hit after hit, for decades on end.

Clapton got his public start in The Yardbirds, that mid-60s spawning-ground for guitar legends, in which both Jimmy Page and Jeff Beck were to follow. He left The Yardbirds when they became too pop for his taste and joined John Mayall's Bluesbreakers, where he laid down some classic tracks on the 1966 album *Blues Breakers With Eric Clapton*. Next he achieved immense success with his bands Cream, Blind Faith, and Derek & The Dominos—and then launched a celebrated solo career that is entering its fifth decade.

For the *Blues Guitar Handbook* CD I've created a song in the style of Clapton's Cream era, reminiscent of the song 'Cross Road Blues (Crossroads).' The fiery solo style Clapton used in this song was truly played from a rock'n'roll, not a blues, point of view. Yet the song and solo use blues chord progressions, scales, and classic blues motifs throughout. It's really the same old blues, but Eric just put a little fire under it all. Count the measures to hear how the solo works.

In the first two measures of the solo we find ourselves playing A major pentatonic at the second fret, then shifting up to the fifth fret for a more typical A (minor) pentatonic riff in the third measure. A brief visit to "B.B.'s Box" at the eighth fret takes place in the eighth measure, before we drop back into the main pentatonic pattern at the fifth fret.

Eric Clapton is very fond of soloing in the fourth pentatonic position, especially in songs in the key of A, so we'll visit this territory as the second chorus begins, remaining there for much of the next 12 measures.

For the rhythm part of this Cream-era Clapton style rocker (opposite), we're pumping away at power chords and the classic A5/A6 move, over the I chord, followed by similar action over the D (the IV chord) and E (the V chord). This one will test the stamina of your pinky.

The pride and joy of Austin, Texas

The late, great Stevie Ray Vaughan (1954–1990) left us far too soon, tragically losing his life in a helicopter accident just minutes after finishing a concert in which he tore up the stage alongside Eric Clapton, Buddy Guy, Robert Cray, and his older brother Jimmie Vaughan. Fans who were there say Stevie's playing was completely unbelievable that night. Vaughan had come on to the international music scene less than a decade before, breathing life into both a blues scene in sadly failing health and a rock scene in which 80s pop gloss had almost erased many music fans' memories of what a real guitar and amp actually sounded like.

His fiery playing first caught our attention with the 1983 release of the album

Rhythm track in the style of Eric Clapton

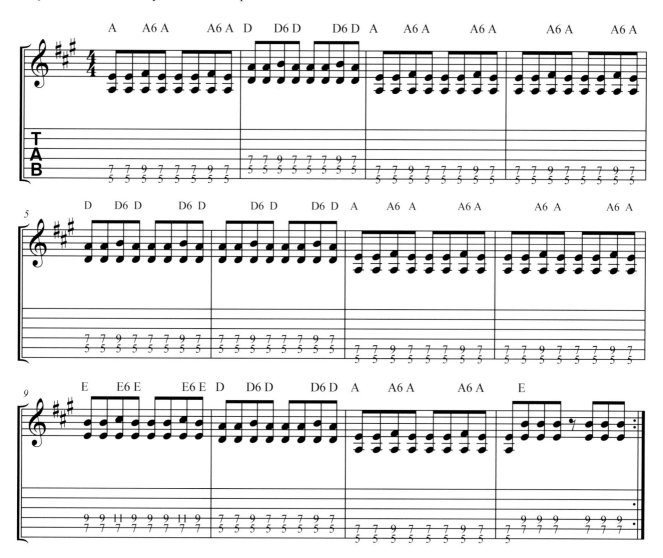

CD TRACK 86

Example 8.7

S E C T I O N I I PART **3**

Texas Flood, largely recorded live in the studio—and in just three days. The album was so out of step with the rest of the rock scene of the era that it simply could not be ignored. Stevie Ray Vaughan may be one of the bluesiest players ever to find regular rotation on the television channel MTV, then just starting out; his humorous video for his hit song 'Cold Shot'—not to mention his immense skill on the guitar strings—made a huge star out of him in very short order.

On the *Blues Guitar Handbook* CD I've laid down a track reminiscent of Stevie's 'Pride And Joy,' which itself is simply a familiar stride-piano 12-bar blues riff transferred to the guitar. Though Stevie played pretty much everything with the guitar tuned down a half-step to E♭, I have recorded this track in standard E tuning.

The opening is a trademark lead technique borrowed from as far back as the Delta stylings of Charley Patton or Robert Johnson. It begins with unison notes, then moves to a minor third bent major in the second measure, then back to the unison figure.

We quickly jump into a series of double-stops in measure five to truly kick off the solo. Vaughan followed this with some Chuck Berry-style riffs in measures eight and nine, before he hit us with a flurry of bends. Quick open-string playing was one of Stevie Ray Vaughan's trademarks, and he drops into the E minor pentatonic in the open position halfway through the first chorus.

The second half of the solo re-introduces the opening unison and bent-thirds salvo before thickening things up a bit with an open high E-string played against a series of thirds on the second and third strings. Eventually Stevie would drop back into the open position again, as we see in the seventh measure of the second chorus, a position he would often stay in at length.

The rhythm guitar for this track (opposite) is based on piano trends of the 20s, particularly the stride techniques and walking bass lines that came out of Harlem, New Orleans, St. Louis, and the ragtime movement. This pattern of alternating the walking bass line with a high-string chord is also found in country music, and having grown up in Texas, Stevie Ray Vaughan was certainly aware of classic country techniques.

Rhythm track in the style of Stevie Ray Vaughan

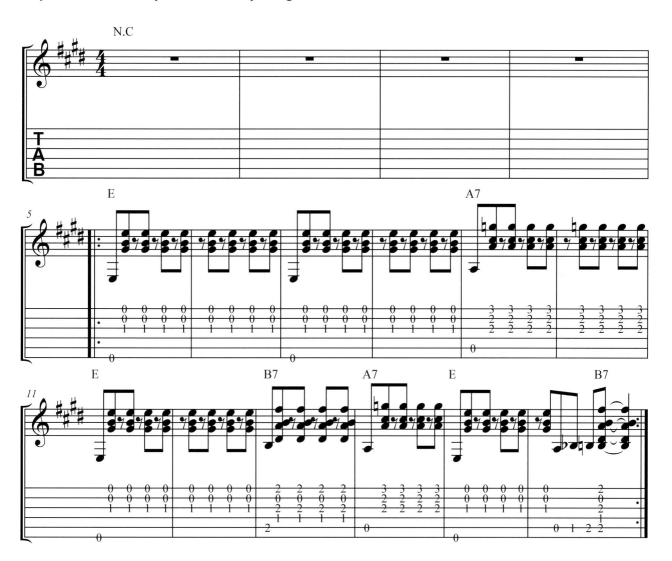

SECTION II PART **3**

Jazz blues

Blues and jazz have been mingling since the earliest days of either genre. The process began with big-band guitarists such as Charlie Christian, Freddie Green, and T-Bone Walker, carried on through the jazz combo playing of Kenny Burrell and Wes Montgomery, and has continued into the modern jazz-blues-rock and jazz-fusion stylings of players such as Robben Ford and Scott Henderson. In this section of *The Blues Guitar Handbook* I'll explore the way in which two influential players use the blues as a guideline for more jazzy fretboard explorations.

Boppin' the blues

Blues chord progressions, riffs, and phrasing have found their way into jazz music since the early 1900s. Many early jazz guitarists moonlighted in the world of blues on their jazz bands' off-nights, picking up common licks and turnarounds. Later they twisted those ideas into a more sophisticated format to use in a jazz setting. The big-band and swing eras, featuring the orchestras of Duke Ellington, Benny Goodman, and Count Basie among others, brought even more bluesy playing into what was then mainstream music.

Big-band guitarists—relegated to the rhythm section until guitars went electric—soon became highly regarded soloists alongside the brass and woodwind stars of the day. Charlie Christian, who played with Benny Goodman from 1939 to 1941, is often credited as being the first big-band guitarist to go electric, and his fluid solo lines are credited by some (including famed producer John Hammond) as the best improvisational turns of the entire swing era. Christian's fretwork inspired others, including T-Bone Walker (who was mentored by Christian as a teen), to follow. They in turn influenced folks such as B.B. King, Chuck Berry, Jimi Hendrix, and The Allman Brothers.

During the years of World War II, swing began to be replaced by newer jazz strains, such as bebop and later cool jazz, both of which make up a broader category known as modern jazz. Despite this change from what was essentially dance music to musical styles more suited to virtuosity and attentive listening, blues guitar phrasings and progressions remained part of the jazz vernacular.

With the bebop movement, horn players such as John Coltrane and Charlie "Bird" Parker set the standard, and both included blues in their repertoire. Charlie Christian is often cited as a bebop guitarist as much as a swing guitarist—though he straddled both genres.

When cool jazz—often referred to as West Coast jazz—arrived around 1950, horn players such as Miles Davis and Stan Getz were considered leaders of the movement. They brought blues mannerisms forward yet again, and they were matched by guitarists such as Kenny Burrell, Wes Montgomery, Tal Farlow, and Herb Ellis.

Beginning in the late 60s and into the 70s, jazz and rock combined to form jazz-fusion, a tag that is still relevant today. From the guitar side, pioneers in jazz-fusion include Jeff Beck (particularly his *Wired* and *Blow by Blow* discs), Al Di Meola, and John McLaughlin. In turn, these monumental players were followed by the likes of Robben Ford, Frank Gambale, Allan Holdsworth, and Scott Henderson.

In this section of *The Blues Guitar Handbook*, I'll demonstrate and examine the styles of two jazz-blues players: one is a swing guitarist, the other a contemporary jazz-fusion cat.

The T-Bone shuffle

Aaron Thibeaux "T-Bone" Walker (1910–1975) was born in Texas to a musical family, and learned guitar, banjo, ukulele, violin, mandolin, and piano at an early age. By 10 he was guiding blues great Blind Lemon Jefferson—a family friend—to his gigs, and by 15 he was playing professionally and serving an informal apprenticeship with Charlie Christian.

T-Bone married and moved to Los Angeles in the mid 30s, where he found work in jazz bands and became a featured performer in the popular Les Hite Orchestra, working L.A.'s hoppin' Central Avenue nightclubs. It was around 1940 when T-Bone amplified his guitar, formed his own combo, and hit the clubs. His style leaned toward the blues on which he had been brought up, and his stage antics—playing with his teeth, behind his back, while doing the splits—soon earned him acclaim.

Walker began his recording career shortly after that, and his smoky blues style, flavored with a taste of swing jazz in his fluid lead lines, quickly became popular. B.B. King has often claimed that he decided to get his first guitar after hearing T-Bone's 'Call It Stormy Monday.'

On the *Blues Guitar Handbook* CD I've included a jam reminiscent of 'Call It Stormy Monday' and other slow blues tunes T-Bone recorded. It gives us the chance to examine a variety of his jazz-inspired blues licks. This slow blues groove, in the key of G, is laid-back and a great exercise in restraint. Full of tasty licks that became the standard for blues guitarists such as B.B. King—and everyone who followed—it's a perfect introduction to jazz-blues phrasing.

The solo kicks off with a standard blues opening in the main pentatonic pattern, followed by a series of easy bends. Then we hit the trademark T-Bone lick: a quick flurry of 16th-notes in the second measure, which adds the ninth of the scale to the main pentatonic pattern. This ninth interval added to otherwise straight pentatonic licks is a big part of the T-Bone Walker sound and an easy jazz tone to add to any blues solo. Walker (and, later, players from B.B. King and Chuck Berry to Jimi Hendrix and Stevie Ray Vaughan) would use this exact move in countless solos.

Over the IV chord (C9) in measure five, we slide up into what would essentially be the main pentatonic pattern in C, at the eighth fret, adding the major third at the ninth fret of the third string for a simple Mixolydian phrase. T-Bone would then partially mimic this phrase back on the I (G) chord in measure seven. Heading into the jazzy turnaround in measure nine (beginning at the end of measure eight) we find a series of simple bends which bring us back to the I, and more of the T-Bone phrasing that so clearly influenced Chuck Berry.

In the second chorus we encounter much of the same phrasing, with T-Bone's classic flurry off the main pentatonic, including that jazzy ninth. Over the IV chord in measures 17 and 18 we alternate chord and passing tones of the C9 chord by simply adding E at the fifth fret on the second string, the third of the C9 chord. At the turnaround we again play with this E note, bending it a half-step and releasing it to serve as both the flat third (when bent) and the ninth of our V chord (D). Simple yet elegant phrasing, with a few jazz tones thrown in, equals classic T-Bone Walker.

The rhythm part of this jam (opposite page) is primarily played using the standard blues ninth chord. T-Bone loved to slide this chord chromatically, especially a half-step above and below the I chord. In the turnaround we encounter a trademark jazz ii-V-I, here Am-D7-G.

The blues fusion experiment

California-based blues and jazz-fusion guitarist Robben Ford (born 1951) grew up in a musical family, picking up sax at age 10 and guitar by 13. He played in a band through his teens with brothers Mark (harmonica) and Patrick (drums). Called the Charles Ford Band, it was named in honor of their father. By 18, Ford and the family band had recorded two albums and begun a stint as backup band for a noted blues harp player, Charlie Musselwhite.

Robben eventually left the family group—though it has reunited from time to time over the years—and launched a critically-acclaimed career involving collaborations, tours, and recordings with artists such as The Allman Brothers' Gregg Allman, The Grateful Dead's Phil Lesh, blues singer Jimmy Witherspoon, and jazz legend Miles Davis. Robben joined Tom Scott's L.A. Express in time to serve as backing band on George Harrison's 1974 U.S. tour, and then as Joni Mitchell's live and studio band (Ford is the guitarist on Mitchell's *The Hissing Of Summer Lawns* and *Miles of Aisles*).

Ford went on to form jazz-fusion pioneers The Yellowjackets in 1976, and by the early 80s began releasing a series of outstanding blues-based solo albums (some attributed to Robben Ford & The Blue Line), and jazz-fusion records with the group Jing Chi, among other recordings.

Rhythm track in the style of T-Bone Walker

CD TRACK 88

Example 8.9

S E C T I O N 12   PART **3**

On the *Blues Guitar Handbook* CD I've laid down a track in the style of Ford's 'Misdirected Blues,' in the key of C. Count the measures to hear what is happening in the solo. It jumps back and forth between C Mixolydian and C major pentatonic riffs in the first two measures before jumping up to the fourth pentatonic pattern in measure four. He tweaks the pattern slightly, however, for a repetitive riff that is diminished in nature. It works because the I chord is, at this point, serving as the V chord of the upcoming IV chord (F), which we hit in the fifth measure. Jazz-fusion players are fond of throwing diminished riffs over a V-I chord change, and Ford often jumps at the opportunity.

Most of the solo involves the major blues or Mixolydian sound and uses licks from the main pentatonic pattern throughout. Some of the tastiest phrases are found over the chord changes, where Ford exercises a bit of jazz theory. Check out the arpeggiated riff over the E♭ chord in measure six, and the cool turnaround riff in measures 21 and 22 over the G7 and F7 chords. This solo retains its blues flavor, but adds the occasional jazzy gem, common in the work of Ford and other jazz-fusion players.

Rhythm guitar parts on jazz-fusion tracks, particularly those which lean toward blues, often include typical blues "comping" patterns, spiced up with a few tasty chords here and there. On this track (opposite page) we're playing a straight shuffle-type blues pattern throughout, except for measures four through six, and again in the same spot the second time through the progression.

The track relies on a C5/C6 move over the I chord until the fourth measure of I, where we throw in a very jazzy sounding C7♯9♯5 chord (which is easier to play than it sounds). This chord then simply slides down one fret to become our IV chord (F6/9) and then two more frets to cover the E♭ chord, which we're substituting in place of the second measure of the IV chord. The rest of the track is a standard blues shuffle rhythm part.

Rhythm track in the style of Robben Ford

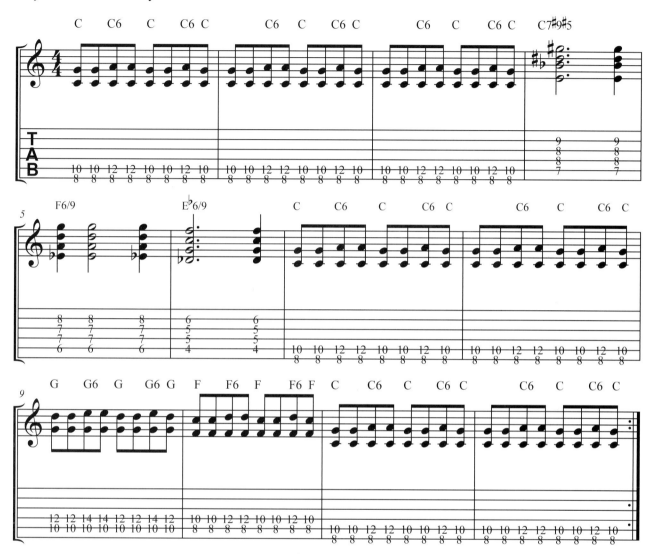

Example 8.10

SECTION 12 PART **3**

On the CD

Some of the CD tracks consist of several musical examples played one after the other.

CD TRACK 1: Tuning
CD TRACK 2: Examples 4.24-4.26
CD TRACK 3: 4.27-4.29
CD TRACK 4: Example 4.30
CD TRACK 5: Examples 4.31-4.33
CD TRACK 6: Example 4.34
CD TRACK 7: Example 4.35
CD TRACK 8: Example 4.36
CD TRACK 9: Example 4.37
CD TRACK 10: Examples 4.38-4.39
CD TRACK 11: Example 4.40-4.42
CD TRACK 12: Example 4.43
CD TRACK 13: Examples 4.44-4.45
CD TRACK 14: Example 4.46
CD TRACK 15: Example 4.47
CD TRACK 16: Example 4.48
CD TRACK 17: Example 4.49
CD TRACK 18: Example 4.50
CD TRACK 19: Example 4.51
CD TRACK 20: Examples 4.52-4.53
CD TRACK 21: Examples 4.54-4.55
CD TRACK 22: Examples 4.56-4.57
CD TRACK 23: Examples 4.58-4.60
CD TRACK 24: Examples 4.61-4.62
CD TRACK 25: Examples 4.63-4.65
CD TRACK 26: Examples 4.66-4.67
CD TRACK 27: Example 4.68
CD TRACK 28: Example 4.69
CD TRACK 29: Examples 4.70-4.71
CD TRACK 30: Example 4.72
CD TRACK 31: Example 4.73
CD TRACK 32: Example 4.74
CD TRACK 33: Example 4.75

CD TRACK 34: Example 4.76
CD TRACK 35: Example 4.77
CD TRACK 36: Examples 5.1-5.3
CD TRACK 37: Example 5.4
CD TRACK 38: Example 5.6
CD TRACK 39: Examples 5.8, 5.10
CD TRACK 40: Example 5.11
CD TRACK 41: Examples 5.12-5.13
CD TRACK 42: Example 5.14
CD TRACK 43: Example 5.15
CD TRACK 44: Example 5.16
CD TRACK 45: Example 5.17
CD TRACK 46: Example 5.18
CD TRACK 47: Example 5.19
CD TRACK 48: Example 5.20
CD TRACK 49: Example 5.21
CD TRACK 50: Example 5.22
CD TRACK 51: Example 5.23
CD TRACK 52: Exercise 1
CD TRACK 53: Exercise 2
CD TRACK 54: Exercise 3
CD TRACK 55: Exercises 4-6
CD TRACK 56: Example 6.1
CD TRACK 57: Example 6.2
CD TRACK 58: Example 6.3
CD TRACK 59: Example 6.4
CD TRACK 60: Example 6.5
CD TRACK 61: Example 6.6
CD TRACK 62: Example 6.7
CD TRACK 63: Examples 6.8-6.10
CD TRACK 64: Example 6.11
CD TRACK 65: Example 6.12
CD TRACK 66: Example 6.13

CD TRACK 67: Example 6.14
CD TRACK 68: Example 6.15
CD TRACK 69: Example 6.16
CD TRACK 70: Example 6.17
CD TRACK 71: Examples 6.20-6.21
CD TRACK 72: Example 6.22
CD TRACK 73: Example 6.23
CD TRACK 74: Example 6.24
CD TRACK 75: Example 6.25
CD TRACK 76: Example 6.26
CD TRACK 77: Example 6.27
CD TRACK 78: Example 6.28
CD TRACK 79: Example 6.29
CD TRACK 80: Example 8.1 Robert Johnson style
CD TRACK 81: Example 8.2 Brownie McGhee style
CD TRACK 82: Example 8.3 Muddy Waters style
CD TRACK 83: Example 8.4 Elmore James style
CD TRACK 84: Example 8.5 John Lee Hooker style
CD TRACK 85: Example 8.6 B.B. King style
CD TRACK 86: Example 8.7 Eric Clapton style
CD TRACK 87: Example 8.8 Stevie Ray Vaughan style
CD TRACK 88: Example 8.9 T-Bone Walker style
CD TRACK 89: Example 8.10 Robben Ford style

246

Discography

Perhaps more than any other form of music, the blues has been repackaged, remastered, and reissued, making for a bewildering and labyrinthine recorded history. And the earlier the artists were active, the more complicated their audio legacy becomes. Blues players working in the 20s and 30s generally made scattered 78s for various labels, the tracks from which have since been compiled in many different combinations. Some of these people never recorded again, while others were forgotten for a while before being "rediscovered" by a succession of folk and blues revivals in the 50s and 60s, when they began recording again. Even these later recordings, and recordings by artists who started their careers in this period or afterward, have since been frequently repackaged and added to, making it hard to create definitive discographies. Taking that into account, what follows is a selected discography of the 50 key artists named in part one of this book.

Luther Allison
Luther's Blues
Motown
1974

Luther Allison
Soul Fixin' Man
Alligator
1994

The Allman Brothers Band
The Allman Brothers Band
Atco
1970

The Allman Brothers Band
At Fillmore East
Capricorn
1971

Barbecue Bob
Chocolate To The Bone
Yazoo
1992

Chuck Berry
One Dozen Berrys
Chess
1958

Chuck Berry
The Anthology [boxed set]
Chess
2000

Michael Bloomfield & Al Kooper
*Live Adventures Of Michael Bloomfield &
Al Kooper*
Columbia
1969

Lonnie Brooks
Bayou Lightning
Alligator
1979

Lonnie Brooks
Hot Shot
Alligator
1983

Big Bill Broonzy
All The Classic Sides 1928–1937 [boxed set]
Jsp Records
2003

Big Bill Broonzy
Big Bill Broonzy Sings Folk Songs
Smithsonian Folkways
1989

Big Bill Broonzy
Amsterdam Live Concerts 1953 [boxed set]
Munich
2006

The Butterfield Blues Band
Butterfield Blues Band
Elektra
1965

The Butterfield Blues Band
East-West
Elektra
1966

Eric Clapton
From The Cradle
Reprise
1994

Albert Collins
Ice Pickin
Alligator Records
1978

Albert Collins, Robert Cray & Johnny Copeland
Showdown
Alligator Records
1985

Albert Collins
Cold Snap
Alligator Records
1986

Robert Cray
Strong Persuader
Mercury
1986

Robert Cray
Shoulda Been Home
Rykodisc
2001

Papa John Creach
Filthy!
Grunt/RCA
1972

Cream
Disraeli Gears
Polydor
1967

Rev. Gary Davis
Pure Religion & Bad Company
Smithsonian Folkways
1957

Rev. Gary Davis
Say No To The Devil
Obc
1961

Rev. Gary Davis
Little More Faith
Obc
1999

Delaney & Bonnie & Friends
On Tour With Eric Clapton
Atlantic
1970

Derek & The Dominos
Layla & Other Assorted Love Songs
Polydor
1970

Bo Diddley
Bo Diddley's Beach Party
Checker
1963

Bo Diddley
The Definitive Collection [boxed set]
Geffen/Chess
2007

Willie Dixon
I Am The Blues
CBS
1970

Willie Dixon
Chess Box [boxed set]
Chess
1990

The Fabulous Thunderbirds
The Fabulous Thunderbirds
Chrysalis
1979

Robben Ford
Talk To Your Daughter
Warner Bros
1988

Robben Ford
Handful Of Blues
Blue Thumb
1995

Buddy Guy
A Man & The Blues
Vanguard
1968

Buddy Guy
Blues Singer
Jive
2003

John Hammond Jr
Country Blues
Universe
1964

John Hammond Jr
Hot Tracks
Vanguard
1970

John Lee Hooker
It Serves You Right To Suffer
Universal
1966

John Lee Hooker
Endless Boogie
MCA
1971

John Lee Hooker & Canned Heat
Hooker N Heat [boxed set]
Capitol
1991

Lightnin' Hopkins
Complete Aladdin Recordings [boxed set]
Capitol
1991

Lightnin' Hopkins
Lightnin' & The Blues: The Herald Sessions
Buddha
2001

Lightnin' Hopkins
Country Blues
Tradition
1960

The Hour Glass
The Hour Glass
Liberty Records
1967

Son House
The Complete Library Of Congress Sessions, 1941–1942
Travelin' Man
1996

Son House
Father Of The Delta Blues: The Complete 1965 Sessions
Sony
1992

Howlin' Wolf
Moanin' In The Moonlight
Chess
1959

Howlin' Wolf
Howlin' Wolf
Chess
1962

Elmore James
Blues After Hours
P-Vine Records
1961

Elmore James
Sky Is Crying: The History Of Elmore James
Rhino
1993

Skip James
Hard Time Killing Floor Blues
Biograph
2003

Skip James
Devil Got My Woman
Vanguard
1968

Skip James
Complete Early Recordings
Yazoo
1994

Blind Lemon Jefferson
Complete Recorded Volumes 1 – 4
Document
1994

The Jimi Hendrix Experience
Are You Experienced?
Track
1967

The Jimi Hendrix Experience
Electric Ladyland
Reprise
1968

Robert Johnson
The Complete Recordings [boxed set]
Sony
1990

Albert King
Born Under A Bad Sign
Stax
1967

Albert King
King Of The Blues Guitar
Atlantic
1969

Albert King
I'll Play The Blues For You
Stax
1972

B.B. King
Live At The Regal
ABC
1965

B.B. King
Completely Well
MCA
1969

B.B. King
Blues On The Bayou
MCA
1998

Freddy King
Let's Hide Away And Dance Away With Freddy King
King
1961

Freddie King
My Feeling For The Blues
Friday Music
1969

Huddie "Leadbelly" Ledbetter
Bourgeois Blues: Lead Belly Legacy, Vol. 2
Smithsonian Folkways
1997

Huddie "Leadbelly" Ledbetter
Gwine Dig A Hole To Put The Devil In
Rounder / Umgd
1992

Huddie "Leadbelly" Ledbetter
Lead Belly's Last Sessions [boxed set]
Smithsonian Folkways
1994

Little Charlie & The Nightcats
Disturbing The Peace
Alligator
1988

Little Charlie & The Nightcats
Shadow Of The Blues
Alligator
1998

Taj Mahal
Taj Mahal
Columbia
1968

Taj Mahal
An Evening Of Acoustic Music
Tradition & Moderne
1994

John Mayall & The Bluesbreakers
Blues Breakers With Eric Clapton
Deram
1966

John Mayall
Blues From Laurel Canyon
Deram
1968

Mississippi Fred McDowell
Mississippi Fred McDowell
Rounder
1971

Mississippi Fred McDowell
I Do Not Play No Rock 'N' Roll: The Complete Sessions
Capitol
1969

Brownie McGhee
Brownie McGhee: The Folkways Years, 1945–1959
Smithsonian Folkways
1992

Keb' Mo'
Keb' Mo'
Okeh/550/Epic
1994

Keb' Mo'
Suitcase
Red Ink
2006

Charlie Patton
Complete Recordings 1929–34 [boxed set]
Jsp Records
2002

Bonnie Raitt
Give It Up
Warner Bros
1972

Bonnie Raitt
Nick Of Time
Capitol
1989

Jimmy Reed
I'm Jimmy Reed
Vee-Jay
1958

Jimmy Reed
Jimmy Reed At Carnegie Hall
Vee-Jay
1961

The Rising Sons
Rising Sons Featuring Taj Mahal & Ry Cooder
Columbia/Legacy
1992

Duke Robillard
After Hours Swing Session
Rounder
1990

Duke Robillard
Stretchin' Out Live
Stony Plain
1999

Otis Rush
Right Place, Wrong Time
Hightone
1976

Otis Rush
Mourning In The Morning
Atlantic
1969

Son Seals
Midnight Son
Alligator
1976

Son Seals
Live And Burning
Alligator
1978

Kenny Wayne Shepherd
Ledbetter Heights
Giant
1995

Kenny Wayne Shepherd
The Place You're In
Reprise
2004

Hubert Sumlin
Heart & Soul
Blind Pig
1989

Sonny Terry & Brownie McGhee
Backwater Blues
Fantasy
1991

Sonny Terry & Brownie McGhee
Midnight Special
Universal
1978

George Thorogood & The Destroyers
George Thorogood & The Destroyers
Rounder
1979

George Thorogood & The Destroyers
Bad To The Bone
EMI
1982

Derek Trucks
Live At The Georgia Theater
Sony
2004

Derek Trucks
Songlines
Sony
2006

Jimmie Vaughan
Strange Pleasures
Epic
1994

Jimmie Vaughan
Do You Get The Blues?
Epic
2001

Stevie Ray Vaughan
Texas Flood
Epic
1983

Stevie Ray Vaughan
In Step
Epic/Legacy
1989

T-Bone Walker
T-Bone Blues
Atlantic
1959

T-Bone Walker
Imperial Recordings
Capitol
1991

T-Bone Walker
Stormy Monday
LRC Ltd
2009

Muddy Waters
Fathers & Sons
Chess
1969

Muddy Waters
Can't Get No Grindin'
Chess
1973

Muddy Waters
Hard Again
Blue Sky
1977

Junior Wells & Buddy Guy
Hoodoo Man Blues
Delmark
1965

Johnny Winter
Second Winter
Columbia
1969

Johnny & Edgar Winter
Together: Johnny & Edgar Winter Live
Blue Sky
1976

ZZ Top
Tres Hombres
Warner Bros
1973

ZZ Top
Eliminator
Warner Bros
1983

Other great books in this series:

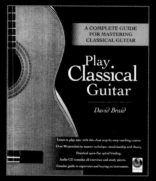

PLAY CLASSICAL GUITAR
ISBN 978-0-87930-657-1

THE FOLK HANDBOOK
ISBN 978-0-87930-901-5

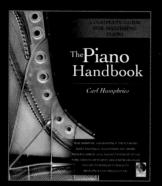

THE PIANO HANDBOOK
ISBN 978-0-87930-727-1

THE FIDDLE HANDBOOK
ISBN 978-0-87930-978-7

PLAY ACOUSTIC
ISBN 978-0-87930-853-7

**THE PIANO IMPROVISATION
HANDBOOK**
ISBN 978-0-87930-977-0

THE BASS HANDBOOK
ISBN 978-0-87930-872-8

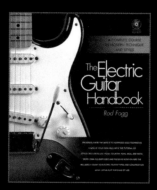

**THE ELECTRIC GUITAR
HANDBOOK**
ISBN 978-0-87930-989-3

Acknowledgements

I'd like to thank all the people who helped make this book a reality, including Tony and Nigel from Jawbone Press, and of course my editor John Morrish (nice Skypeing with you)—thank you all for your incredible patience! Thanks also to my music journalism friend and mentor Jon Chappell for his insight and guidance at so many points in my writing career, and for recommending I contact Tony Bacon about this book in the first place. Thank you also to the folks at Backbeat Books and Hal Leonard for your efforts to make this book (and my many previous books) a fun and popular title out there in the music universe. I'd also like to thank all the blues and rock artists I've interviewed, learned from, and been inspired by through the years, and all those who helped mold my guitar playing. And a final word of thanks to my wife and kids for putting up with a musician and a stressed-out author in the house, and to my father, Mel, for getting me started with guitar lessons all those years ago ... Thank you all!

Adam St. James

For more information about the author go to www.adamstjames.com

ARTIST PICTURES

Images were supplied by Getty Images, London. **Getty** photographers/collections are indicated by the following key: **AL** Andrew Lepley/Redferns; **BS** Brian Shuel/Redferns; **CG** Charlie Gillett Collection/Redferns; **CH** Charles Paul Harris/Michael Ochs Archives; **CM** Chris Morphet/Redferns; **EG** Erika Goldring; **FD** Frank Driggs Collection; **GP** Gilles Petard/Redferns; **HA** Hulton Archive; **HH** Harry Herd/Redferns; **JA** Jorgen Angel/Redferns; **KF** Keystone Features; **LH** Larry Hulst/Michael Ochs Archives; **MC** Matt Carmichael; **MO** Michael Ochs Archives; **PN** Paul Natkin/WireImage; **PS** Peter Sherman/Michael Ochs Archives; **RA** Richard E. Aaron/Redferns; **RJ** Robert Johnson Estate/Hulton Archive; **RV** Lipnitzki/Roger Viollet; **SC** Stephen J. Cohen; **SR** Simon Ritter/Redferns; **TC** Tom Copi/Michael Ochs Archives; **TE** Tony Evans; **VW** Val Wilmer/Redferns.

Pictures and photographers are identified by bold-type page number, subject, and photographer/collection key (see above): **5** Johnson RJ; **6** Jefferson HA, McTell MO; **7** Davis TE, McGhee GP; **8** Berry FD, Lockwood MO; **9** Beck VW; **10** Winter HH, Raitt RA; **11** Harris PN, Mo' SR; **12** Sumlin MC, Shepherd SC; **15** Broonzy FD; **16** Vaughan PS; **17** Patton MO; **18** Leadbelly MO; **19** McDowell MO; **20** Crayton TC, Reed MO; **21** Guy VW; **22** King CG; **23** Hopkins MO, Rush CH; **24** Hooker MO, Wolf MO, Mahal EG, Bloomfield MO; **25** Korner BS; **26** Mayall AL, Green KF; **27** Hendrix RV; **29** Fuller MO; **31** Allman MO; **32** White CM, Clapton LH; **34** Waters TC, Taylor JA.